How Wives & Daughters
Really Lived in Country House
Society Over a Century Ago

Undeserved sneers have been directed at the Lady of the Manor who blandly dispensed soup and blankets, but it must be admitted by any impartial observer that she was often the one who urged her husband to carry out the work of repairing cottages ... The Lady of the Manor lent her garden for Church fêtes and heroically saw the public trampling down her lawns, or her drawing-room for Church sales, or her dining room for the Sunday School play.

It was all part of a pattern of country life that seemed then as immutable as the laws of nature.

Susan Tweedsmuir, *The Edwardian Lady* (1966)
(Lady Tweedsmuir was born in 1882, married in 1907, and died in 1977)

How Wives & Daughters Really Lived in Country House Society Over a Century Ago

Pamela Horn

AMBERLEY

This edition first published 2012

Amberley Publishing
The Hill, Stroud
Gloucestershire, GL5 4EP

www.amberley-books.com

ISBN 978 1 4456 0832 7

British Library Cataloguing in Publication Data.
A catalogue record for this book is available
from the British Library.

Typeset in 11pt on 14pt Palatino.
Typesetting and Origination by Amberley Publishing.
Printed in the UK.

Contents

I

Ladies in Landed Society

Mrs Transome was anxious to run estate affairs ... Like all eager-minded women who advance in life without ... tenderness or any large sympathy, she had contracted small rigid habits of thinking and acting ... and had learned to fill up the great void of life with giving small orders to tenants ... [She], whose imperious will had availed little to ward off the great evils of her life, found the opiate for her discontent in the exertion of her will about smaller things ... She liked that a tenant should stand bareheaded below her as she sat on horseback. She liked to insist that work done without her orders should be undone from beginning to end. She liked to be curtsied and bowed to by all the congregation as she walked up the little barn of a church. She liked to change a labourer's medicine fetched from the doctor, and substitute a prescription of her own.

George Eliot, *Felix Holt, The Radical* (Warwick Edn of George Eliot's Works, 1901), 28, 33–34 and 42–43.

In many ways George Eliot's fictional Mrs Transome conformed to the traditional picture of a nineteenth-century lady of the manor. Busily engaged in organising her household and servants, she was none the less closely involved in the daily routine of the wider village community. This might range from visiting the sick and aged poor in their cottages or inspecting the school, to running benefit clubs and presiding over the annual fête or flower show. In return, she expected to be greeted with respect and deference by the villagers. She might also derive a good deal of satisfaction from her leading social role. The newly married Louisa Yorke, wife of the squire of Erddig near

Wrexham, was certainly not alone when she happily recorded in her diary one special occasion in the summer of 1902:

> This was a great day. I felt like a Queen. We drove in the Dog Cart ... to Marchviel where a Tea was given in honour of our marriage. A triumphal arch was made. I was presented with an exquisite bouquet by the school-master's little girl, aged two, & we had speeches & all kinds of nice things, a band, cheers, etc.[1]

To Florence Nightingale, whose father owned estates in Derbyshire and Hampshire, caring for the cottagers offered an early opportunity for the exercise of her nursing skills. In July 1843 when the family moved north to Lea Hurst, she decided to spend most of her days in the village and was soon badgering her mother to supply medicines, food, bedding, and clothing. When the time came for them to leave, she wanted to stay behind to continue her work. 'It breaks my heart to leave Lea Hurst,' she confided to her aunt in September. These tasks had given a sense of purpose to an otherwise sterile existence.[2]

Another real life counterpart of Mrs Transome was Rosalind, Countess of Carlisle, who not only took in hand the direction of her husband's extensive estates in Cumberland and Yorkshire but involved herself in a multiplicity of charitable and political ventures in the parishes surrounding them. She also ruled her family with a rod of iron. 'My mother was an Olympian,' wrote a younger daughter, 'and her presence in the house was diffused through a priesthood of governesses, tutors and hand maids.'[3]

Equally dominant was Lady Jocelyn, who held that 'duty to one's neighbour' meant visiting the sick and caring for the poor on the family estate. According to her granddaughter, there was no one

> at Tullymore or in the surrounding villages whom she did not know intimately. She used to spend long days driving in her jaunting car from one outlying cottage to another, carrying her baskets filled with bottles of medicine and embrocation and three-cornered shawls crocheted by herself – so many of these were distributed that they became almost a uniform in the district ... We were taught that to waste money on oneself was inexcusable.[4]

However, while these accounts of strong-minded benefactors illustrate some aspects of the lives of country-house ladies in Victorian and Edwardian England, they by no means represent the whole truth. A closer analysis reveals that the role and the status of such women were both more ambiguous and less independent than this simple view suggests.

First, like other upper and middle-class females at this time, the wives and daughters of the landed elite were influenced by current Victorian opinions on the 'natural' separation of the male and female spheres in life, and the importance of hearth and home as the centre of female existence. They were expected to cultivate their character, mind and abilities for the benefit of those around them rather than for themselves. In this way they would be pleasant companions to their husbands and careful mothers to their children. Some wives, indeed, took these injunctions so seriously that like Lady Ebury of Moor Park, their 'whole life was unobtrusively lived for others'.[5] The same was true of gentle Harriet Grey of Falloden, Northumberland. Her concern 'to make life go smoothly' was such that, according to her son, she 'shrank ... from argument and ... was always prepared to efface herself. This made it possible for the arrangement for a joint home between my Grandparents and Parents to work smoothly.'[6]

The common attitude towards this Victorian cult of domesticity was expressed by the Revd Charles Kingsley in an 1855 'Lecture to Ladies' when he declared that a woman's 'first duties [were] to her own family, her own servants'.[7]

Yet, paradoxically, while so much emphasis was placed on the importance of female responsibilities within the domestic domain, in other areas of their lives they were treated as frivolous subordinates to their male relatives. This meant they were deemed incapable of conducting business or financial matters on their own account or of making rational judgements on important issues. That even applied to such personal matters as their own marriage settlements, an issue we shall discuss in a later chapter. Negotiations over these involved the fathers of the bride and groom, as well as the prospective husband, since it was 'considered commendable in a man to be concerned about the financial aspects of marriage', although 'reprehensible in a woman'.[8] Even intelligent girls like Lady Maud Cecil felt it necessary to disclaim all knowledge. 'I am so sorry your Father should be worried about those tiresome settlements just now,' she wrote to her fiancé shortly before their marriage in 1883. 'I do not ... know much about money or what is usual in settlements but I should think the investment question is merely made by the lawyers ... I don't see why trustees are necessary at all ... but as I said before I know nothing about it, & am probably therefore talking nonsense.'[9] Nevertheless she sent a discreet note to her father on the subject – which may have been what her future husband intended – and the problems were quickly resolved.

Eleanor Glyn, herself the wife of a minor Essex landowner, pinpointed the general approach towards women when she described how George

Curzon, who had grown up at Kedleston Hall, Derbyshire, treated the females of his class:

He likes their society for entirely leisure moments – they are of no real importance in his scheme of things. He likes them rather in the spirit in which other men like fine horses or good wine, or beautiful things to embellish a man's leisure, but not as equal souls.[10]

It was in such circumstances that wives and daughters were expected to amuse and entertain guests at country-house weekends or to give glamour and gaiety to an otherwise solemn dinner party. They thereby not only acted as arbiters of what was considered proper conduct in their circle but they made comfortable and congenial the day-to-day social contacts between members of that grouping. 'In a gathering of people selected by a really clever hostess,' wrote Lady Tweedsmuir:

there might be one or two Cabinet Ministers who welcomed the opportunity of quiet conversation, or there might be a Viceroy or high official from a far-off corner of the Empire, anxious to make someone in the government of the day realise a little more the difficulties of a particular experiment that Britain had delegated to him to carry out. These parties often included … a painter, and almost certainly a musician who played to some of the company in the evenings. Besides these eminent people there was usually a sprinkling of women famous for their beauty or wit, or both, who either gave the conversation a sparkling turn, or were wise enough not to interrupt good talk, and who accordingly sat looking statuesque or flower-like.[11]

Within their local communities, these women were expected to act as bridges between rich and poor, through their role as dispensers of charity and other aid. In this way they were able to assure villagers of the interest and sympathy of their social superiors. It was with this 'Lady Bountiful' role in mind that Victoria Sackville-West resolved, on moving to Knole with her father in 1889, that she would 'try to get to know all the families on the place and hope to see that they are comfortable'.[12] Likewise Lady Leconfield, who was born in 1846, remembered that during her youth, although 'social work was not organised … there was full scope for individual energy, especially in the country, where parish life was a continual round of activity. A very pleasant feeling of fellowship united those who were thus grouped together.'[13]

Significantly, too, when this role seemed to be neglected, especially by younger women, older relatives were likely to remind them of their responsibilities. It was in this spirit that Lord Rosslyn reproved his step-daughter, Lady Brooke (the future Countess of Warwick) for succumbing to the temptations of a too energetic social round shortly after her marriage. As Frances Maynard, Lady Brooke had inherited Easton Lodge, an extensive property in Essex, from her paternal grandfather when she was only three, and it was in this context that Lord Rosslyn commented sourly on her current frivolity:

> The society of women whose only thought is dress and gossip, who paint their faces and disfigure their heads ... palls after a time – but it is so difficult to get rid of. Once adopted in youth you dance through life a sort of dance of death – knowing how wrong things are ... yet without the courage to free yourself from the thraldom of early acquaintance or early habit ... For work, have you not yr poor yr hundreds who depend more or less upon you – yr servants & domestic affairs ... and as appears probable ... children of yr own to educate? Can you hesitate?[14]

Although Lady Brooke certainly did not abandon her gay social round (her relationship with the Prince of Wales became notorious in the 1890s), neither was she deaf to such appeals. Throughout her life she proved a conscientious benefactor to her 'tenants and dependants'. Not only was the housekeeper instructed to send blankets, coal and food to pregnant mothers, the old and the sick, but at Christmas distributions of bread and meat were made by Lady Brooke personally, aided by the parson.[15]

Another country-house lady who combined an active social life with her charitable duties was Margaret, Countess of Jersey. As she told a friend wryly, the most appropriate epitaph for her tombstone would be, 'She Gave Away Prizes', so greatly was she in demand to distribute awards to schoolchildren from parishes around the family seats at Middleton Stoney in Oxfordshire and Osterley near London. At the end of her life she claimed there was scarcely a child in Middlesex who had not received a gift from her hands.[16]

For their part, the recipients of this largesse were expected to display humble gratitude. Many genuinely welcomed the help they received and were flattered that their social superiors should devote time to them. One woman, a former cook who had married the gamekeeper on an estate and lived in the lodge, confided that she always kept her baby 'nice because you never knew who they (the Gentry) were bringing in'. A particular lady guest at the Hall frequently called when out walking the dog, 'didn't matter what time of day it was, she'd go and fetch baby out of her cot. And she'd say, I'm never afraid to fetch her out of her cot because she's kept as well as if she was in my own nursery. I did hear her say that ... and I thought, oh ... that's a feather.'[17]

However, others recalled the social control exercised with a sense of bitterness. 'You were under and you dussn't say anything' was how one cottager put it.[18] At Helmingham in Suffolk, for example, the dowager Lady Tollemache encouraged the establishment of coal and clothing clubs in that village and its neighbour, while cottages were kept in good repair and allotments provided. But in return, boys were expected to touch their cap or forelock and girls to curtsey when they met members of the Tollemache family. One girl who failed to offer the requisite mark of respect to Lady Tollemache remembered being caned for it in school the next day.[19] It was a system which, at the end of her life, the Countess of Warwick condemned severely, comparing it to 'something akin to serfdom':

> The landowning classes expected a certain fealty, a certain acceptance of the view of those who gave the 'dole'. Blankets, soup, coals, rabbits, and the rest were all paid for, though not in cash – because the recipients were the poorest of the poor – but in subservience, in the surrender of all personality, and in a certain measure of humility from which there could be no escape.[20]

However, this was written in the 1930s, when such practices were already seen as outmoded. In the Victorian and Edwardian years, attitudes were very different. Then the role of 'Lady Bountiful' was expected of the wives and daughters of all landed families who took their social responsibilities seriously. Linked with this was a feeling among many of them that their personal behaviour should provide an example to the working classes. Hence the elaborate observance of Sunday as a day of rest in some households. Even card playing was banned because it provided a bad example to the servants, and in a few households the spirit of Sabbatarianism was so strong that no cooking was permitted on that day.[21] Regular family attendance at church on the Sabbath was also part of the same process, as was the practice of some girls, like Alice Harbord, Lord Suffield's daughter, of playing the organ in the village church for Sunday services.[22] In this way moral standards could be visibly maintained in the community.

Among older women, meanwhile, the opportunities for social leadership also led to the laying down of norms of behaviour to be observed by younger members of their own class. Lady Tweedsmuir remembered the sense of inferiority induced by the dominant dowagers she encountered as a girl at her first balls:

> Any good looks or social graces one possessed shrivelled away under

the raking searchlight of the *lorgnons* ... I often felt worthless and out of place, ... any charm or usefulness I had in daily life vanishing like a wreath of mist in a chill wind ... But the serried ranks of dowagers sitting bolt upright on gilded chairs or sofas round the room underneath glittering chandeliers intimidated much bolder spirits than mine.[23]

An allied activity which these older ladies took up with zeal was the art of matchmaking. Lord Suffield, for one, claimed that his marriage at the early age of twenty-three was engineered entirely by his widowed mother and her friend, Mrs Baring, mother of the prospective bride. 'My wooing was not long a-doing,' he later wrote, 'for both the mothers greatly desired the match. So our engagement was very brief, all the arrangements being made by the parents, as was the custom in those days, nothing being left to us but to follow them dutifully.'[24]

About half a century later, the matchmaking preoccupations of Lady Minto were made very clear when in 1906 she asked her sister, Louisa Antrim, to 'scan the peerage' for suitable young men to introduce to her daughters. Lady Antrim speedily cooperated, producing a list of possible candidates:

Why not Lord Glamis – nearly twenty-two – he is quite delightful in every way ... I believe the Alfred Fitzroy son is nice – I don't know what age but he might be worth thinking of. Zena also says Lord Compton is ... perfectly delightful. Why not ask him out as a cousin. Lord Lucas I know you are prejudiced against and also I think he is surly and sober and has only one leg ... I suppose Ed. Wood is no good ... Young Curzon I should certainly ask – I like his face.[25]

In the event, one Minto daughter married the Earl of Cromer, another took Lord Lansdowne's younger son as her first husband and Lord Astor of Hever as her second, while a third girl, after being prevented from marrying an 'unsuitable' candidate of her own choice eventually settled for the sixth son of the Duke of Buccleuch.[26] Daughters were soon made aware by their mothers as to who was, or was not, regarded as an acceptable partner. Lady Constance Primrose noted drily that her mother had been 'in a fidget' when she spent 'a great deal' of time in conversation with a Mr Morill.[27] A month or two later Constance became engaged to Henry Wyndham, son and heir of the wealthy Lord Leconfield, and hence a thoroughly eligible spouse from her mother's point of view.

It was against this background that Lord David Cecil considered that in his youth at the turn of the century, 'the life of family and personal relations ... was looked upon as being just as valuable and important as public life, and ... [it] was the women who were responsible for it. They ruled in family and social life as much as the men did in public life and they were eminent for the qualities that made private life and personal relations precious; sensibility, imaginative sympathy, social ease, and often instinctive wisdom'.[28] Nonetheless, while countless 'ladies of the manor' enjoyed the outer trappings of power and authority within their own circle, at a deeper level these impressions of dominance and control were misleading. In a majority of cases the wives and daughters of aristocratic and gentry families, like their middle-class counterparts, were dependent for status and material well-being upon their close male relatives, be they father, husband, brother or cousin. Of course, a few strong-minded dowagers like Frances Anne, Marchioness of Londonderry, and Sarah, Countess of Jersey, were able to control their own financial and business affairs with single-minded determination and efficiency. Lady Jersey had inherited a good deal of the Child banking fortune and was able to retain power over it even following her marriage. She was a director of the firm for most of her life, and several years after her death in 1867, a newly married granddaughter-in-law discovered that around the family seat at Middleton Stoney her influence was still strong:

> The fear and awe of her seemed to overhang the village, and the children were still supposed to go to the Infant School at two years old because she had thought it a suitable age ... But she was ... exceedingly good to the poor people on the property ... One old woman ... told me how she had heard of her death soon after receiving a present from her, and added, 'I thought she went straight to heaven for sending me that petticoat!'[29]

At her death Lady Jersey's personal estate was valued at approaching £300,000.

However, women such as she were the exceptions. For most ladies this degree of self-assertiveness not only conflicted with the expected norms of aristocratic behaviour but was impossible on monetary grounds. Despite the creation of family trusts, designed to protect a wife's financial position and to provide a jointure should she be widowed, and the passing of Married Women's Property legislation in 1870 and 1882, the purse strings of the vast majority of females were in male hands. Under the terms of large numbers of marriage settlements, the bulk of the annual income was held by the husband while the wife received only pin money. This was reinforced, especially in the early and mid-Victorian years, by the women's ready acceptance of their subordinate position. Typical of many was Lucy Arkwright who wrote to her husband in 1867, 'I cannot bear to *think* or *do* anything that you do not like. I am glad to have somebody to think for me & to take care of me.'[30]

It was, indeed, in economic and political affairs that the essentially 'derivative' role of women was seen at its clearest, as compared to that of their male relatives. Not only were ladies of the manor, like all other females at that time, debarred from exercising the parliamentary franchise, but they were excluded from the magistracy, too, until after 1918. Admittedly some of them began to play an active part in local government, especially from the 1890s, but they were always heavily outnumbered by the men. In other cases, as with Lady Randolph Churchill, or Rosalind Howard, the future Countess of Carlisle, canvassing on behalf of a husband or male family member gave an opportunity for the exercise of political talents. In 1885, Lady Randolph masterminded the campaign for her husband's re-election for the Woodstock constituency when, as was customary in those days, he had to re-contest the seat on being given office in the then Conservative government. Randolph himself decided to take no part in the electioneering, so it was left to his wife and his sister, Lady Georgiana Curzon, to rally support. The constituency was centred around the Churchill family seat, Blenheim Palace, and Lady Randolph's experiences indicated both the scope – and the frustrations – of this kind of vicarious female involvement in parliamentary politics. The Conservatives had their headquarters at the Bear Hotel in Woodstock and Lady Randolph was soon at work:

Revelling in the hustle and bustle of the committee-rooms, marshalling our forces, and hearing the hourly reports of how the campaign was progressing. I felt like a general holding a council-of-war with his staff in the heat of a battle ... Sometimes with these simple country-folk a pleading look, and an imploring, 'Oh, please vote for my husband; I shall be so unhappy if he does not get in' or, 'If you want to be on the winning side, vote for us, as, of course, we are going to win,' would be as effective as the election agent's longest speeches ... Lady Georgiana Curzon, who was a beautiful driver, brought down her ... tandem, and we scoured the country with our smart turnout, the horses gaily decorated with ribbons of pink and brown, Randolph's racing colours. Sometimes we would drive into the fields, and getting down, climb the hayricks, falling upon our unwary prey at his work ... Party feeling ran high, and in outlying districts we would frequently be pursued by our opponents, jeering and shouting at us...

At the end of a tiring fortnight, Randolph was returned at the head of the poll. From the window of the Bear Hotel I made a little speech to the crowd, and thanked them ... I surpassed the fondest hopes of the Suffragettes, and thought I was duly elected, and I certainly experienced all the pleasure and gratification of being a successful candidate. I returned to London feeling that I had done a very big thing, and was surprised and astonished that the crowds in the streets looked at me with indifference.[31]

Despite the efforts of reformers, not until 1918 were women able to stand for parliament in their own right. Soon after, in November 1919 a country-house lady – the American-born Lady Astor – became the first female to take her seat as an MP. In this context her nationality was probably no accident, for transatlantic peeresses were widely considered to be more independent-minded and self-confident than their home-grown counterparts.[32]

In economic matters the subordinate position of female members of the landed elite was equally obvious. As Lawrence Stone and Jeanne Fawtier Stone have pointed out, daughters were often regarded with disfavour by parents because of the financial burden they represented. They were 'expensive to maintain in clothes and finery and to equip with fashionable educational polish like dancing and French, and were even more expensive to marry' because of the portion that had to be found for them if they were to make an appropriate match. Barbara Tasburgh (later Charlton) of Burghwallis Hall, Yorkshire, was certainly not alone when she bitterly recalled that although she was her mother's favourite, she 'certainly was not my father's, who ... thought a third daughter a superfluous addition to his family'.[33] Similarly Lady Maud Cecil, eldest child of the 3rd Marquess of Salisbury, remembered being 'very much offended' when, at the age of three, shortly after her eldest brother was born, she heard 'so many people say when addressing the baby, "It is a good thing it *was* a boy this time." From that period,' she added, 'I began to look at life from a feminist standpoint'.[34]

This view of daughters as second-class citizens was, often enough, accepted by mothers, and found expression in their anxiety to bear sons rather than daughters, in order to secure the male succession for family and estate. Lady Mosley, third daughter of Lord Redesdale, recalled that when she was born in June 1910, her mother cried. 'She was to have seven children, six of them girls, and she wanted only boys. I was the fourth child, and in my case it was particularly annoying because had I been a boy the family would have been nicely balanced: two of each.'[35]

Tina Lucy of Charlecote Park, Warwickshire, experienced similar emotions when in March 1870 her third daughter came into the world. According to Mary Elizabeth Lucy, her formidable mother-in-law, she 'could not at all be reconciled to her disappointment that this new baby was not a boy. She kept crying and saying, "Oh! What will Spencer [her husband] say to me for having another girl."'[36] In the event, the Lucys did not have a son and on Spencer's death the estate passed to another branch of the family.

The position of Henrietta Bankes of Kingston Lacy, Dorset, was even more galling until a son was born to her in 1902, after two daughters. There were rumours that her husband's mistress had already borne him two healthy and good-looking boys – the elder of them named after him. But all was forgiven when the much-desired heir appeared. According to his sister, the 'great bell in the stables … resounded at the moment of birth and wild celebrations began. Oxen were roasted whole, bonfires lit, fireworks exploded into the balmy air. Excitement and relief flooded house, farm and estate, at the long-awaited leap into life of my … brother.'[37]

Failure to produce a son and heir was, then, regarded as a serious fault on the part of any wife in landed society. Equally unsatisfactory was the failure of a girl to marry at all. Although by the 1880s and 1890s demographic change and the tendency for younger sons to enter colonial or military service abroad were reducing the opportunities for country-house daughters to marry, the old attitudes persisted. The two unmarried Grosvenor sisters of Moor Park, Hertfordshire, were regarded as mere ciphers by other members of the family. They 'had reached middle age without it having ever apparently occurred to them to start homes of their own,' wrote a sister-in-law. 'They migrated with their parents from Moor Park to London and back again … twice yearly. To a certain extent they had made a life of their own among their neighbours both rich and poor, but they were essentially dependent on their parents, and had nominally neither control nor freedom.'[38] When parents died, the predicament of such women could become even worse, unless they had sufficient means to establish a household of their own. For all too often, with the loss of their father they became 'enforced and unwelcome pensioners on the bounty of brothers or more distant relatives,' as an American commentator put it in the mid-1880s.[39] Yet, at the end of the nineteenth century it has been estimated that about a third of peers' daughters remained single. This was seen not merely as social failure but as likely to lead to uterine disorders and even mental problems as these women grew older.[40] 'Marriage,' as Leonore Davidoff has pointed out,

> was not so much an alliance between the sexes as an important social definition; serious for a man but imperative for a girl. It was part of her … duty to enlarge her sphere of influence through marriage … A girl's

whole life from babyhood was oriented to the part she had to play in this 'status theatre'.[41]

Where spinsters were dependent upon male relatives for financial backing, that could lead to personal exploitation. And after the death of a father or the marriage of a brother for whom they had acted as hostess, they were faced with the possible loss not only of a home but of their domestic function as well. Some, like Margaret Wyndham, Lord Leconfield's youngest daughter, spent much time visiting family and friends or engaging in charitable activities. But the regular round of country-house visits could pall. 'I got here yesterday, & as I expected the party is not a very amusing one,' Margaret wrote to her mother during one such visit in November 1912. 'Teddy Campion is the nice feature, the others are strangers to me.'[42] This visit was followed by one to her eldest sister. Then came preparations for a Red Cross demonstration at the home of another relative, and two further country-house visits, before she returned to the family seat, Petworth, now occupied by her brother, for a shooting party on 3 December.[43]

Sometimes an unmarried daughter would make her home with her widowed mother, as did Theodora, youngest daughter of the 2nd Marquess of Westminster. And when, in her late thirties, Theodora at last married, her mother remained with the couple, lavishing on her new son-in-law the devotion she had once given to her husband.[44]

Very different was the experience of Lady Leigh's unmarried daughters. Their mother, towards the end of her life, made them feel their inferiority by demoting them 'to a position where they could be arbitrarily silenced' should she wish to hear the opinion of her newly married granddaughters, who, although only in their twenties, yet had the status of matrons'.[45] 'Spinsters,' wrote Lady Muriel Beckwith of her Victorian youth, '... were compelled to keep up attitude. Their hair might turn grey, and their cheeks become wrinkled, but they remained girlish, simpered, walked delicately.'[46]

Only the fortunate few were able, like Louisa Jebb, to find a niche in the household of a married brother where they were welcomed and valued. Louisa ran the household for her sister-in-law and was regarded as a second mother by the six Jebb children, who were born between 1872 and 1881. She was 'the companion of pranks, the inspirer of dreams' and remained an important figure in the lives of the children until her death in 1925.[47]

The inferior economic position of women in country-house society was, however, at its most obvious in the matter of land ownership itself. As a result of the application of the principle of primogeniture and of patrilineal descent, it was rare for property to pass to or through the female line. Between 1840 and 1880, for example, it has been suggested that only about eight or ten per cent of property transfers were made to women, because of a failure in the male line. If properties transferred through women were added, the proportion still amounted to only around twelve to fifteen per cent.[48]

This is confirmed by John Bateman's survey of *The Great Landowners of Great Britain and Ireland*, the fourth edition of which was published in 1883. It revealed that of fifteen landowners with annual incomes from land of £100,000 or more at that time none was female; and of fifty-one with an income of between £50,000 and £100,000 only one – Lady Willoughby d'Eresby – was female. She had inherited the family estates as a result of the death of an unmarried brother in 1870 and when she herself died in 1888, the property passed to her only son and heir. Four years later he was created Earl of Ancaster.[49] At her death, Lady Willoughby d'Eresby left a personal estate valued at £188,306.

On a national basis, the Bateman survey revealed that just under seven per cent of the country's major landowners (that is, those holding 3,000 acres or more) were women; of the minor landowners (those holding between 2,000 and 3,000 acres or receiving between £2,000 and £3,000 a year rental from estates of over 3,000 acres) about eight per cent were female. Pride in their family name and a desire that it should continue led many landowners to ensure that, where possible, property passed to collateral male relatives. They were then expected to adopt the family name, if necessary, and thus secure a continuation of the 'historical association of family and estate'.[50]

Linked to this was the essentially male-dominated nature of the British peerage itself. Out of 580 peers in 1880, only seven were females holding a title in their own right.[51] Because of their sex, none was able to sit in the House of Lords.

As a result of these attitudes, where there were both sons and daughters in a family, it was normal for the estate and the bulk of any cash assets to pass to the heir, while younger sons and daughters received comparatively modest capital sums, and the widow was provided for through a jointure or annuity charge on the estate.[52] Hence when Lord Leconfield died in 1901 the bulk of his £1.8 million estate was inherited by his eldest surviving son, Charles. The four younger sons received £150,000 apiece, plus a share in some further smaller amounts, and on their mother's death her home at Great Stanhope Street in London was to be sold and divided equally among them. The three daughters received only £32,000 each, plus a small additional sum of just over £2,000. Two elder girls, who were both married, had received their £32,000 under the terms of their marriage settlement. The youngest girl, Margaret, who was unmarried, obtained her inheritance on her father's death.[53]

A similar arrangement occurred, albeit on a far smaller scale, when Simon Yorke of Erddig died in 1894. The bulk of his £29,000 estate went to the heir, Philip, although he had to provide his mother with an annuity of £700 for life. But Philip's two sisters received just £1,500 apiece. If invested at the then going interest rate of four per cent, this would have secured each of them precisely £60 a year. Perhaps fortunately, both women were already married when their father died.[54]

Concern to secure a male inheritor for their estates did not, ironically, prevent landowners from regarding a wealthy wife as a possible means for an heir to restore the family's fortunes, if these were at a low ebb. Lord Monson, after succeeding to the title in 1841, repeatedly urged his eldest son 'to find a girl with a fortune to rescue the house of Monson from its predicaments, which were mainly caused by the prolonged burden of two dowagers until 1851 and one survivor until 1891'. One candidate considered in 1850 was reputed to enjoy an annual income of £9,000 – subsequently increased to £15,000: 'there are two younger daughters of £40,000 each, not bad but the first is the large prize. I should be very sorry for you to marry for money but a nice wife with it would not be bad.' The following year he reproved his son because although an aunt had recommended many rich girls to him he had not selected any of them. 'Lord have mercy on you if she does ferret out a young heiress.'[55] In the event the Monson heir did not marry until after his father's death and then he chose the widow of the Earl of Yarborbugh.

Small wonder, in such circumstances, that the *Sixpenny Magazine* of 1861 should run an article entitled 'Heiress Hunters' in which it claimed that men with 'an old name and a young face' could 'ferret out dowries, scent a mile off a wealthy father-in-law, and fall at a dead set before the rich heiress'.[56] These tactics became all the more necessary in the final quarter of the nineteenth century when the effects of agricultural depression led to a decline in rental income for many landed families. It came at a time when the financial demands imposed by an increasingly luxurious and pleasure-seeking social life were increasing, thereby adding to the pressures to find extra revenue. Hence in 1896 when the future Marquess of Bristol married Alice Wythes, daughter of a former contractor for public works, a trustee of the Bristol estate congratulated him on the move: 'It is most fortunate that the large fortune which your fiancée has, and will inherit, renders … further encumbrances unnecessary.'[57] Likewise Lady Meath, a daughter of the 11th Earl of Lauderdale, openly admitted that her dowry had been essential for her husband's ambitious social reform plans. 'Just eight years since the death of my father,' she wrote in 1886, '... It is his economy that has enabled us to do much which otherwise would have been quite an impossibility.'[58]

But while Lady Meath was happy for such arrangements to continue, other critics condemned the mercenary attitudes which they induced. Among them was the writer, Marie Corelli, who in 1898 attacked the whole spirit behind this aristocratic marriage market:

> It is an absolute grim fact that in England, women – those of the upper classes, at any rate – are not today married, but bought for a price. The high and noble intention of marriage is entirely lost sight of in the scheming, the bargaining and the pricing.[59]

Although exaggerated, the complaint had some validity. Consuelo Vanderbilt, an American heiress, recalled bitterly that soon after her marriage to the 9th Duke of Marlborough he bluntly informed her that he had married her for her money. Under the terms of the marriage settlement, her father had provided an income of $100,000 a year for herself and the Duke, plus a further $100,000 a year for her 'separate use'.[60] Marlborough had 'made up his mind to marry me and to give up the girl he loved, as he told me ... For to live at Blenheim in the pomp and circumstance he considered essential needed money, and a sense of duty to his family and to his traditions indicated the sacrifice of personal desires.'[61] Consuelo, for her part, had married the duke largely because of pressure from her socially ambitious mother, and similar motives led to a number of other marriages between well-to-do American girls and British peers in the half-century before the First World War.[62]

Although not all transatlantic marriages were made for such blatantly materialistic motives as those of Consuelo Vanderbilt and the Duke of Marlborough, they were certainly not unique. Fortunately few bridegrooms went as far as the Earl of Yarmouth, heir to the Marquess of Hertford. In 1905 he married Alice Thaw, daughter of a Pittsburgh millionaire, and when the marriage was annulled three years later it was revealed that the earl had demanded payment of the dowry in advance. This had temporarily delayed the wedding ceremony. After the annulment, the countess agreed to continue paying her former husband an allowance of $40,000 per annum. 'Allegedly, this was in return for the earl's agreement to the nullification of the marriage; he did not contest the decree, which was granted on grounds of non-consummation.'[63]

It was events like these that led Marie Corelli to claim dramatically in 1905 that there was always a British title going a-begging – always some decayed or degenerative or semi-drunken peer, whose fortunes are on the verge of black ruin, ready and willing to devour, monster-like, the holocaust of an American virgin, provided bags of bullion are flung, with her, into his capacious maw.[64]

Such, then, were the undercurrents and concerns which affected the lives of Victorian and Edwardian ladies of the manor. As they look out from their photographs, serene and assured, it is easy to forget the nagging anxieties and frustrations that many of them experienced and the responsibilities they bore. The beautiful Consuelo, Duchess of Marlborough, despite personal unhappiness, did not neglect her duties as mistress of an important landed estate. Not only did she bear two sons in the first three years of married life, thereby assuring the succession, but she carried through her role as 'Lady Bountiful' with grace and conviction. This included visits to the poor, listening to old ladies 'whose complaints had to be heard and whose infirmities had to be cared for', and reading to the blind. Each day after family prayers the curate told her of any sick or poor people who needed her personal attention, and at Christmas there were trees to be provided for the schoolchildren and teas for the older people: 'Every morning, with my sisters-in-law and the housekeeper, I made up bundles of clothing and gifts to be taken to the poor.'[65] In the villages around Blenheim Park, Consuelo came to be much loved. When the coach and four was heard in the distance, writes one historian of the family, 'cottagers popped in for a spotless apron, to pop out in time to drop a curtsey as the ducal equipage passed; but personal visits by the … Duchess … made red-letter days'. Years later an old woman described how the previous night she had dreamt that Consuelo had called and had told her that hers was the cleanest cottage she had ever been in. 'Such visits and such dreams were treasured in a way which nowadays might easily be despised; yet treasured they were and they made for happiness and self-respect,' was this writer's somewhat complacent conclusion.[66]

But while many country-house ladies followed Consuelo's example and performed the duties expected of them conscientiously, there were some who bitterly resented the narrowness of their lives and the limitations of the patriarchal society in which they lived. Of none was this more true than Florence Nightingale. 'Ladies' work has always to be fitted in,' she wrote bitterly in 1841, 'where a man is, his business is the law.' Just over a decade later, when in her early thirties, she compared the restraints placed on female development with the freedom allowed to men:

Women are never supposed to have any occupation of sufficient importance *not* to be interrupted … In a country house, if there is a large party of young people, 'You will spend the morning with us,' they say to the neighbours, 'we will drive together in the afternoon, tomorrow we will make an expedition, and we will spend the evening together.' And this is thought friendly and spending time in a pleasant manner. So women play through life … They are taught from their infancy upwards that it is a wrong, ill-tempered, and a misunderstanding of 'woman's mission' (with a great M) if they do not allow themselves *willingly* to be interrupted at all hours … The actual life is passed in sympathy, given or received for a dinner, a party, a piece of furniture, a house built or a garden laid out well, in devotion to your guests … in schemes of schooling for the poor, which you follow up perhaps in an odd quarter of an hour, between luncheon and driving out in the carriage – broth and dripping are included in the plan – and the rest of your time goes in ordering the dinner, hunting for a governess for your children, and sending pheasants and apples to your poorer relations … The time is come when women must do something more than the 'domestic hearth', which means nursing the infants, keeping a pretty house, having a good dinner and an entertaining party.[67]

Fortunately, the vast majority of females accepted their lot with more philosophy and better grace than did Miss Nightingale. After all, they had been conditioned to it from childhood.[68]

2

Growing Up in a Country House

I had a nurse I very much disliked ... When annoyed she had a habit of shaking me, & I remember thinking her thoroughly unreasonable ... In the summer holidays we usually went to the seaside, sometimes in England, more often in France, & granny & the aunts sometimes came to the same places ... Till I was ten I had very little education. Daily governesses of a transitory character, & a few classes like dancing & gymnastics. I learnt to read, & I think read a good deal, as when I was ten I first made acquaintance with Macaulay's essays ... Boys went to preparatory schools & then on to public schools ... but it was not at all usual for girls of the upper class to go to boarding schools.

Recollections of the Countess of Selborne, the former Lady Maud Cecil (b. 1858), eldest child of the 3rd Marquess of Salisbury.[1]

The daily routine of most country-house girls was strictly regulated so as to instil in them the correct moral, social and religious attitudes. One of Estella, Countess Cave's earliest memories was of a hymn resolutely

sung by the nurse, we children having to sing as best we could after her:

Round the throne of God in Heaven
Thousands of children stand;
Children whose sins are forgiven,
A holy, happy band.

Such youngsters were taught that the privileges they inherited carried with them certain responsibilities, and they were reminded of the importance of upholding the reputation and traditions of the family. Years later Lady Aberdeen remembered how as a child she had had 'an abiding fear of bringing the names of my parents and their forebears into disgrace'.[2] While Vita Sackville-West's governess stressed the obligation to lineage and kin when she tried to encourage decorous behaviour in her young charge by reminding her of the ancient line to which she belonged, saying, 'My child, remember who you *are*.'[3] This sense of family identity was strengthened by the houses in which many of the children lived, with their impressive architecture, sculptures, furniture and ancestral portraits. 'We had ... a solid base to set forth and face the world with,' was Lady Muriel Beckwith's comment.[4]

From an early age little girls learnt the importance of their role as a future 'Lady Bountiful'. They accompanied their mother or other female relatives on charitable excursions, and carried out specially assigned tasks, such as sewing baby clothes and flannel petticoats for cottage families, or distributing food to the needy. Mabell Gore remembered that when she and her sisters stayed with their paternal relatives large gallipots were brought into the dining-room each day after luncheon and

> into them were ladled the remains of the most succulent dishes, to be taken to invalids. We children used to cast wistful eyes on our favourite puddings as they were whisked off the table ... With appetites still unsatisfied we used to set out immediately after luncheon, on foot or in the jaunting car, to deliver the gallipots to the chosen recipients.[5]

In addition, on Sundays they spent the time between breakfast and the morning service in painting religious texts, 'dreadfully printed and embellished with stiff floral sprays – to be taken back to London and wrapped round the pennies which we were encouraged to distribute to beggars'.[6] As a further stimulus to their charitable instincts they were also given 'a continuous supply of tracts to read, varied by books such as *Daisy in the Field* and *Ministering Children*, which had a prominent place in most well-conducted schoolrooms ... as fostering the spirit of charity, and affording the necessary insight into the conditions of the poor'.

The diaries of Cecilia (Lily) Harbord likewise reveal frequent visits to cottagers on the Suffield estate at Gunton, Norfolk. On 2 February 1877, shortly before they were due to go to London she and two younger sisters carried out a round of charitable calls on elderly tenants: 'took a bundle of clothes to Whitwood & some wine etc. to old Mrs Barber'.[7] Each of the older girls also 'adopted' a daughter of one of the cottage families from nearby Thorpe, for whom they made clothes and provided other gifts. In August 1877, Cecilia went with twelve-year-old Winifred to 'choose her child. We selected Amelia Sexton, little Mrs Sexton's youngest daughter – aged three yrs. – a nice little thing with curly golden hair. Frida is delighted.'[8]

At Aston Clinton, Buckinghamshire, there was yet another variation on the theme, when Constance and Annie de Rothschild were allowed by their mother to help with the teaching at the village school. Constance developed 'a passion for teaching' when she was eleven, and she and her sister enjoyed themselves 'immensely' instructing the little girls.[9] Both of them also helped Lady de Rothschild distribute clothing and blankets to the poor.

On a broader basis, however, the part played by parents in the education and training of their children was more limited. While Augusta, Lady Midleton and Julian, Lady Radnor taught their children to read, and Edith Cropper 'leaped about the furniture with her children, played the piano while they danced, sang to them, read aloud, and showed them her treasure cabinet', other mothers remained remote or indifferent.[10]

Both tradition and an active social life ensured that much maternal supervision of children in landed society was intermittent. Even affectionate mothers, like Lucy Arkwright of Hampton Court, Herefordshire, often left their children at home or with relatives while they went on a series of visits.[11] Hence it was upon nannies, governesses and other servants that the responsibility for bringing up the children largely devolved, until they were ready to enter the adult world or, in the case of boys, were old enough to go away to school. Nurses might have sole charge of large families for weeks at a time while parents were away and, often enough, were expected to escort them on unaccompanied holidays to the seaside or the country. Close relationships might be formed with other servants, too, especially cooks and housekeepers who gave treats such as chocolate, cakes, and ices to add variety to the monotonous nursery diet, or younger maids who were inveigled into joining in impromptu games. Susan Tweedsmuir recalled that the servants' lives 'appeared to us to be so much more ... alluring than that of the elders in our family', while the Grosvenor cousins enjoyed visiting the servants' quarters because

> the atmosphere behind the baize door was one of jokes and laughter, and from a child's point of view far preferable to that of the drawing-room where we found it only too easy to knock something over ... [The] vivid and interesting life going on below stairs was like the difference

between eating plain bread and rich cake...[12]

Even when they were at home, many parents took the view that children should be seen and not heard. As Lady Muriel Beckwith observed, 'signs of individuality in the young, if observed, were firmly nipped in the bud ... the child was only permitted to think under supervision'.[13] In such cases contacts between mothers and offspring might be limited to formal daily visits – the so-called 'children's hour' – for which the youngsters were carefully prepared. B. L. Booker, who grew up in London during the 1890s, recalled meeting her mother only once a day, after tea, in the drawing-room: 'We lived upstairs in a different world and were at the mercy of our nurses.'[14]

Vita Sackville-West also resented her mother's lack of sympathetic interest in her; her mother even told her as a little girl that she 'couldn't bear to look at [her] because [she] was so ugly'. Vita was afraid of Lady Sackville's quick temper, too, but the latter none the less tried to impart to her daughter her own shaky moral principles. 'One must always tell the truth, darling, if one can, but not *all* the truth; *toute vérité n'est pas bonne à dire*.'[15] However, Lady Sackville's attitude may have been influenced not only by her daughter's tomboyish character but by the fact that she had been excommunicated because, a Catholic herself, she had refused to bring up her only child as a Roman Catholic.

However, one of the strangest examples of this lack of intimacy between parents and children involved Viola Bankes of Kingston Lacy, Dorset. In 1904, when she was four, her father died at home. Neither she nor her sister, who was about two years her senior, realised what had happened. They only learnt the truth five years later when a governess inadvertently revealed that he was not in India, as they had believed, but had been dead for a long time.[16] Nearly eight decades later Viola still remembered the shock this sudden discovery had been.

Such remoteness between family members was, of course, reinforced by the large size and complex layout of the houses in which they lived, with the children's nursery and schoolroom usually situated on the top storey, well away from the adults' main living quarters. To small children, these large mansions, lit by candles, oil lamps or gas, could easily become gloomy labyrinths when it grew dark. At Stanway, Lady Cynthia Charteris found the downstairs rooms 'seemingly vast, and for a long time uncharted regions'.[17] While Susan Tweedsmuir on a childhood visit to Castle Howard, remembered being 'constantly lost. I wandered in a sort of bad dream, crying for my nurse and my parents, among the legs of endless gilded tables in wide passages hung with tapestries and pictures.'[18]

Often, where a family owned several properties, or where the parents were in London a great deal, perhaps in connection with a father's political career, youngsters did not even live in the same house as their parents for several months of the year. May Harcourt, whose husband was a member of the Liberal Government, described one such arrangement in 1909. She herself had spent some days at Nuneham Park, the Harcourt family seat in Oxfordshire, while the children stayed at her mother's home, Mymms Park, Hertfordshire. On her way up to London she planned to spend two nights at Mymms 'to see the children', then two nights in London, before going to her husband's constituency in north-east Lancashire.[19] Earlier in the year, while taking a lengthy 'cure' at Bad Nauheim in Germany, she had reported that the children were 'entertaining a series of guests on their own' at Nuneham, under the supervision of their nurse, their father remaining in London.[20] But in her case a partial explanation for these frequent separations lay in her belief that the youngsters were healthier in the country than in London. '[They] have come up from Mymms in teeming health & spirits,' she wrote on one occasion. 'I feel quite guilty in having them in London [where] they will begin to get white & peeky but they are a great joy.'[21]

Far more painful problems of childhood isolation arose when parents' marriages broke down. This was Nancy Cunard's unfortunate fate. She was born at Nevill Holt, Leicestershire, in 1896. Her beautiful, American-born mother soon grew tired of the limitations of English country life and the sporting preoccupations of her middle-aged husband. Furthermore, as Nancy's biographer drily observes, in Lady Cunard the maternal instincts 'were not strong', and from an early stage she was happy to hand over the care of her only child to servants. Lady Cunard professed 'a deep distaste for motherhood, which she called "a low thing – the lowest"'.[22] Hence much of her time was spent with friends in London and at country-house weekends, or in travelling abroad, while Nancy's father, Sir Bache, pursued a sporting round in which his daughter had little part. The little girl spent long periods alone with the household's forty or so domestic staff, interspersed with sudden invasions by her mother and a weekend party. 'My picture of Holt,' recalled Nancy fifty years later,

> is one of constant arrivals and departures during half the year, of elaborate long teas on the lawn with tennis and croquet going on, of great winter logs blazing all day in the Hall and Morning Room, with people playing bridge there for hours on end.[23]

Her own role in all this was peripheral, although she was allowed to put flowers in the guests' bedrooms and to help check that the writing desks were fully equipped with pens, ink, and paper. She was also befriended by some of the guests, including the author, George Moore, who was on intimate terms with her mother. But as she grew up her relations with Lady Cunard worsened, and in adolescence one of her main objects in life was to escape from her mother's influence.

Clearly, then, household structures and the personalities of parents all contributed to the kind of relationship which grew up between adults and offspring.

Another factor was, as Osbert Sitwell cynically noted, the parents' awareness that children could be noisy nuisances. Consequently,

> a whole hedge of servants, in addition to the complex guardianship of nursery and schoolroom, was necessary, not so much to aid the infant as to screen him off from his father and mother, except on such occasions as he could be used by them as adjunct, toy or decoration.[24]

This segregation applied to all aspects of the children's lives. Meals for the nursery and schoolroom were prepared separately from the rest of the household, and the dietary requirements specified by a nanny for her young charges often led to ill-feeling between her and the kitchen staff. Food was frequently monotonous. One woman employed as a nursemaid in a large household in Yorkshire remembered nursery luncheons as consisting of jellied soup, fish or chicken, followed by a milk pudding, while tea comprised thin bread and butter, jam and sponge cake. Milk, sterilised in the nursery's own steriliser, was drunk, and all water used was boiled; no child was allowed to drink from a tap. In this house the nursery even had its own china, silver and linen, and when the children were old enough to go downstairs for Sunday tea they took their mugs, plates and table napkins with them.[25] Small wonder that May Harcourt in 1908 considered that in any household it was 'always nurseries, children & governesses which make the difficulties & it certainly adds enormously to the work ... in every department'.[26]

Larger houses had both day and night nurseries, as well as separate bedrooms for the older children. The head nurse normally slept in the same room as the most recent baby. Furnishings were often handed down from one generation to the next and might be very shabby. They contrasted sharply with the luxury to be found in the rest of the house. This was partly for practical reasons, so that the youngsters could romp freely without damaging valuable articles, but it also seems to have been the custom to use the nursery as a repository for items of furniture not wanted elsewhere. Lucy Lyttelton, second daughter of the 4th Lord Lyttelton, remembered her London nursery in the

1840s as containing a battered dirty red work-table with a hole in it, through which she used to poke her finger, a massive white wardrobe for clothes, and a high white cupboard where the toys were kept. A dark wood cupboard stood against one wall and in it were stored the breakfast, dinner and tea things as well as some cold plum pudding left on one side from the servants' supper![27]

The girls' toys normally included a doll's house, a rocking-horse, and 'a screen decorated with cut-out pictures and old Christmas cards'.[28] Only tomboyish girls like Vita Sackville-West could boast a bow-and-arrow, soldiers, a fort, and 'swords and guns'.[29] Far more typical was Viola Bankes who remembered creaking up and down on a huge, dappled rocking-horse, or rearranging miniature furniture in the doll's house her father had given her. Her older sister, Daphne, would embroider 'in the corner of a white cotton square, in huge, vivid stitches', while they listened to the singing of the canary. Viola's favourite toys were a black golliwog with a blue coat and scarlet trousers, and a 'plump stuffed dog called Leo', which she used to drag along for walks up and down the long nursery on a leather string.[30]

But in less prosperous households conditions could be much more austere. To the end of her life Barbara Tasburgh recalled the discomfort she and her brother and sisters had experienced at Burghwallis, their Yorkshire home:

> I especially remember having *soi-disant* pet animals in our nursery which was for night as well as day … On one sill was a cage containing a pet squirrel, let loose at times for our diversion, and on the other was a canvas box enclosing caterpillars … This was by way of instructing us in natural history and to this day I can smell the fetid odour of corruption and decay that emerged from that detestable collection…
>
> For playthings we had a stand-up barrel organ and a large rocking-horse, but no toys whatever except those given to us by stray visitors … We were allowed so few enjoyments as children that to dine downstairs on Christmas night … was an unforgotten landmark in our lives…
>
> When my sisters were old enough they had a nursery governess … who was sister to Aunt Anne's [lady's] maid. She may have helped me with my letters, but what I best remember is that she let me play in her room, even when my sisters' lessons were in progress, and I felt very grateful towards her for releasing me from the smelly caterpillar atmosphere.[31]

The clothing worn by well-to-do children for much of the Victorian and Edwardian period was cumbersome and uncomfortable. Little girls wore numerous petticoats – flannel in winter and stiffly starched cotton in summer. For outdoor excursions there were black-buttoned boots, ornate hats, and coats or pelisses, embellished with tucks, frills or pleats.[32] There was also a large amount of 'dressing up' to cope with. According to Sarah Sedgwick, who was a nanny in several large households, winter clothing was worn until the end of May no matter how hot the weather, and summer clothes were retained, irrespective of the temperature, until late September. In winter, the girls wore a vest, 'a woollen binder, drawers, a bodice, a flannel petticoat, and a cotton petticoat; and on top flannel dresses'. Summer saw the flannel petticoat exchanged for one of lighter weight, 'the binder was cotton instead of wool, and the frocks cotton, linen or muslin'. The same clothes were never worn both morning and afternoon and a further complete change was required before the youngsters went downstairs for the 'children's hour'. At that time, Sarah claimed

> no little girl went outside the house without gloves of wool or cashmere … Children were very disciplined in those days. On walks the little girl would hold on to the pram, and never think to run about, and all the children, if they were dressed up for a party, quite understood being tied on to their chairs, or when older sitting perfectly still, so that nothing would get creased.[33]

Many youngsters, needless to say, failed to conform to this virtuous ideal. Vita Sackville-West delighted in getting muddy when playing with local farm children and admitted that at the age of ten she was 'an unsociable and unnatural girl with long black hair and long black legs, and very short frocks and dirty nails and torn clothes'.[34] Frances Maynard from an early stage was permitted to keep a variety of pets, including birds, kittens, rabbits, dogs, and even toads and frogs. She climbed trees 'like any sailor lad, and was able even to reach the nest of golden-crested wrens that built at the top of the highest fir trees'. But her 'best joy of all' were the horses. She began to ride at the age of five and later claimed that she could hardly remember the time when she was unable to do so.[35]

Frances also recalled with deep chagrin that, although a considerable heiress in her own right, she had to wear dresses made from her mother's cast-off gowns until she was about sixteen. Her hair was dragged back from the face and put in numerous small hard plaits, so that on Sunday morning it stood out in an unbecoming mop of crinkly waves.[36] This was apparently to ensure that she did not develop undesirable traits of vanity. Similar moral preoccupations also applied to the Sabbath itself, with the children having to attend church twice a day. 'In place of our usual toys, our religious sensibilities were cultivated with the aid of a Noah's Ark, while a book on the Collects replaced our favourite authors. Like many another child of my era, I hated the dreary humbug of it.'[37]

In those families where contacts between parents and the younger children were restricted to the 'children's hour' the youngsters were brought down by their nurse to the drawing-room and were escorted back to the nursery at the expiration of that time. Maud Cecil recalled how she tried to defeat this rigid routine by creeping downstairs when her nanny was occupied with her baby brother. There she joined her mother in the drawing-room and while the latter wrote letters, she played her own games quietly, hoping her mother would say when the nurse came in pursuit that she 'was quite quiet & might be left'.[38]

In such circumstances mothers could easily come to be seen as distant beings only to be admired from afar. 'You didn't have ... the intimacy that people have with their mothers now,' confessed Joan Poynder (b. 1897) of Hartham Park, Wiltshire, in the mid-1970s. Certainly the young Winston Churchill regarded his mother as a 'fairy princess ... possessed of limitless riches and power ... [She] shone for me like the Evening Star.'[39] While Lady Victoria Buxton's children revered her as a saint – 'something radiant and rather apart, something beautiful and inspiring'. Yet she was seldom demonstrative and rarely used any terms of endearment when they were with her.[40]

Lady Leigh, although small, frail and often in poor health, exerted an almost unbounded influence over her children. 'As middle-aged men and women we have often laughed over the way in which we have still accepted "mama said" so-and-so as a final verdict,' wrote her daughter.[41]

But sometimes these strictly rationed contacts between mothers and children (and especially daughters) were less happy. Nancy Cunard was not alone in resenting her mother's indifference towards her, and one of Estella Mathews' earliest memories of her mother was of being 'slippered' by her because she was noisily defying her nurse when her parents were due to depart for a dinner engagement:

> She put me away from her, saying, 'You naughty little girl, you have completely spoilt my evening,' and ran out of the room to join a shouting papa. 'Come along at once and leave that little wretch alone; we shall be late for dinner,' and the front door slammed.

Most girls were aware that they were regarded as less important than their brothers. This attitude was typified by May Harcourt's comment on hearing that a friend had borne a fifth daughter:

Poor Mildred Chelsea isn't it *cruel* luck. five girls!!! What an infliction. She will now say, 'Not only have I got five girls (instead of four) but I have got to find five fools to marry them,' which was her speech when she was blessed with four daughters.[42]

At this time May herself was pregnant with her second child. She was destined to bear three daughters before the desired son and heir made his appearance.

It was on these gender grounds that Edith Sitwell claimed to have been 'unpopular' with her parents from birth: 'I was in disgrace for being a female, and worse, as I grew older it was obvious that I was not going to conform to my father's standard of feminine beauty.'[43] She recalled her mother as being in a 'constant' rage with her and of once taunting her that as the daughter of the Earl of Londesborough 'she was better born than Edith, whose father was a mere baronet. This Lady Sitwell considered to be the lowest thing on God's earth.'[44]

Still more unfortunate, however, was the Sitwells' reaction to the discovery that their daughter had curvature of the spine. All parents at this time placed great stress upon girls having good deportment – so that a future Duchess of Westminster was made by her mother to wear 'a mahogany backboard ... strapped round her arms and ... tightened and buckled at the back' to prevent her from stooping.[45] Likewise when eighteen-month-old Doris Harcourt was found to have a weak leg she was subjected to electric shock treatment as well as having steel supports in her boots. 'She is ... having her electricity with a new machine which intermits the current & it is therefore *more* of a *shock* than the continuous current.'[46] Doris was presumably too young to make known her dislike of these indignities. But in the case of Edith Sitwell things were very different. A visit to a London orthopaedic surgeon resulted in her being incarcerated in what she called 'a sort of Bastille of steel'. Her imprisonment began under the arms and extended to her legs and ankles. At night these and the soles of her feet were locked up in an excruciating contraption. A device was even produced to straighten her nose. This resulted in one nostril being blocked and breathing made very difficult.[47]

Happily the eccentric relationships which applied in the Sitwell family were absent from most other landed households. Lady Leith, for example, brought up her children in a pleasantly casual and unstructured manner. As a contemporary observed, she allowed 'her family to grow up as best they may while she goes to London with one daughter or two and brings them out.'[48] Sometimes, as with Lady Suffield, Lady Lyttelton and Lady Leconfield, bonds of deep affection united mothers and children. The diaries of Lady Suffield's eldest daughter, Cecilia, abound with loving references to her mother and to the influence she had upon the family. Similarly Lucy Lyttelton referred to the 'gentle and loving care' displayed by her mother even though, like Lady Suffield, she rarely intervened directly in the children's education. In her case, the frequency of her pregnancies would have made this difficult anyway. At the Lyttelton home at Hagley the schoolroom was flanked on one side by their father's study and on the other by their mother's boudoir and thus formed a sort of passageway between the two. As Lucy recalled many years later,

> it always gave me a happy feeling when I heard Mamma's little cough outside the door, or saw her tall and graceful figure passing through the room … it was nice to feel that they were so close to us.[49]

When Lady Lyttelton died in 1857, shortly after the birth of her twelfth child, the grief of the older children was intense. Lucy never forgot that terrible time, as her older sister, Meriel, then just seventeen, tried to take her mother's place. For the next few years she and Lucy shared the care of the younger children between them.[50]

In the case of Lady Leconfield, not only did she join in the children's games and take them for walks, or in the winter, skating, but she gave them lessons and catechised them on Sundays. On 15 September 1877, she described a typical daily routine:

> Walked with … the children in the garden … George has worked at a French & an arithmetic paper … Tiny [her daughter, Mary] has worked at arithmetic, not quite so well as usual, & has begun compound addition … She has also done a little French, & Needlework, & both children have read daily (except today) the *Child's Roman History*. I have begun reading to them *Sandford & Merton*.[51]

Even the recruitment of a French governess and the return of George's tutor from holiday did not end her active participation in the children's education. On 3 December she noted that she had arranged with the governess

> to take Tiny's arithmetic, as it did not get on in French. She now comes to me from 12.30 to 1.30 daily, when she does dictation, arithmetic and English History. She then goes to the schoolroom till 2 o'cl. to do her music. George does lessons with Mddle. B. for ¾ of an hour (12.30 to 1.15) on Tuesdays, Thursdays, & Saturdays & for an hour 12.30–1.30 on the other days of the week. Charlie does a little work with a picture book in the afternoon.

A few weeks earlier, while recuperating from the birth of her fourth son, she noted with satisfaction that during the time she had been

> laid up the children have always been down twice in the day. In the evening they have generally amused themselves with transfer pictures, or with threading beads, & now they have taken violently to pricking outlines on paper, & then working them in wool. Maud [her second daughter] has been much engrossed with the baby, whom she insists upon nursing whenever the opportunity occurs. On Sunday I took up *Sunday Echoes* again ... & began the third part of the *Fairchild Family* in the evening.[52]

If her children were ill, she helped with the nursing, as on 4 June 1876, when she was looking after her eldest son, George, 'who had been in bed three days with a violent sore throat, approaching diphtheria'. About six months later, it was Maud who was giving cause for concern: 'she was so flushed & restless & her breathing so hurried, that Cole [the nanny] sent down for me after dinner, & we sent for Mr Hunt, dreading inflammation of the lungs. After a poultice had been applied, she grew better.'[53] Even when her children were grown up, she took a hand in their nursing during serious illness. In 1899 for example she spent several months in Ireland looking after her third son Reginald, when he was suffering from typhoid.

Nor was the lighter side of life neglected by Lady Leconfield. At a children's party on 10 January 1877, arrangements were made for the fitting up of a mock post office:

> (with screens) in one corner of the white and gold [drawing-room], & a parcels Delivery Office in the other. Miss Evelyn Barttelot dressed up as the postmistress & Mr Robinson [the tutor] as the parcels clerk, & each child first went to the Post Office to receive a letter, & then to the parcels office for his parcel. Afterwards we hid a number of little things about the room for the children to hunt for, as a variation of bran pie.

Altogether she considered that the whole thing had gone off 'very well indeed'.

But few country-house mothers devoted as much time and attention to their children as did Lady Leconfield. When she died in 1939, aged ninety-three, her obituary in *The Times* pointed out that despite her many years as chatelaine of Petworth and its associated estate, 'the task of bringing up her large family of six sons and three daughters' was 'of far more absorbing interest to her than the social round'.[54]

Elsewhere, older sisters would supervise the lessons of younger siblings, as both Lucy Lyttelton and Cecilia Harbord did, while in the Jebb family it was the children's unmarried aunt, Louisa, who took their education in hand. Although she was strict about their applying themselves to lessons, she readily shared in their games, teaching them 'how to make and use boomerangs, kites, popguns, bows and arrows, toboggans, stilts and fishing-nets, and – supreme joy – over her bedroom fire – to melt lead and cast bullets'. According to a niece, she also used an empty back bedroom as a workshop, 'where she introduced those who had a wish to carpentry, wood turning, glass-cutting and glazing'.[55] When they were staying at their holiday cottage in Wales, they were expected to make their own beds, wash-up, and even help with the cooking – practical skills which few country-house girls learnt at that time.

In most households, however, it was the nanny rather than a member of the family who was the pivotal person in a child's early life. Davis, Edith Sitwell's nurse, remained with the family until Edith was fifteen. She gave her young charge the affection and stability which were otherwise lacking in what was often an unhappy childhood. Davis took the children boating on the lake at their Derbyshire house, Renishaw, and taught them the names of wild flowers. She was the one wholly reliable adult in their lives and when she left after a disagreement with Sir George Sitwell, they were heartbroken.[56]

Margaret Leigh, too, had happy memories of her nanny, Mrs Gailey, who joined the household when the little girl was four. Previously she had been employed by the Duke of Norfolk but had left when the duchess became a Roman Catholic. Prior to 'Gailey's' arrival, Margaret had been cared for by her wet nurse, Brownie, who had stayed on until her marriage to the Leighs' coachman; presumably 'Brownie' had been an unmarried mother when she was first recruited as a wet nurse. When Mrs Gailey arrived, Margaret bluntly told her that she would never love her like Brownie, but soon all such reservations were forgotten. Gailey was not only an excellent nurse and stimulating companion, she

> could tell stories by the hour and knew all sorts of old-fashioned games which we played in the nursery on holiday afternoons, The great joy of the schoolroom children was to join the little ones after tea and to sit in a circle while she told us either old fairy tales, or more frequently her own versions of novels which she had read.[57]

She stayed with the Leighs until she retired.

For Dorothy Beresford-Peirse, the only daughter in a family with five older step-brothers, her beloved Scottish nanny was 'a most wonderful naturalist. She knew where the birds were likely to nest,' and on occasion she and Dorothy would take out an old kettle and hide it in a suitable place so that it could be used as a nesting site by robins.[58]

Where family networks were large and contacts well maintained, there were also frequent exchanges of visits between cousins and other relatives to break the monotony of the daily routine. Three daughters of the Duke of Abercorn, for example, married the Earls of Lichfield, Durham and Mount Edgecumbe, respectively, and produced numerous offspring. The families then exchanged 'hospitality on a wholesale scale' for weeks at a time. 'The effect of the triple alliance,' remembered one child, 'was that we grew up more or less as one gigantic family of thirty-nine with a plurality of residences.'[59] A similar situation existed with Mary Lyttelton, Lucy's mother, who eventually had twelve children, and her sister, Catherine Gladstone, who had eight (of whom seven survived into adult years). Great cavalcades of nurses and children travelled between Hagley, the Lyttelton home, and Hawarden and London, where the Gladstones lived. On 1 January 1857, Lucy noted that the 'whole tribe of Gladstones poured into the house … and we made up the goodly number of eighteen children under seventeen'. The following day she described the house as 'choked, overflowing, echoing with children'. For breakfast they were divided between two tables, with the governess, Miss Smith, and Lucy presiding at one table and Meriel, her eldest sister, at the other:

> The noise pervading the room, as much from scolders as scolded, from bellowers as bellowed at, from children, boys, women, girls, may be imagined, mingled with clatter of crockery, pouring of tea, hewing of bread, and scrumping of jaws.

Soon they were all 'fizzing' in a whirlpool of excitement as they decided to put on a play to entertain the adults. 'All … are getting up their parts in different ways; rehearsals are ceaseless, lessons droop, disorder prevails.'[60]

On another occasion Lord Lyttelton commented on finding 'seventeen children upon the floor, all under the age of twelve, and consequently all inkstands, books, carpets, furniture, ornaments, in intimate intermixture and in every form of fracture and confusion'.[61] Over this disorder and turmoil the much-loved Lyttelton nanny, 'Newmany' presided, making sure that things did not get too far out of hand.

In April 1856 the cousins even went together with their respective mamas to attend a Queen's ball for children at Buckingham Palace in honour of Princess Alice, whose birthday it was. Fourteen-year-old Lucy recorded the great event in her diary:

We got out, and were ushered up the ... grand staircase, on either side of which were masses of flowers, and through a door which led into an ante-room; when lo from a side door issued a 'gallant train'. First Her dear little gracious Majesty ... Down went our curtseys, and we had her smile and bow all to ourselves. After the Queen came the Princes and Princesses. Down went our curtseys. Then came the fat Royal Duchesses. Down went our curtseys, Then the rest of the company. We fell in with them, and moved on to the Throne Room ... [The] dancing began, and I danced very nearly every one thing ... Aggy [Gladstone] ... danced with Prince Alfred, and talked to Princess Alice, happy girl! There was supper ... and I had wine and seltzer water, and ices, which were delicious.... The ball was over at about half-past twelve, when the Queen came down from the dais, and made a lovely curtsey to everyone ... Then came the National Anthem. Then we managed to find our belongings and went home.[62]

Most youngsters were fortunate in having a nanny like the Lytteltons' 'Newmany', who was concerned with their welfare. Thus Sarah Cole, who was head nurse to Lady Leconfield's children, regularly sent reports to her employer about their daily doings, and particularly about their health, when she took them on unaccompanied holidays to the seaside. In March 1873, for example, she wrote from St Leonards to report that while 'Mr George and baby [were] quite well, ... I do not think the cod liver oil suits Miss Tiny'. She asked whether it was to be discontinued and, if so, whether 'Tiny' was still to take her tonic. In total, she sent seven letters to Lady Leconfield about the children between 7 March and 3 April, when they returned to Petworth.[63] A similar pattern was followed when they went on other holidays to Eastbourne and Ramsgate. Likewise, May Harcourt considered Hales, the nanny, to have been 'quite splendid' when her baby suddenly developed bronchitis; 'no fuss, most efficient, devoted & quiet' were other tributes paid to Hales' skills.[64]

However, a few unlucky youngsters had cruel and tyrannical nurses and also parents who were too preoccupied with their own affairs to appreciate their offspring's parlous position. Viola Bankes of Kingston Lacy recalled how the happy nursery regime enjoyed by herself and her brother and sister was destroyed when Nanny Turrell departed and was replaced by grim Nurse Stanley.

Life seemed ... to have turned into a series of deprivations. Her one aim was apparently to make us miserable. I suppose all children had their fingers painted with bitter aloes when they gnawed their nails, but Nurse

Stanley revelled in giving us the purgative powder, undoing the little paper wrapper with great relish. It was probably true, too, that sweets would have been bad for our teeth, but Nanny took an unnatural delight in banning them. We did not have iced cakes, except for birthdays … Even our Mama was cowed into submission.[65]

Salvation came only when Ralph, the son and heir, became so pale and sickly that a London specialist was called in. He discovered that the boy was not being fed properly under Nurse Stanley's eccentric régime, and her unlamented departure followed soon after. Stability then returned to the nursery in the form of 'efficient brisk Nurse Startin. Director of her own nursing home in Bournemouth and not very keen to leave it, she took pity on my desperate mother and came to stay at Kingston Lacy, coaxing Ralph back to health with real food … My mother once more began to smile.'

But even the departure of an unloving nanny could be a traumatic event for some children. Cynthia Charteris experienced a deep sense of bewilderment when her nurse left. 'Without that familiar, all-pervading presence, I felt as if my whole known world were dissolving around me – my very sense of me-ness crumbling back into nothingness.'[66] Or as Joan Poynder put it, 'grown-up people never realised how much it meant' when a nanny who had been with a child for years suddenly moved away.[67]

When girls reached the age of about five or six they would be handed over to a governess to be educated. The position of governess in a country house was not an enviable one. While she was regarded as the social superior of the servants, she was not accepted on terms of equality by her employers. Indeed, according to Loelia, Duchess of Westminster, ladies despised their governesses; 'they thought them tedious and had no wish to see them more than necessary'.[68] Hence their existence was often very lonely and their relationship with their pupils strained. This was aggravated by the fact that many women lacked appropriate academic qualifications for their post, like Frances Maynard's first teacher, Miss Phillips, who was also so nervous that she was terrified of a cow or a mouse. Nevertheless she taught the little girl to play the piano and to read with ease. Later came Miss Blake, who was as 'inexorable as any *grande dame* … on matters of etiquette and manners' but was a superb teacher of French, German, and Italian, all of which were essential 'accomplishments' for a young lady in mid-Victorian England. She was a good teacher of history, too, although science amounted to little more than a 'timid nibbling at botany, geology' and astronomy, and geography was also neglected. Miss Blake had catholic tastes in music and the arts and took Frances to concerts at the Albert Hall and on visits to the Royal Academy and the National Gallery. In order to prepare her pupil for future tours of the art galleries of Paris and Florence, Miss Blake encouraged her to study the catalogues of the relevant galleries.

'In this way the names of the great world-pictures became intelligently familiar to us before we actually saw them.'[69] But, as Frances' biographer has pointed out, this unstructured education produced little more than 'a superficially cultured veneer' designed to match 'the requirements of upper-class society'. To the end of her life, despite her native intelligence, she 'retained some of its butterfly characteristics'. Nevertheless, Miss Blake gained her affection and eventually retired to a cottage on her former pupil's Easton Lodge estate.

Nancy Mitford too had a well-loved French governess whom she considered the sole civilising influence in her childhood. She was recruited when her future pupil, then aged four, was taken by the mother to see the formidable Blanche, Countess of Airlie. Lady Airlie was horrified to learn that her young visitor had not begun to learn French. 'There is nothing so inferior,' she pronounced in magisterial tones, 'as a gentlewoman who has no French.'[70]

But not all girls were so fortunate in their instructors. Mary Gladstone, who was born in 1847, wrote decades later of the 'lifelong depreciation' she had experienced when she was given 'the impression that I was "wanting", i.e. half-witted. My governess, from ten to seventeen years, continued to treat me as half-witted, so I grew up a nonentity. I have never outgrown it.'[71] Throughout her childhood, Mary's governess gave her young charge no word of praise or encouragement – only criticism and disapproval. Neither she nor her two sisters ever learned to study systematically. Instead her mind 'was kept like a kind of domestic pet, to be fed upon literary tit-bits'.

Her cousin, the sweet-tempered Lucy Lyttleton, also had unhappy clashes with some of her governesses. With one, Miss Nicholson, she was 'horribly naughty; sly, obstinate, passionate, and very stupid'. But she blamed this partly on the governess's 'over-severe' attitude, 'apt to whip me for obstinacy when I was only dense … and punishing too often. So I was always labouring under a sense of injustice.' On one occasion when they were at Brighton. Miss Nicholson took the little girl along the parade with her hands tied behind her, with Lucy terrified they would meet a policeman. 'At home my usual punishment was being put for a time into a large, deep, old fashioned bath that was in one corner of the schoolroom, before which hung curtains, so that I was partially in the dark.'[72] In 1848, when Lucy was seven, the severe Miss Nicholson was replaced by the lenient Miss Crump. By this time there were six children, and Miss Crump's indulgence was soon rewarded with defiance and disobedience. 'We "shirked" duties, and became untruthful, disobedient, and self-conceited.' Three years later came Miss Pearson, who took a much sterner moral line and insisted on truth and openness as the first of human virtues. But she was often ill and the children were left to work on their own at poetry, the

'Christian Year', 'bits of Shakespeare and Milton, and long things out of a book of collections'. In September 1855, a very stout French governess was recruited but she, too, ran into discipline problems. Not until June 1856 did 'ladylike and pleasant-looking' Miss Smith join the household and impose order in the school routine. She 'has begun us … well,' wrote Lucy approvingly:

> Our week divided into Monday and Thursday for Italian, Tuesday and Friday for French, Wednesday and Saturday for English, with a half-holiday on the latter day. Our studies are learning of Goldoni's plays, Italian conversation, verb, translation and reading Metastasio, writing translation of *Le notti Romane*, hour's music a day, small hand copy, reading and writing abstract of Arnold's *Rome*, translation of Bossuet's *Histoire Universelle* to English and back again, translation of *Pigeon Pie* (Miss Yonge), drawing, repetition of Racine's poetry, and Campan's *Fr. Conversations*, reading of Lamartine's *Gironde*, Fr. dictation, writing of English composition, arithmetic, repetition of Cornwall's geography, Longfellow's poetry, Mangnall's Fr. dates, reading of Reed's *English History*, and poetry, definition of words, and mental arithmetic. We ought to get on, I think.[73]

Miss Smith also shared the girls' leisure hours, including teaching them 'a nice Irish game' called croquet.

Half a century later, much the same kind of academic regime applied in the schoolroom at Kingston Lacy. 'During the reign of Miss Tidmarsh,' recalled Viola Bankes, 'the Arts flourished.' However, a gesture was made towards science in that on clear nights the governess would lead her young charges round the windows of the house so that they might learn to identify the stars and constellations. In the spring she took them to a pond, where they could catch tadpoles to study in the schoolroom until they turned into frogs. 'Sometimes, we would painstakingly dissect a flower … or make collections of wild flowers, meticulously labelling their delicate forms in simple, picturesque vernacular and more pompous Latin.'[74] But to Viola, one of the biggest disadvantages of a governess was that a pupil could never escape from her surveillance.

> Being naughty in lessons always led to reprisals in the rest of your life. It was bad enough being made to stand in the corner with your face to the wall, totally humiliated if the manservant came in with a bucket of coal. Even more annoying was the fact that you could not leave your school self behind at the end of the day … but had to carry it with you till bedtime, which could be advanced by several hours to make up for some satisfying but short lived insurrection, or some unintentional accident.[75]

Her feelings were shared by Dorothy Beresford-Peirse: 'you are watched day and night by a gov.' was her memory of the 'rather strict government' she experienced in the Bedale schoolroom.[76]

The relentless diet of 'accomplishments' thus administered was designed to equip girls to be amusing companions to the young men they would meet when they left the schoolroom. Any more demanding programme was rejected by most parents on two grounds. First, it was felt that an over-educated girl would be regarded as an unattractive bluestocking who would frighten away potential suitors. It is significant that the young Rosalind Stanley during her first London Season felt it necessary to deny vehemently that she had ever learnt Greek or Latin: instead she claimed her favourite pursuits were music and literature.[77]

A second factor for those approaching puberty was the widespread belief that an over-rigorous academic regime would have undesirable physiological side effects which would damage a girl's future reproductive processes. Although educational reformers firmly rebutted these views, in the upper echelons of society and in certain sectors of the medical profession they continued to be widely held. Hence the frustration of girls like Florence Nightingale who wanted to study 'masculine' subjects like mathematics, Greek, Latin or science. In 1840, Florence appealed to her parents to allow her to have a mathematics tutor, but this was firmly rejected. Her mother expressed the view that it was her daughter's destiny to marry, and 'what use were mathematics to a married woman?'[78]

These attitudes doubtless contributed to parental reluctance to allow daughters to attend the reformed girls' schools which were being established on an increasing scale in the second half of the nineteenth century. However, also relevant in this regard may have been a desire to protect them from striking up undesirable friendships with social inferiors. 'Girls' schools were looked upon with horror in the 1870s,' declared Mabell, Countess of Airlie, 'and none of our contemporaries went to one with the exception of our cousins the Ashley girls who attended a High School. They reaped the benefits of a wonderful education but the fact of their doing so was always deplored, so strong was the prejudice.'[79]

Instead parents preferred to engage visiting masters to polish up the accomplishments of their daughters in dancing, singing and painting, or to send them to exclusive day schools for brief periods during the London Season, where they would associate with girls of a similar class. This was true of Joan Poynder, who supplemented the instruction of her much-disliked foreign governess by classes at Miss Wolff's school in Mount Street while her parents were in London:

I was asked questions about things I'd never been taught ... like dates of the English kings ... I made wild answers and then they all laughed ... And my governess was so furious about this that she made me lie on a backboard ... and she made me learn the kings of England and their dates from William the Conqueror.

There were also literature and English classes but Joan attended too briefly to make much progress. Instead she had to concentrate on French and German, 'one language one week and one the other'. As an only child she was desperately lonely and pleaded with her parents to send her away to school, but they refused. 'I don't think they bothered much about girls' education,' she ruefully observed.[80]

This conclusion was underlined, from a transatlantic perspective, by Consuelo Vanderbilt, the future Duchess of Marlborough. She contrasted English upper-class schooling unfavourably with that in the United States. 'I pitied the limited outlook given by so restricted an education, and wondered what chance a girl so brought up had against a boy with a public school and college background. Later on I was to find that English girls suffered many handicaps, and I came to realise that it was considered fitting that their interests should be sacrificed to the more important prospects of the heir.'[81]

Hence although Cheltenham Ladies' College became established as a superior day and later boarding school for girls in the 1850s, and new public schools like Roedean (1885) and Wycombe Abbey (1896) appeared with the intention of attracting the daughters of the upper classes, their success was limited. Loelia Ponsonby, whose father had been Equerry to Queen Victoria and who subsequently became Head of the Royal Household, remembered that her parents felt self-consciously 'modern' when they sent her to school during the First World War.[82] At Cheltenham, too, where mathematics, science, Latin and Greek were gradually introduced into the curriculum during the 1860s under the influence of a pioneering headmistress, Dorothea Beale, aristocratic recruits were few in number. One of Miss Beale's prized pupils in this regard was Mary Tribe, the future Duchess of Bedford – 'our own Duchess,' as Miss Beale called her. But, significantly, Mary was the daughter of a clergyman, Archdeacon Tribe of Lahore, and had met her husband, then serving in India, when he was only a second son and therefore not likely to succeed to the title. According to her grandson, when she did come to England after her marriage she received a 'pretty frigid welcome' from her aristocratic in-laws.[83] Consequently, although by the 1890s Cheltenham boasted that it catered particularly for 'the daughters of gentlemen', it had some way to go as regards attracting the offspring of major landed families. They still relied upon governesses. Indeed, as late as 1912, May

Harcourt reported the arrival of a new daily governess for her second daughter, who was having difficulty with her reading. 'The other girls are full of drawing, elocution, fencing, dancing, German (I have a German lady for the whole of Wednesday afternoons...) singing & skating ... education is in full swing.'[84]

So it was that most girls emerged from the schoolroom with a superficial knowledge of languages, literature, music and drawing, and with little else besides. They were taught to behave in a ladylike manner and to defer to the menfolk of the family. Some spent a year or so at a finishing school, usually in France, Germany or Switzerland, as Joan Poynder did, so that they might improve their linguistic skills and their social graces. Cynthia Charteris and Emily Jebb both went to a finishing school in Dresden, where they studied art and German literature, and enjoyed the experience greatly. 'There was nothing specially good about the teaching,' wrote Cynthia, 'but formal education was a very small part of the value of those golden months in Dresden ... How impossible to convey the twofold bliss of that Dresden time; twofold because, while with music, poetry and pictures swimming into your ken, day-to-day life with all its fun and companionship was such delight.'[85] At the end of the last century, it has been said, the streets of Dresden 'were filled with crocodiles of English school-girls, easily recognised by their shirts and sailor-hats'.[86]

But these experiences apart, most young ladies were trained 'for courtship ... not for the more practical requirements of marriage'. Few had much knowledge of how to keep household accounts or even to check up on tradesmen's bills. There were, of course, exceptions. Elizabeth Yandell was taught cookery, housekeeping and needlework by her nurse and the cook, while Lady Radnor took her children with her when she interviewed the housekeeper and the cook about domestic affairs.[87] But Cynthia Charteris summarised the position of many:

> Our helplessness equalled our want of independence ... Everything was done for us. I was never so much as taught how to mend or wash – let alone make – my clothes. I couldn't even pack for myself. Of cooking I knew no more than the art of navigation. Absurd upbringing, for even had conditions remained as they were, how can you criticise a cook if you know nothing of her craft?[88]

Ironically it was Princess Louise, one of Queen Victoria's daughters, who instructed her sister-in-law, a daughter of the Duke of Argyll, how to sew a button on her father's coat.[89]

But the majority of girls well understood the rationale for their inferior education and, despite some regrets, most accepted it. 'It was generally thought that girls were less capable of being educated than boys and that any but a smattering of accomplishments made them less likely to be good wives and mothers.'[90] Even talented girls accepted the 'domestic ideology' which dominated their lives, although a few like Florence Nightingale, Mary Gladstone and, to a lesser degree, Cecilia Harbord, attempted to compensate for their lack of formal learning by pursuing a campaign of self-education. Many more benefited from the wider cultural ambience of the family, with distinguished guests invited to dine or to stay. When they 'came out' into adult society such girls were able to listen to erudite discussions on a wide range of literary, philosophical and political issues, and thus supplement their own meagre knowledge. At Hatfield, for example, the Cecil children were encouraged to pursue their own interests. 'Politics … and current events were all discussed and dissected to the root over the breakfast table, with such concentration that the breakfast dishes had sometimes to be moved to the side table so that luncheon could be laid.'[91]

Many girls also enjoyed opportunities to travel abroad not merely for education but for pleasure. Joan Poynder stayed in Fiesole on the outskirts of Florence on one such tour and persuaded her governess to dispense with formal lessons so that she might go round the Florentine art galleries instead.[92] And in the first half of the nineteenth century, Margaret Leigh's mother was taken by her father, the future Lord Westminster, on a Mediterranean cruise in his yacht. Years later she remembered a sweetmeat seller in Constantinople who had wiped his hands on the back of his cat between serving customers and the way in which she and her sister, aged respectively twelve and thirteen years, had been allowed to go on early morning rambles by themselves in Rome.[93]

The diaries of another young traveller – ten-year-old Lady Constance Primrose (the future Lady Leconfield) – reveal a surprising maturity as they describe the journey of herself, her older sister, and two brothers, with their mother, step-father, and an entourage of servants through France and Italy in 1856. Constance's father had died when she was only four. Just over three years later, in 1851, her forceful mother had married Lord Harry Vane, later the 4th Duke of Cleveland. He proved a generous step-father to the four children. Hence Constance's diaries describe not only the cultural experiences she enjoyed but also the excitements of the journey and the luxury of some of the hotels in which they stayed. In Paris they were accommodated in an 'enormous' building with '700 rooms & 200 servants including 28 cooks & scullions'. In Turin, which they reached on 13 October, they stayed at the 'Grand Hotel d'Europe', opposite the king's palace. Here, too, the dining-room was 'something quite splendid; it reminds us of Francis 1st Gallery at the Louvre'. Lord Harry acquired a diligence for them to cross the Alps, and they had the frustrating experience of being held up twice on the journey by a broken axle tree. After it had been replaced the second time, the party started off 'surrounded by the whole village whose sympathy had been awakened by our misfortunes'.[94] Such experiences gave children a knowledge of the world far wider than anything they could gain from schoolroom studies. As girls grew up, there were gradual attempts to integrate them into adult society in readiness for their 'coming out' at the age of seventeen or eighteen. This might involve joining parents and their friends for luncheon or accompanying their mother when she paid calls. Cecilia Harbord recorded in her diary during 1877 the first occasion when she and all her six sisters joined their parents for luncheon; at that time the youngest daughter, Bridget, was only about seven. And Constance de Rothschild recalled that although her mother 'never looked with an eye of favour ... upon children's balls and parties' while her daughters were in the schoolroom, she nonetheless encouraged them to join in conversations between their parents and adult guests: 'the lessons we learnt ... were culled from people as well as from books'.[95]

But other mothers shared the attitude of the Countess of Warwick (formerly Frances Maynard) when she frankly admitted that as daughters grew older, women who were conscious of their own age and beauty had somewhat ambivalent feelings towards them. 'We were good mothers in those days, but preferred to keep our children young,' she confessed, 'for the younger generation, we knew, would date us.'[96]

This was a theme taken up in Vita Sackville-West's novel *The Edwardians*, when the attractive Lady Roehampton reluctantly accepted the need for her daughter to 'come out' because she had reached the age of eighteen. Nevertheless, she determined that this would interfere as little as possible with her own social life, and proposed to leave the duty as far as she could to her husband's sisters, who had daughters of their own of about the same age.[97]

Meanwhile, for the girls themselves, the transition from schoolroom to adult world was fraught with anxiety and uncertainty which they had to overcome, or conceal as best they might. 'I do not think that, in spite of my love of dancing, I was very eager to leave my happy schoolroom life, and make my appearance as a young lady in Society,' wrote Constance de Rothschild.[98] Her reservations were shared by many other country-house daughters at that time, even though they accepted the need to conform to the social conventions of their world. Most relied on their mother to act as their guide and mentor in this new situation, and they, for their part, became their mother's constant companion and concern. 'The *strongest* feeling of my heart,' declared Louisa Sneyd to her daughter, '*is* the wish that you may look upon me as your attached friend.'

3

'Coming Out' & Marriage

'Unless a girl was quite exceptional – which I was not – her fate was decided by her first impact on society. Anyone who failed to secure a proposal within six months of coming out could only wait for her second season with diminishing chances. After the third there remained nothing but India as a last resort before the spectre of the Old Maid became a reality.' … This being the accepted point of view, mothers, aunts and married sisters rallied round the débutante, fresh from the cloistered atmosphere of the schoolroom. The ice was always broken for her by a series of visits to country houses. All her relations and married friends invited her in turn to stay with them, gave parties for her … and rounded up the eligible bachelors of their acquaintance.

Jennifer Ellis ed., *Thatched with Gold: The Memoirs of Mabel, Countess of Airlie* (1962) (As Mabell Gore, Lady Airlie came out in the mid-1880s).

It was generally accepted in the upper ranks of society that when a girl reached the age of seventeen or eighteen she was ready to leave the schoolroom for the responsibilities – and the pleasures – of the adult world. No longer was she restricted to occasional forays like parental luncheon parties or calls upon family friends with her mother; she must be groomed to participate fully in the social calendar of her circle, with its balls, banquets, country house visits and similar events. Hair had to be put up, skirts lengthened, and a new wardrobe acquired. A change of behaviour was also needed, as one Victorian débutante recalled:

Suddenly to emerge from the schoolroom, where your word was law to the little ones, into a world where you were generally the youngest and least important personage was sometimes a little chilly. On the other hand you had the honour and glory of breakfasting at nine instead of eight, sitting in the drawing-room, dining out and going to bed with the elders, and talking to whom you pleased. This last was a real emancipation, for, though the schoolroom girl appeared at luncheon when neighbours came over or there was a party in the house, woe betide her if she ventured to say more than 'Yes' or 'No' to remarks addressed to her – as for a joke of any sort it was unthinkable! From the opposite side of the table a gorgon-eye would be fixed upon her plainly intimating that she was transgressing the proprieties and freezing her to silence.[1]

But once she 'came out' things were very different. 'What previously had been called reprehensible ... was now a virtue.' As a member of Society it was her duty to contribute to the general pool of conversation and to be entertaining and amusing. No longer were vivacity and light-heartedness faults to be frowned upon. 'I was fêted, feasted, courted, and adored, in one continual round of gaiety, and I lived in and for the moment,' remembered the Countess of Warwick, who as Frances Maynard 'came out' in the spring of 1880.[2] The following June her engagement to Lord Brooke, heir to the Earl of Warwick, was announced. He had fallen in love with her when she was only sixteen but, in deference to the wishes of her mother and step-father had concealed his feelings until she made her official debut. Even then he had been discouraged for a time, as it was thought possible that Frances might be chosen as a bride by Prince Leopold, the Queen's youngest son. As soon as it became clear that the prince wished to marry someone else, Lord Brooke was allowed to propose, was accepted, and in April 1881 they were married.[3]

Nevertheless, if certain rules of conduct were relaxed for a débutante as compared to her schoolroom days, others remained very strict. One of the firmest of these related to chaperonage. Chaperons were required not only to accompany girls to balls and parties but to oversee their partners and ensure that they did not compromise themselves by sitting out a dance with a young man, unless this was approved by the chaperon for strategic marital reasons. That was the case with Margaret Leigh, who had attracted the attention of the young 7th Earl of Jersey. He did not dance and so although 'sitting-out' was 'not then the fashion,' Margaret remembered, 'we somehow found a pretext – such as looking at illuminations – for little walks'. Once indeed, a helpful chaperon physically barred the way into the ballroom, insisting to the young couple that the fairy lights at the other end of the garden ought not to be missed![4] On the twelfth meeting the earl proposed and on 18 July 1872, they were engaged. The sheer speed of the courtship and of others like it – the 2nd Duke of Sutherland proposed to Lady Harriet Howard eight days after she began her Season and the 4th Duke's future bride was only sixteen when they became engaged – suggests that a girl's suitable social status, financial circumstances and beauty were the decisive factors in the choice rather than 'the real knowledge of character and well-tested affections' produced by a longer courtship.[5]

Such cases apart, however, the restrictions placed on unmarried girls remained severe. In April 1861 Lucy Lyttleton felt 'scampish' when she walked alone on the pier at Brighton, despite her twenty years. Two days later when returning by herself from an afternoon church service she 'pretended to belong to two elderly ladies in succession, who I don't think found out that they were escorting me'.[6] Even in 1912 Lady Diana Cooper discovered that although in her second Season she 'was allowed more liberty and choice' she was

> still forbidden to be alone with a man except by chance in the country. A married woman must bring me home from a ball. For walking and shopping and even driving in a taxi, a sister or a girl was enough protection. I could go to the Ritz but to no other London hotel.[7]

Often on shopping expeditions or charitable excursions a governess or lady's maid would act as chaperon, as the diaries of girls like Cecilia Harbord and Constance Weld make clear. 'Shopped with Mademoiselle nearly all the morning,' Cecilia recorded typically on 7 June 1877.[8] 'Mademoiselle' was one of the two governesses employed by Lord and Lady Suffield for their daughters. Similarly, Louisa Roffey, officially engaged by the Earl of Arran to act as young ladies' maid for his three daughters, was soon combining this with 'the roles of duenna, companion and friend'.[9]

The symbol of a girl's entry into adult society was her presentation at Court – an event which took place at one of the official drawing-rooms held by the Queen. Without this, declared *Etiquette for Ladies* (1900), 'a girl has no recognised position … Prior to this important function, she is a "juvenile", but after making her profound curtsey to Royalty she leaves the magic presence a "grown up"!'[10] During the final twenty years of Queen Victoria's reign the number of presentations more than doubled, necessitating the addition of a fourth drawing-room in 1880 and a fifth in 1895; it was an indication of the importance of 'coming out' for a girl's future social success.

Many débutantes prepared for the great event by making preliminary visits to relatives and friends before the beginning of the Season in early May. These gave a girl valuable experience in meeting her elders on terms of equality and thereby promoted an easy manner in social intercourse. For all too often when girls emerged from the schoolroom their sheltered upbringing left them 'shy, silent, uninformed', lacking opinions of their own, and painfully gauche when in the presence of young men.[11]

This smoothing of social rough edges was the more necessary because of a general recognition that the Season's major purpose was to act as a marriage mart for the well-to-do. Most débutantes were well aware that if they had not achieved their goal of matrimony by the end of their second or third Season, the chance of making a good match would sharply recede. 'A girl's prospects of marriage, even her entire future, may well depend upon her conduct at this most important juncture of her youth,' warned *The Lady's Newspaper* solemnly. 'Any false step may prove disastrous.'[12]

Some, like Frances Maynard and Lady Harriet Howard, were engaged during their first Season. Others, like Lady Wilhelmina Stanhope, had to wait a good deal longer. 'London is emptying fast,' wrote Lady Wilhelmina in her diary on 16 July 1843,

> & in a week or two we shall be migrating to Chevening, & thence to Walmer. I hope all the neighbours there are not so much wearied of me as I am of them. I think they must be *rather* sick of seeing me return, year after year, the same Lady Wilhelmina that I went, & I agree with them, that some new name might form an agreeable variety.[13]

Happily her time of waiting was almost at an end. On 8 August, Lord Dalmeny, heir to the 4th Earl of Rosebery, proposed and, following one of the brief courtships common in aristocratic circles, they were married a few weeks later, on 20 September. Arrangements were finalised during the serious illness of Lady Wilhelmina's mother and amid a flurry of negotiations over settlement terms and similar financial matters.

Cecilia Parke, whose father was a leading member of the judiciary and who came out in 1837, aged seventeen, was one débutante who benefited from an introductory tour to prepare her for entry into Society. She and her sister, Mary, were taken by their parents on a visit of Switzerland, Austria and Hungary, where they stayed with Prince Esterhazy. They returned by way of Paris and there she was able to purchase her 'coming out' trousseau. As she excitedly told her aunt, they had returned with a 'pile of three large cases' and other luggage:

You would be surprised if you saw Mary and me now, for we have got some new French stays and are become such wonderful shapes that every time I see myself in the glass I open the *eyes of astonishment* and lift up the voice of *admiration*. We are also *bejacketted* in a very tight fitting style and altogether our appearance is very wondrous to behold.[14]

Lucy Lyttelton, too, went on several preliminary visits before she formally 'came out'. In June 1858, shortly before her seventeenth birthday she accompanied her widowed father to a dinner at the Bishop of Worcester's in London, where 'for the first time I was bowed at to leave the room, and taken in by the Bishop! I didn't know if I was on my head or my heels.' Soon after, still aged sixteen, she ordered dinner at Hagley (her home) for the first time in her life. Then on 21 September, about a fortnight after she had reached the magic age of seventeen, she commenced her country-house visits. They began at Hams, the home of Sir Charles Adderley. Although this was not far from Hagley, she found the experience unnerving. 'I am exhausted with behaving properly, and feel as if we had been away from home for a week!' she confided in her diary the following day. It was with evident relief that she returned to the peace of Hagley on 25 September: 'Three cheers, we came home, having been much pleased and amused with our visit. I am amused at everything, dulness and all, and in part it has been very pleasant … [But] the refreshment of coming into the glowing evening beauty of Hagley after three days of country … as dull as ditchwater!'[15]

This respite proved short-lived, for soon she, her sister, Meriel, and their father were again on the move, staying with a cousin, Lady Wenlock, at Escrick, where, among other things, Lucy played cards for money for the first time and recorded modest winnings. She also enjoyed the musical evenings, and when she reached Hagley once more on 11 October, admitted that it had given her 'a very happy launch into the world. I have enjoyed it greatly and kept quite clear of all scrapes. In fact C[ousin] Ebbett has paid us both compliments as to our manner, etc. This is very nice to hear: it is what would have pleased Mamma.'[16]

Other visits followed and on 30 December she and Meriel attended their first ball at Stourbridge, where they were chaperoned by Lord Lyttelton and one of their aunts. 'We were not in bed till past three, nor up next morning till half eleven! I felt so dissipated.'[17]

Nonetheless Lucy did not feel really 'out' until she had experienced her first London Season. It began on 18 May 1859, when the Lytteltons travelled up in the open britschka on what proved to be 'a most smutty journey'. Her father ended up with 'the complexion of a stoker, having faced wind, rain, and dirt on the box'. After visiting Aunt Catherine Gladstone, Lord Lyttelton and Meriel went out to dinner, but Lucy was 'begged off, being the colour of a blotchy turkey-cock from having to wash my face with cold water'.[18] Almost a week later, she went to her first ball: 'We danced much more than I expected: M[eriel] six times and me four … It was fearfully crowded.' Another ball, at Lady Derby's, was described as 'truth to tell … very dull: hot crowds of chaperons and old gentlemen, and the dancing a fierce struggle with all-surrounding petticoat, and I only danced once, at about two … when I had quite given up. This was pleasant, for the room was thinned, and we had the space of a hearthrug.' Her first visit to the opera took place around the same time and was apparently permitted by her father only because it included no ballet, of which he disapproved. But this too, she found disappointing. She also attended several 'drums', or evening parties, as well as concerts, cricket matches and picture exhibitions. At one of these she expressed disgust at the pre-Raphaelite paintings on display: 'every face bright pink, and every sky of lilac, tin leaves and grass like coarse stuffs … The result is like the sign of an inn; a laboured and vulgar finish.'[19]

Her presentation at Court took place on 11 June. All débutantes awaited this with trepidation, in case they committed a *faux pas* which would disgrace them before their mother and their peers. Constance de Rothschild remembered 'being first amused at the idea of a Court train and feathers, and then thinking that we were all wasting much time over a good deal of nonsense'. But when the day of presentation actually arrived, she was as nervous as any other girl. She and Lady de Rothschild joined a large number of débutantes and mothers, whom she compared to a flock of sheep, at St James's Palace. There was a long wait in the ante-room before their names were called out and then they entered the queen's chamber. There she made a deep curtsey and kissed the royal hand, before being hurried on to join her mother, who had gone ahead.[20]

Cynthia Charteris, a daughter of the Earl of Wemyss, had similarly mixed emotions when she described the ritual:

The metamorphosis called Coming Out was supposed to be effected when you were presented at Court, where the wand was officially waved over your head, The picturesque rites of this social baptism were preceded by weeks of trepidation – weeks busied with long lessons in deportment … and panic-stricken rehearsals of my curtsey … then there were endless wearisome hours of trying-on.[21]

For Mabell Gore and Edith Brodrick the worst aspect of the whole business was the long wait they had to endure between their arrival at the palace at 1 p.m. and the official commencement of the drawing-room at 3 p.m. 'A scrappy lunch had generally been consumed in the intervals of dressing,' remembered Edith, 'and as you did not get home till about five the whole proceeding was exceedingly fatiguing … the result was that ladies unable to bear the strain of the long standing had been known to faint; and we none of us looked our best by the time we went through.'[22]

Lucy Lyttelton had pleasanter memories. After 'all the … awestruck anticipation … it was a moment of great happiness to me. The look of interest and kindliness in the dear little queen's face, her bend forward, and the way she gave her hand to me to be kissed, filled me with pleasure … that I wasn't prepared for.' She was especially touched because the queen had made clear that she knew Lucy was being presented by her aunt, Catherine Gladstone, because her own mother was dead.[23]

Constance Weld, by contrast, found the whole affair an embarrassing nightmare. She was the deeply religious daughter of a major Roman Catholic landed family from Dorset, and only arrived in London, with her two sisters, Agnes and Eleanor, and their governess, on the day before the presentation was to take place. Like the Lyttelton girls, the Welds had lost their mother at an early age and Constance and Agnes were therefore to be presented by a family friend. Soon after reaching the capital, the two elder girls hurried to the Bond Street dressmaker who was making their Court dresses so that these could be tried on. Then on 5 May, 1874, the

long dreaded Presentation day … arrived … our dresses came very late & fitted atrociously – I never suffered such a fearful day in my whole life – Charlotte Horningold presented us. We started from her house at twelve & didn't get to Buckingham Palace until after three. The Presentation was a very different thing to what I had thought – I did all sorts of wrong things – seized hold of the queen's hand for one thing … when we had left the royal presence came the most fearful part of the day – down at the entrance the pushing, shoving & want of order altogether was dreadful – we didn't get away until 6.30 – quite tired & exhausted we both were.[24]

It would doubtless have been of little consolation to her to know, either, that should her social status change, for instance by marriage or, after that, by her husband succeeding to a higher title, she would have to be re-presented. Lucy Lyttelton underwent a second ceremony in May 1865, eleven months after her marriage to Lord Frederick Cavendish, a younger son of the Duke of Devonshire. One of her husband's aunts presented her and she 'went in gorgeous array of white lace (my wedding lace) and white *moiré* train, with my beautiful diamond tiara on my head'.[25]

Meanwhile, a fortnight after Constance Weld's ordeal was over she described with mixed pleasure and irritation the daily round she and Agnes had been pursuing since their arrival in town:

> We have not ceased shopping & everlasting leaving of cards ... we have dined with Carry [a married sister] twice ... we had one very pleasant day down on the *Agincourt* [a yacht]. We were invited down by Mr Bruce to see the landing of the Czar at Thames House, instead of that he went aground at Flushing & went to Dover ... we enjoyed ourselves immensely on the *Agincourt* ... we lunched on board & afterwards danced all the afternoon until five when we went back to London ... Miss Fitz [the governess] & I payed [sic] Louise Blundell a visit during her music lesson ... Today I drove out with Carry & her ponies in the park ... Most nights we go to the evening service and benediction at the Oratory after dinner.[26]

As Constance's diary suggests, the London Season involved much more than balls and dinner parties, even if they provided the main focus of maternal matchmaking activities. There were also numerous opportunities for self-improvement. The diary of twenty-one-year-old Cecilia Harbord reveals that she regularly attended literature classes, took music and singing lessons and joined a choral society.[27] The literature class involved 'homework' in the form of a weekly essay, and she spent at least an hour a day reading. Among the topics covered were reports of parliamentary proceedings in the newspapers, which would presumably help her to join in political discussions at the dinner table. She also had her portrait painted and took drawing and painting lessons. Her mother was at this time Lady of the Bedchamber to Alexandra, Princess of Wales, and so was not always at liberty to chaperon her daughter. On one occasion at least this meant that Cecilia and the next eldest daughter, Alice, were unable to fulfil an evening engagement as they had planned, because there was no adult male member of the family or older married woman relative to act as chaperon. During the late morning or late afternoon Cecilia often went riding in the park with her brother, Charles, who was an army officer, and there were also frequent visits to the homes of friends and relatives – to say nothing of the formal ritual of leaving cards which so exasperated Constance Weld.

Ideally, when leaving a card a lady would sit in her carriage and allow her servant to take the card to the door, where he would hand it to a footman. The latter would take it to his mistress and she could then decide whether or not she was 'at home' to the caller. According to Maude G. Cook in her *Manual of Etiquette* (1896),

> the stress laid by Society upon the correct usage of these magic bits of paste-board, will not seem unnecessary, when it is remembered that the visiting card, socially defined means, and frequently is, made to take the place of one's self.[28]

Another important part of the London ritual, as Lady Muriel Beckwith recalled, was the frequent changing of clothes – at least three changes a day:

> The morning was sacred to a linen or muslin, or a fawn woolly material – this was worn when we walked up and down the Row, a daily ceremonial, when the débutante … felt her wings socially, watched the people riding, met her friends, and discussed with girlish enthusiasm the delights of Lady Somebody's ball the night before.

This occupied the time until 11.30 a.m. when 'everyone … sped, with as much despatch as was consistent with dignity, to Hyde Park Corner or Albert Gate, to see the Guards march back to barracks after drilling in the middle of Hyde Park'.

Then came luncheon, which was

> always at 2 p.m. in London, and gave one plenty of time to change to an afternoon dress, which was correct for leaving cards and calling … In the afternoon we went driving. To be seen on your legs at this hour wasn't the thing. After tea we strolled in the park again, but generally sat on the chairs for an hour until it was time to go and dress for dinner.

This was at 8.15 p.m.

> If one dined at home there was a terrible wait before going to a dance, as eleven o'clock was the usual time. The carriage was never ordered before this hour … The débutante did not drink champagne and would not have dreamed of smoking … The excitement of sugary lemonade or a strawberry ice was the height of her modest ambition.

Lady Muriel herself attended three balls a week – that was 'my limit, unless on occasion there was something very special. We were always home by three, as it was considered rather second-rate to be swept up with the crumbs.' As a daughter of the 7th Duke of Richmond, there was, of course, nothing 'second-rate' about Lady Muriel.[29]

Some girls, however, deeply disliked the social round which the London Season entailed and the ceaseless round of balls, dinners, riding in the park, and afternoon calls which it involved. For those who had 'not attracted a sufficient quota of partners', balls could prove a particular ordeal. 'The chaperons kindly tried to talk to us and we tried to look gay and animated,' remembered Susan Tweedsmuir, 'but it was painfully obvious that we deserved that horrid word "wall-flowers" … there were evenings with very painful memories.'[30] Indeed, in April 1867, Constance Primrose had 'to comfort her [mother] … all the way home' because she had 'danced only three times'. 'I … was plainly told by Mama that we had better go away as soon as possible, as it was no good remaining.'[31] And one of Constance Weld's great regrets was that after having the 'luck … of going to the opera with the Andertons' at Covent Garden, she had been obliged to follow this up with attendance at 'the Petre's ball … I had much sooner have gone home with the lovely airs running in my head. However, we left early I must say to my great relief.'[32]

The highly religious Florence Sitwell shared these reservations about many of the events in which she was expected to take part when visiting London with her mother in 1877. She noted disapprovingly that 'Aunt Puss' (her mother's sister) talked 'a good deal of people who have made or were on the point of making "brilliant marriages"' – a subject in which she took little apparent interest.[33] Then there were débutantes like Betty Lytton who in 1887 'was not an easy girl to please and disliked the common routine of balls etc.'. Lady Constance Malleson likewise sourly described her experiences in 1905 as 'the same people, the same talk, the same eternal round of so-called gaiety … I'll swear I never met an intelligent man during my whole London Season.'[34]

Some parents also disliked the upheaval involved in setting up an establishment in London, even though most realised that the effort must be made if their daughters' matrimonial prospects were to be promoted. Only minor gentry families, like the Yorkes of Erddig and the Wilkes of Elmdon, who lacked the means or the interest to participate, neglected the expected social round. Instead they concentrated upon local contacts, even though this had its matrimonial penalties. In the second half of the nineteenth century both of the Yorke daughters married country clergymen of modest means, and the same was true of Elizabeth Wilkes of Elmdon.[35] Elizabeth's husband was, indeed, a mere curate, although her father subsequently presented him to the family livings of Elmdon and Wenden Lofts.

More typical were Lord and Lady O. in Vita Sackville-West's novel *The Edwardians*. They were 'martyrising themselves' by taking a house in Belgrave Square for the Season

> for the sake of what they considered to be their duty towards their daughter. Of impeccable respectability and historic lineage, they had long looked forward with dread to this year when it would be necessary to … devote themselves for three months to the task of taking their Alice 'out', involving not only weariness for them, but also a constant irritating anxiety as to possible contact with things and people of whom they would disapprove.[36]

Lord and Lady O. had their real-life counterpart in Mary Elizabeth Lucy, who had been widowed in 1845. Two years later she reluctantly left her beloved Charlecote Park in Warwickshire, to launch her daughter, Emily, upon Society. As Mrs Lucy's brother encouragingly suggested, shortly before they departed, it was to be hoped that 'dear Emy' would soon 'find her head in a circle of rosebuds without any sharp points in the wires to prick her'.[37] Escorted by her brother, Fulke, and often enough with her mother and younger sister, Caroline, also in attendance, Emily enjoyed her Season and on 28 July, shortly after returning to Charlecote, was duly proposed to by one of her admirers, then staying with the family. He was accepted and the wedding took place on the following 21 October. The party travelled to the small church in the park in twelve carriages. The 'village bands of Charlecote, Hampton Lucy and Stratford united drumming and fiddling along the road as we passed, to the great danger of frightening the horses,' remembered Mrs Lucy. A double arch of evergreens decorated with flowers 'waved over the Park gate and an archway of evergreens and flowers was erected from the churchyard gate to the church porch'. When the couple left church to return to their carriage the path was strewn with flowers by the village schoolgirls, who were dressed in pink frocks, white tippets, and straw hats with pink ribbons for the occasion. The bride received a diamond bracelet from the tenants of the estate and at 3 p.m., after the family's own wedding breakfast, every cottager was regaled with beef, plum pudding, and

> good ale in the new Loft over the Stables … at nine o'clock the Tenantry, their wives and sons and daughters began to arrive for a Ball, they danced in the large Dinner Room and Supper was laid in the Great Hall. There was an excellent Band and everything went off well, and dancing was kept up with great spirit till four o'clock in the morning.[38]

However, things proved more difficult when it came to making a match for Mrs Lucy's second daughter, Caroline. The situation was complicated by the fact that early in 1852, when she was already about twenty-four, Caroline had been involved in a *cause célèbre* in Warwickshire. One day, while walking back to Charlecote alone, she was overtaken by members of the local hunt, riding home after a shortened day's hunting. One of them, Colonel Shirley of Ettington, offered to escort her and on the way they engaged in a lively, perhaps flirtatious, conversation. Then they came to a muddy spot in the lane and in order to avoid dirtying her shoes, Caroline climbed on to the grass bank. A local labourer later claimed to have seen her there, lying on the ground with her petticoats around her waist. She did not appear to be struggling, although she later claimed this was because she had fainted. According to her, Colonel Shirley had attempted to 'salute' her and this had brought on an hysterical fit. Once the matter came to light Caroline's uncles instituted a legal enquiry into the affair and a local jury decided that the labourer had only made his statement in an attempt to blackmail the Lucys. The case was dismissed and Caroline was taken by her mother on a visit to relatives in Wales to allow the episode to fade away. Nevertheless, it is likely that it damaged Caroline's chances of matrimony and in 1859, at the age of almost thirty, she was still unmarried. Her great opportunity to avoid the stigma of becoming an 'old maid' was, however, about to materialise.

In May of that year Mrs Lucy again took a house in London even though she had 'no heart to enter into any gaieties'. It was left to her second son, Spencer, to act as Caroline's escort and at one of the dinner parties they attended Caroline met Captain Pawlett Lane, the eldest son of a small Oxfordshire landowner. Soon after, his mother invited the girl to Brighton, and when Mrs Lucy followed a few days later she discovered that Caroline and Pawlett had fallen in love. They pleaded for her consent to their marriage, but for some time she resisted on the grounds that the captain lacked the means to support a wife. Caroline responded that her own fortune, which amounted to around £14,000, would suffice and that 'she was willing to make any sacrifice in order to become Pawlett's wife'. After further pressure, the Lucys agreed to the match, and the two were married at Charlecote on 2 September.[39] As before, the tenants joined in the celebrations and presented her with a diamond bracelet and other items.

For the Lucy girls, therefore, the London Season served its purpose as a marriage mart, although, in the case of Caroline, only after much delay. But many girls were not prepared to accept the first suitor who asked for their hand. Mary Glynne aroused the ire of her aunt Neville because she refused to marry the eligible Lord Gairlie. To her plea that she did not love him, her aunt responded tartly:

> Women are not like men, they cannot chuse, nor is it creditable or lady-like to be what is called in love; I believe that few … well-regulated minds ever have been and that romantic attachment is confined to novels and novel-readers, ye silly and numerous class of young persons ill-educated at home or brought up in boarding-schools.[40]

Fortunately, Mary was able to satisfy both her family and herself shortly afterwards when she became engaged to the young and attractive 4th Lord Lyttelton. She and her sister, Catherine, who married William Gladstone, had a joint wedding ceremony on 25 July 1839, and then spent most of the honeymoon together in Scotland, including a good deal of time in Fasque, the Gladstone family home.

Cecilia Harbord's diary for 1877 recounted the embarrassment which could arise in rebuffing an unwanted suitor. Lord Grimston, the admirer in question, began by sending a 'lovely bouquet of lilies' on 14 March. About a month later he and Cecelia's mother 'had a talk together – poor little mother. I am dreadfully sorry for her but it is a great relief to me!' However, the matter was not quite ended, for two days later, on 13 April, her mother had another interview 'with Lord G. and then I had to go down. It was *very dreadful* but I am thankful it is over.'[41]

By contrast, her relations with Lord Carrington, whom she married the following year, proceeded smoothly and speedily. Although he was a member of her wider social circle, he did not feature prominently in her diary until 28 May 1878, when she attended Mrs Naylor's ball:

> Contrary to our expectations we shall always look back to this … ball with very great pleasure. We did not know many people there but after a short time Lord Carrington arrived, danced with me, & then something took place which has made me very very happy. I went to mother & whispered to her ear 'I have won the jacket' (one that Mother worked and put aside for the first one of her girls who married). I ought indeed to be grateful for this great happiness, & I *am*. There is no one like him in all England & Father & Mother are *very* fond of him.

Unlike Captain Pawlett Lane, there were no financial objections to Lord Carrington from the prospective bride's family. He was a major landowner, owning about twice as much land as Lord Suffield, himself a large property owner. Between 1865 and 1868 he had been Liberal MP for High Wycombe, where his principal seat, Wycombe Abbey, was located, before succeeding his father to the title. Later, at the end of the 1890s, when Lord Suffield's profligacy had led to serious financial embarrassment, he was associated with plans to rescue his father-in-law from the disgrace of possible bankruptcy.[42]

Meanwhile, the day after the proposal, Cecilia called her sisters, her maid and the housekeeper to her room very early in the morning to give them the good news. Later she went walking with Lord Carrington and received a 'beautiful diamond ring' from him. 'We then went to see Lady Carrington, who was so kind to me – for Charlie's sake of course – that I shall *never* forget it ... We all dined at Mrs Campbell's house in the evening. I am more & more happy every moment.' She continued to be showered with gifts by her fiancé, including several expensive pieces of jewellery and a pair of ponies for her to drive.

They were married on 16 July, with Cecilia's six sisters acting as bridesmaids, and with the Prince and Princess of Wales among the guests. The ceremony took place at the Chapel Royal, Whitehall, and after the reception they went to Barleythorpe, Lord Carrington's Rutland hunting lodge. There they remained on honeymoon until 27 July, when they returned briefly to London, before travelling on to High Wycombe. Here further celebrations had been prepared, with the mayor and crowds of townspeople waiting to receive the young couple:

> The whole town was decorated, every balcony & window was full of people & there were three beautiful Arches. After four Addresses had been given & Charlie had answered two, the horses were taken out of the carriage (the phaeton) & the Fire Brigade pulled us all through the town up to our door. I shall never forget our reception, there were thousands of people! We fed 300,000 [sic] children in the park etc. After dinner we went out ... to see a large bonfire & then on to the balcony of some old people called Grove ... Directly we came out ... we were known. It was a heavenly night.[43]

Later their wedding presents were displayed in the Town Hall where those interested could inspect them for a small fee. The proceeds, which amounted to £57, were handed over to the Cottage Hospital.[44]

Cecilia Harbord's romance was, in many respects, the 'ideal' at which matchmaking mothers aimed. Her husband, then in his mid-thirties, was still young; he was also titled, well-to-do, and a prominent member of the same social circle as Cecilia herself. But, of course, many couples were less fortunate. Some were the victims of over-ambitious, scheming parents. Lady Zouche, married at eighteen, believed 'her mother had forced the marriage on Robin (Zouche), who did not love her'.[45] The marriage was unsuccessful, and she eventually left him. Others, like Lady Ferrers, accepted a proposal from a man they did not love in order to secure a home of their own. As Lady Ina White she had kept house for ten years for a bachelor brother but when he suddenly married, she decided to accept an offer from Earl Ferrers, a long-standing admirer. The marriage proved 'disastrous'; he was extremely possessive, 'never let her go anywhere without him, enforcing upon her the kind of life he approved of, which was dull and socially very formal'. According to a friend, she 'realised almost at once that she could never escape, and that feeling and the climate [at Staunton Harold, where they lived] shattered her health'.[46] There were no children and Lady Ferrers died in 1907, after about twenty-two years of marriage.

But these problems apart, three impediments in particular might stand in the way of a painless path to marital bliss. They were unsuitable social rank or connections; poor health; and lack of appropriate financial resources.

As regards rank, it is clear that most marriages involving landed families were 'in-marriages', with both spouses coming from a similar social class. Within the upper echelons of the peerage, especially prior to the 1870s, this caste-consciousness was especially strong. Hence when dukes, marquesses or their heirs married they were likely to follow the rule of 'rank endogamy'. This meant that even the daughters of barons and viscounts were *not* regarded with favour as potential spouses by members of this most exclusive grouping.

Up to the last quarter of the nineteenth century about two-fifths of all marriages by heirs to titles were to the daughters of fellow members of the peerage. Of the remaining three-fifths, the vast majority were from landowning or military families, who themselves often had strong landed connections. Only after 1880 did this change, as agricultural depression reduced aristocratic incomes from landed estates at a time when the owners' increasingly luxurious lifestyles were intensifying the pressures upon those incomes. Some of the largest owners, like Lord Leconfield or the Duke of Westminster, were rich enough to shrug off such problems.[47] Others embarked upon a programme of retrenchment and austerity, and others again turned to outside sources of income. These might include company directorships (167 peers figure as directors in 1896)[48] or they might involve marriage to a wealthy wife.

It was against this background that endogamous marriages by peers declined. Already in the 1880s they had fallen to about thirty-two per cent of the total and in the period 1900–9 they fell again, to under twenty per cent. Some looked for brides among business or professional families, but, although those increased during these decades, they remained of relatively minor importance, at least where British-born brides were concerned.[49] An exception to this was banking, with such leading landed families as the Baths, the Lytteltons, the Shaftesburys, the Spencers and the Sutherlands becoming connected with the Baring banking dynasty during the late nineteenth century, and the Earl of Rosebery marrying Hannah de Rothschild. So significant had the trend become that by the end of the century about a quarter of leading City bankers claimed an aristocrat for a father-in-law.[50]

Still more notable was the increase in foreigners, particularly Americans, as aristocratic brides. Girls from overseas comprised nearly nine per cent of all peers' brides in the 1880s and over twelve per cent of those between 1900 and 1909, with more than half of all the foreign brides at the end of the nineteenth century coming from the United States. The scale of the transformation that resulted is seen by the fact that whereas there had been four American peeresses in 1880, that had jumped to over fifty by 1914. In addition, there were American wives of younger sons, baronets and knights to swell further the ranks of the 'titled American elite'. May Burns, niece of the leading American banker J. Pierpoint Morgan and herself a banker's daughter, was one of the wealthiest of the American brides and yet her husband was only a baronet's son. Not until 1916, several years after their marriage, was he raised to the peerage in his own right as the 1st Viscount Harcourt.[51]

To many Englishwomen these American 'invaders' were unwelcome rivals, who were greedily snatching the most eligible young men. Marie Corelli sourly linked the new habits of conspicuous consumption which were percolating through society in the later Victorian era to 'America's … influence on the social world' which taught 'that "dollars are the only wear". English Society has been sadly vulgarised by this American taint.'[52] Susan Tweedsmuir, a granddaughter of Lord Ebury, made a similar point, although in more measured tones:

> When I grew up, Society was expanding and becoming more moneyed, and a less rural standard was creeping in. Society, so called, had also become much larger. Some eldest sons of peers married Americans and other heiresses, which buttressed family fortunes at the cost of bringing in much higher standards of smartness in clothes and equipages.[53]

Yet although certain American wives, like Lady Cunard, were reluctant to carry out the tasks expected of them as 'ladies of the manor', most accepted their responsibilities with as much interest and zeal as their English counterparts. As we saw in Chapter 1, Consuelo Vanderbilt carried out her charitable duties conscientiously when she became

Duchess of Marlborough. And she persisted in this despite the lack of understanding – or appreciation – by her husband's family of her American sensibilities. Early in their acquaintance her mother-in-law, Lady Blandford, displayed a startling ignorance of life in the United States, apparently believing, as Consuelo ruefully remarked, that 'we all lived on plantations with negro slaves and that there were Red Indians ready to scalp us just around the corner'.[54]

May Harcourt, too, played an active part in her husband's political affairs, despite a deep dislike of public speaking. She also organised fêtes and festivities at Nuneham Park, the family's Oxfordshire estate, and at Mymms Park, her mother's Hertfordshire property. 'We are very busy with the Estate Children's Entertainment,' she wrote on 26 December 1900, while staying at Mymms. Four years later, she supervised the packing up of 'all the Xmas dinners' and the distribution of toys to families on her mother's estate.[55]

In the case of American brides such as these, parental rank was no barrier to their acceptance in aristocratic circles. Indeed, their transatlantic origins may have made them easier to absorb since they appeared to pose less of a threat to the exclusiveness of the peerage than would a comparable marriage to a British commoner from a business or commercial background. For the latter would bring in her train unwanted relatives and friends in a way that a foreigner was less likely to do.[56]

Yet the frequent references by contemporaries to the American 'invasion' should not obscure the fact that for every foreigner who married into the peerage, around seven British girls did the same, even in the early twentieth century. And although most marriages took place outside the peerage, the bulk were 'to daughters who already lay within a broad "gentlemanly" class'. That must place in true perspective emotive claims about the effect on the character of the peerage of marriages 'to daughters of businessmen or Americans'. In numerical terms these remained negligible.[57]

Throughout the period there were, of course, always a few 'eccentric' marriages which defied the rule that 'like should marry like'. In 1858, the seventy-year-old Marquess of Westmeath married an attractive scullery maid, Maria Jervis, whom he had met on a train, as she journeyed to London. Four years later, after forming a relationship with a young engineer, she was divorced by the marquess. Again, in 1862 the widowed Lord Montagu, MP for Huntingdonshire, married Elizabeth Wade, his children's nursery maid. But such occasional breaches of accepted practice were attributed to the quirks of character and circumstance of the individuals involved rather than to any serious flouting of customary behaviour.

Rather more controversial were the marriages between peers and actresses which occurred in the late Victorian and Edwardian era, reaching a peak in the heyday of the Gaiety and Gibson Girls in the 1900s. Prior to 1884 only ten peers had married players during the preceding one hundred years, for they were from a class deemed 'quite unsuitable' and as 'little better than prostitutes'. But by the First World War, there had been seventeen such matches. The grooms included the Dukes of Leinster and Newcastle; other peers, like the 2nd Duke of Westminster and the 5th Earl of Lonsdale, had affairs with actresses or other 'professional beauties'. Also significant is the fact that both Newcastle and Leinster were subsequently divorced. As David Cannadine comments, the 'old standards ... were very definitely slipping'.[58]

However, even when girls were born into the 'correct' ranks of society, disreputable family connections might prove a barrier to marital acceptance. Lady Minto was one of many anxious mothers when she warned her rakish eldest son against a too close involvement with Lady Limerick and her daughter: 'the fact of a lady being separated from her husband never tells in her favour ... there are a good many ladies in the world who like to draw young gentlemen on to a point from where it is difficult to retreat with honour'.[59]

Lady Charlotte Bertie, daughter of the 9th Earl of Lindsay, was another victim of this prejudice. When her father died at the age of seventy-four, Charlotte was only six. Three years later her mother was married again to a disreputable clergyman cousin, whom the little girl greatly disliked. As she grew up and especially when the family were in London for the Season, she felt that what was deemed her mother's 'unsuitable' second marriage was preventing her from making the social connections which would normally have been open to an earl's daughter. Eventually, in May 1833, at the age of twenty-one, Lady Charlotte met the leading ironmaster and businessman, Josiah John Guest, a widower in his late forties. Three months later they were married and, despite the difference in age and rank, the marriage proved happy. Nevertheless, Lady Charlotte, who had complained so bitterly about her mother's second marriage, found herself ostracised because she had married a man 'in trade'. A major preoccupation in her early married life was to rectify what she considered her 'unsatisfactory position in Society'. To this end she sought out patrons who could introduce her into the circles where she desired to move. Her persistence was rewarded and on 9 June 1838, she recorded happily in her diary that Lady Lansdowne, wife of the 3rd Marquess, had agreed to call upon her. 'Nothing could be so kind as she was. She recommended my giving a Concert and promised to introduce me to several of the foreign ambassadors and some of the first English families.'[60] About a month later she held a party which Lady Lansdowne helped her arrange. To her relief it was a success. 'I have striven hard to place myself in the situation of life in which I was born … and now I really believe I have accomplished it, and need not henceforth toil through pleasures for the sake of Society,' she wrote triumphantly. 'My children now, I hope and believe, will have none of those struggles, to make which I have felt so much humiliated'.[61]

Apart from problems of rank and family connections, a second barrier to a successful courtship might be the health of the parties. Poor health was seen as a particular handicap in the late nineteenth century, at a time when eugenicists were propounding the view that 'the nation's future citizens should come from the best stock'. Women 'were advised not to marry confirmed invalids' since a wife was ill-equipped to be 'housekeeper, nurse and provider for the family'. Perhaps not surprisingly, the strong-minded Lady Selbourne, who advised her eldest son to 'fall in love with your head as well as with your heart', was one who had very definite views on the subject. In 1906 she considered that a Miss Pratt Barlow 'would have been wiser to postpone her marriage until the doctors could call her well', since according to some people she was 'foolish to marry at all in her state of health'.[62] (It was apparently suspected that she had tuberculosis.)

In the same year the engagement between Alexandra, Lady Carrington's second daughter, and Robin Grant was broken off after three months because of his ill-health. A consultation with Sir Thomas Barlow, the royal physician, confirmed the unfavourable verdict of his own doctor, and he was ordered abroad. Alexandra herself was sent away on a holiday while the two mothers decided that the engagement presents must all be sent back.[63] Alexandra had 'come out' seven years before at the glittering 'Khartoum Ball' held at the Hotel Cecil, which had been attended by well over a thousand people.[64] After this setback to her marital hopes in 1906, over four years were to elapse before she eventually married, at the age of twenty-nine.

Religious differences could also create problems, although they were rarely serious enough to prevent a marriage taking place. In the mid-1850s, Lady Peel was reluctant to allow her youngest daughter to marry Francis Stonor, Lord Camoys's son, because the Stonors were Roman Catholics. However, her friend, Frances, Lady Waldegrave, an inveterate matchmaker, persuaded her to relent.[65]

The Duchess of Cleveland, likewise, was much mortified when her son, Lord Rosebery, became engaged in 1878 to the Jewish heiress, Hannah de Rothschild. She threatened to boycott the wedding unless it took place in a church, complaining that the union was 'on religious grounds' far from acceptable to her.

'You can easily suppose how unhappy I must feel in finding that you have chosen as your wife, & the mother of your children, one who has not the faith & hope of Christ,' she told her son. Her only consolation was that he seemed contented.[66] The previous year, Hannah's cousin, Constance, had also married a Christian, and had soon become identified with the interests of her Christian friends.[67]

But however successful such marriages proved in practice, doubts remained. May Harcourt, in 1908, expressed a not uncommon view when she characterised one mixed wedding she had attended as 'dismal,' adding, 'but that is always so in the case of mixed marriages'.[68]

Perhaps the most serious obstacle along the road to matrimony related to finance, and particularly to marriage settlements. These contracts had long been

> a feature of matrimonial alliances within the landed classes. The business side of [such] arrangements was shrouded under a sacred cloth of tradition an accepted formality, and solicitors were usually left to deal with the legal intricacies. Contributions towards a couple's maintenance and provisions for offspring of the marriage came from the two families involved. The contribution from the wife's family was known as the dowry, or portion, and this was settled on the couple, though the husband usually held control of it, and the wife was allowed a small sum known as pin money.[69]

In order to protect daughters, landed families arranged for trusts to be carefully drawn up so that even before the Married Women's Property Acts of 1870 and 1882 a husband's right to dispose of property which a wife brought into the marriage would be firmly restricted. As a consequence, settlement negotiations could often be prolonged and sometimes bitter. The 5th Earl of Onslow was not alone in complaining of the quite 'absurd wranglings' which took place in 1905 over his engagement to Miss Violet Bamfylde, especially as there 'could be no genuine objection and there was "no real lack of money"'. He considered that 'every sort of difficulty was made over settlements' because 'to get the full fun out of it everyone had to raise objections'.[70] His wedding eventually took place early in the following year.

The negotiations involving Mary Wyndham, Lord Leconfield's eldest daughter, and Ivor Maxse, an army officer and the elder son of Admiral Maxse, also caused distress to the two principal participants. This was compounded by Mary's determination that the wedding should take place before her fiancé departed for South Africa to fight in the Boer War. Olive Maxse wrote to her sister, Violet, to explain the difficulty:

> You know what Papa always is about settlements, and Lord Leconfield is *very* business like and careful about all money investments – so I do not quite know how it will all work out. Lord Leconfield is willing to settle

£1,000 a year on her if Papa will do ditto, but of course he won't, and what is more, I do not think he *can*.[71]

Meanwhile Lord Leconfield was determined that the matter should not be rushed. 'What [the Admiral] offers is by no means satisfactory,' he told his wife, 'but I have endeavoured to eliminate the worst, including one block of shares which would yield no interest.'[72]

Agreement was eventually reached at the last minute and Mary was able to marry. As her sister, Maud, reported, 'one felt all the time so glad & triumphant for [her] sake, it was such a joy to feel that she at last had got what she wanted'.[73] Shortly afterwards she sailed for South Africa with her new husband. To one of the wedding guests, Eleanor Cecil, the ceremony had been 'quite unlike any other I ever went to, and I rather think very much the most attractive – no fuss or snobbery and nothing to take one's attention from the married people themselves'.[74] But for weeks prior to the wedding, Mary's life had been made miserable by the intricate financial transactions involved.

The amount families contributed to a settlement varied with their economic circumstances. Sometimes those of inferior rank but substantial means who were marrying 'above' themselves would be expected to make a larger contribution. Mary Leiter, the rich and beautiful American heiress who married George Curzon in 1895, was provided with a capital sum of £140,000 on marriage, which produced an annual income of £6,300; this rose to £30,000 a year on her father's death. By contrast, Curzon's contribution to the settlement was £25,000, which yielded annual interest of about £1,000. This latter sum was, in fact, the amount aimed at by most rich families for their children. For instance in 1884 when Maud Cecil married William Palmer, the future Lord Selborne, the £26,000 and £25,000 settled on them by their respective families yielded annual interest of around £1,000 in each case.[75] This, as we have seen, was the figure aimed at by Lord Leconfield for his daughter and Ivor Maxse.

But lower amounts were also involved. When Violet Maxse married Edward Cecil, a younger son of the 3rd Marquess of Salisbury, her father settled £10,000 on her while Lord Salisbury's contribution was £25,000. This yielded a joint annual income of £1,600, which Lady Salisbury dismissed as 'love in a cottage', when her son married in 1894.[76]

In the humbler ranks of the landed classes settlement terms could be still more modest. In October 1872, shortly before the Gloucestershire squire, Dearman Birchall, married for the second time, he noted that he had arranged with the bride's father to settle £6,000 on her, while the father provided £4,000.[77] On rare occasions girls without any real financial resources were able to marry into aristocratic or gentry families. Edith Balfour's wedding to Alfred Lyttelton, Lucy's brother, went ahead although Edith disarmingly admitted that she '[hadn't] a farthing'.[78] Elinor Glyn, too, married her landowner husband, Clayton, of Durrington House, Harlow, Essex, even though she had no financial expectations. He apparently considered that her striking good looks made up for other deficiencies.[79]

In yet another instance, Louisa Scott, the daughter of a Wiltshire clergyman of very modest means, married Philip Yorke, owner of Erddig, in April 1902 after an engagement of about two months. His first marriage, to Annette Puleston in 1877, had been arranged to please his father and proved a disaster, Annette deserting him shortly after the wedding. Not until 1899, when she died, was he free to marry again, and after several unsuccessful proposals to other ladies, he asked Louisa to be his bride.[80] She was then in her late thirties and he was in his early fifties, but they soon settled down happily, after spending much of their honeymoon on a cycling tour. When they returned to Erddig, Louisa triumphantly recorded that they were greeted by 'church bells cannoning, crowds of people cheering, two triumphal arches (made by workmen on the estate)'. The servants unharnessed the horses from their carriage and dragged it up to the house themselves. They were then rewarded with a tea and when Philip and Louisa went down to the servants' hall afterwards, 'speeches were made' and she 'was given a bouquet of lovely white flowers'.[81]

While a very few girls only could expect to make an advantageous match without a dowry, it is clear that a too overt anxiety to marry for purely material motives was frowned upon. In 1873, Evelyn Stanhope disapprovingly commented on 'Lord Eliot's marriage to a Miss Heathcote with money which I suppose means Lord Willoughby's plain and middle-aged daughter'.[82] In 1895 Lady Londonderry was equally critical of a bridegroom who had 'married the £10,000 a year as well as the Lady'. It was in this context that some of the American marriages mentioned earlier were condemned.

Where adequate funds were lacking, a marriage would be delayed until parents were satisfied that the young couple were well enough off to live appropriately to their station. Hence the dowager Lady Lyttelton's comment to a relative in November 1849 about 'poor Miss Devereux' whose marriage was to be

deferred for a year owing to want of *means*, as money is now always called. The hitch threatened at first to be lasting, but it has been healed over. I advise you and all such of you who are wishing for pretty daughters to lay in a great stock of good nerves and calm temper against they are grown up.[83]

Sometimes financial uncertainties led to parents refusing to sanction an engagement. Barbara Tasburgh of Burghwallis was prevented from marrying a young army officer of her choice because he was a younger son and hence without either land or means. She subsequently became engaged to the dull but worthy William Charlton of Hesleyside in Northumbria, who was heir to an estate of over 20,000 acres.[84] Even then her father created difficulties over the settlement terms, and the couple eloped to Gretna Green to be married. They were subsequently remarried in more conventional fashion in London and the settlement issue was solved by Mrs Tasburgh agreeing to provide her daughter with £14,000 out of property entrusted to her alone.[85]

Lady Charlotte Bertie was another victim of parental veto when, as a teenager, she fell in love with Augustus O'Brien, a local squire's son. He subsequently became MP for Stafford and Secretary to the Admiralty, but her mother refused to countenance the match, declaring she would rather see her daughter in her grave than married to Augustus.[86] Not surprisingly there was ill-feeling between the two families and Augustus was promised to a young girl who was not yet twelve.[87] It was doubtless to avoid such disputes that Lady Colin Campbell advised any gentleman who had 'little besides love to offer' to adopt the 'more honourable course of seeking the parents' consent before the daughter's' when a proposal was in the offing.[88]

Engagements were usually brief, Lady Salisbury seemingly speaking for the majority when she told her son, Edward, to proceed speedily: 'I am quite against a long engagement and so is your father, and we are quite ready for your wedding at any time!'[89] Marriages often took place towards the end of the Season. An analysis of the date of marriage of over five hundred peers and baronets reveals in 1910 that almost a quarter had chosen June or July for their wedding. April was the third most popular month, with over a tenth of the total; March and May were least popular, presumably because of prohibitions on matrimony during Lent in the former case, and the onset of the Season in the latter.[90]

For brides there was the worry and excitement of acquiring a suitable trousseau. Some, like May Burns, shopped in Paris. 'We are dressmaking madly,' she reported to her to her future stepmother-in-law in April 1899, just over two months before her wedding.[91] Constance Primrose, the future Lady Leconfield, started her 'trousseau labours' about a week after her engagement on 8 June 1867. By 4 July, she reported 'a great deal of trousseau trying on, besides a [riding] habit, & seeking a cook', whom she was trying to engage.[92] Two days later she was 'frightened about [her] simple gowns' by a friend, who presumably favoured a more elaborate wardrobe. 'I have been fidgeting terribly about my trousseau since she dined here,' confessed Constance unhappily. The final week before the wedding on 15 July was so hectic that she was unable to write up her journal, and it was doubtless with relief that she at last arrived at the altar. Her engagement had lasted less than six weeks.

Honeymoons were spent in two principal ways. For those with appropriate connections, the first days after marriage would be spent in a country house belonging either to the family or to a family friend, who had lent it for the occasion. Those who were without these advantages chose foreign travel, and a few, like May Burns and Lewis Harcourt, aimed to combine the two. After their marriage at the beginning of July 1899, the Harcourts travelled down to Nuneham Park in Oxfordshire, where they were soon joined by May's widowed mother. 'It has been such a joy having Mother with us for these two days,' May told her stepmother-in-law on 8 July. After leaving Nuneham they travelled to Malvern to spend a few days with one of Lewis's aunts. But their plans to travel to the United States in September had to be abandoned when May found herself pregnant early in August.[93]

Other couples, too, combined privacy in the immediate aftermath of the wedding with visits to members of the family shortly after. When Lucy Lyttelton married Lord Frederick Cavendish, a younger son of the Duke of Devonshire, in June 1864, they spent the following three days in a house borrowed for the occasion in Chiswick. They then travelled to Bolton Abbey, one of the duke's seats in Yorkshire. On the way north they called at Devonshire House in London so that Lucy might meet her new in-laws: 'I may as well smash the ice at once!' she wrote in her diary. Once at Bolton Abbey, they received visitors, made excursions over the countryside, and began to read 'some books F. chose for the honeymoon; rather an odd trio! Carlyle's *French Revolution*, Butler's *Analogy*, and *Westward Ho!*.'[94]

Henry and Constance Wyndham, the future Lord and Lady Leconfield, spent the first few days of married life at Uppark, which had been lent for the purpose. Three days after the wedding Constance admitted that it had all been 'much more successful & happy … than I anticipated'. They spent the time walking, despite the wet weather, and reading. When it brightened on one afternoon they 'walked down to a little pool where Henry thought of fishing; but as the same idea occurred to three little boys we gave it up, & read *The Mill on the Floss* in the woods instead'. At the end of the week they travelled to the family's nearby seat, Petworth, where they spent the next few days with Henry's sister, Helen. Later Henry's father arrived, as did one of his brothers.[95] For those anxious to avoid family, friends and the responsibilities of managing a house and servants, foreign travel was an attractive alternative. Even then, a bride might have to insist on her desire for privacy, as was the case with Margaret Mackay. In a letter to her future husband in 1913 she pointed out,

The thought of going to Alba and visiting your sister and husband's people alarms me very much, just then I mean. I'd love to go afterwards. It is a comfort to remember that Louise is sure to understand my feelings as *she* put not only the Channel but the length of France between herself and relations for *her* honeymoon![96]

But the evidence suggests that most couples spent their honeymoon in a country house in Britain, often within easy reach of friends and relatives. In this sense the honeymoon served as a transitional stage for the new wives, as they left behind their carefree days as unmarried daughters and assumed the responsibilities of household management which were to be their future lot. The fact that most were ignorant of the sexual act when they married must have meant that lovemaking came as a considerable shock. When Frances Maynard married Lord Brooke in April 1881, her mother sent her lists of 'solicitous instructions' on her honeymoon, but skirted round the main issue. 'Don't get your feet wet my darling, and don't overtire yourself … I like to think of you calm and resting.'[97] Frances became pregnant almost immediately and in the following September suffered a miscarriage.

Even when they loved their husbands, many girls found the sudden break with home and family distressing. Cecilia Carrington confessed to feeling 'very choky & silly all the morning' after she had received letters from her family at Barleythorpe, where she was spending her honeymoon. Happily Lord Carrington 'soon made it all right', and shortly after she was enjoying the peace of the countryside and visiting the stables and the kennels with her new husband.[98] To Lucy Lyttelton, even after more than a month of married life, her first visit to Hagley after the wedding was like 'going home. For so you still are, and so in one sense you ever will be … dear, dear old Hagley! We arrived about seven, and were greeted by a village reception … It all went deep into me … and when we got out upon the old perron, I was trembling all over.'[99]

For some younger brides, like Frances Brooke, Harriet, Duchess of Sutherland, and Consuelo, Duchess of Marlborough, the responsibilities of their new position were particularly sobering, for they were only in their teens when they became mistress of a large household, with all that that entailed. 'I sometimes wished … that my nineteen years had provided me with a greater experience,' wrote Consuelo, decades later, of this phase of her life.[100]

4

Wives & Mothers

One important truth sufficiently impressed upon your mind ... is the superiority of your husband, simply as a man ... For want of a satisfactory settlement of this point before marriage how many disputes and misunderstandings have ensued ... It is to sound judgement ... and right principle, that we must look ... for ability to make a husband happy.

Mrs [Sarah] Ellis, *The Wives of England, Their Relative Duties, Domestic Influence, and Social Obligations* (n.d. *c.* 1843). (Lady Charlotte Guest was one wife who was presented with a copy of this book by her husband.)

Once a girl married it was accepted that her connection with her own family would be loosened and that henceforth she would be closely identified with that of her husband. This transition was symbolised by the fact that were she to be re-presented at Court after marriage, she would be sponsored by a member of her *husband's* family rather than her own.

Inevitably most prospective brides were apprehensive as to how their future in-laws would receive them. Helen Fox was probably typical when she wrote to her proposed sister-in-law, Sarah Angelina Acland, expressing the hope that 'when we meet you will not be disappointed with me. I am sure you will feel with me that it is rather trying for a girl being introduced to her future husband's family.'[1] May Burns displayed similar nervousness when she assured Sir William Harcourt, her prospective father-in-law, of her great affection for Lewis (Loulou), Sir William's only son from his first marriage: 'I feel a dreadful intruder but please Sir William, will you like me a little for Loulou's sake & if you will let me you will only find one more person to love you.'[2] In both cases a warm relationship developed and the girl concerned was quickly absorbed into her new family.

Not all brides were so lucky. Among the less fortunate was Mary Tribe, daughter of the Archdeacon of Lahore, who married Lord Herbrand Russell, younger son of the 9th Duke of Bedford. The wedding took place in India and when the new Lady Russell reached England she received a cool reception from her new relations. 'My family have always thought themselves slightly grander than God,' wrote her grandson,

> and energetic steps had been taken to try to stop the marriage. These had proved unsuccessful, so two of my great-aunts were sent I think to Marseilles, to make sure that my grandmother wore the right clothes and looked respectable before she could be accepted into her new environment. They cannot have sent back a very favourable report as I have heard it said that her mother-in-law walked straight out of the house and never came back again. Be that as it may, the newly married couple soon retired to Scotland for the grouse shooting season.[3]

It was there that their only son was born prematurely in December 1888, in a derelict shepherd's cottage, while husband and wife were out walking across the moors. There was no doctor or midwife present, and the shock of the unexpected birth left its mark on Lady Russell for the rest of her life.[4]

Within a few years, as a result of the death of Herbrand's father in 1891 and of his elder brother two years later, Lord and Lady Russell became the Duke and Duchess of Bedford and took up residence at Woburn Abbey. But even then the duchess was not fully accepted by the family. Her husband assumed responsibility for running not only the estate but the household as well. 'She was told she did not know about such things, so she developed no interest in the house and had nothing to do with it at all. My grandfather even drew up the lunch and dinner menus,' wrote their grandson.[5] Their only joint interests were in certain outdoor pursuits, such as shooting.

In other cases, the position of a new bride could be made difficult because she and her husband were expected to share the parental home. 'It was the era when the rule of the dowager was supreme,' recalled Mabell, Countess of Airlie ruefully:

> Widowed mothers, from Windsor Castle to the humblest cottage, exacted obedience from sons and daughters, no matter what their age.

A son's wife was as much subject to her mother-in-law in Britain as she would have been in India.

My husband's mother had her own house in London, but she – and all her children – regarded Cortachy as her home. Her every wish was law there. The servants were hers and perfectly trained by her. I had no scope for my own initiative. My position as the wife of the head of the family was not recognised.[6]

Lady Airlie was writing of the 1880s, but over half a century earlier Lady Elizabeth Grosvenor had found herself in a similar position when she married the future 2nd Marquess of Westminster in 1819. They did not have a country estate of their own until the 1830s, and huge as was Eaton, the family's Cheshire home, it was not easy for Lady Elizabeth to be a permanent guest in her in-laws' house. Although she remained on good terms with them,

her happiest hours … were those when she was alone there with her husband and when she could write to her mother, 'our life here is so very comfortable and pleasant – quite alone and doing what *we* like …' But it was another matter when she was … with Lady Grosvenor [her mother-in-law] and had to spend the long evening 'listening to Mr Aychbourn reading aloud … in so lachrymose a manner that Dido [her terrier] cried'.[7]

The house's huge vaulted rooms and long unheated corridors added to her discomfort during the winter months. In order to protect herself against the freezing temperature, Lady Elizabeth wore voluminous flannel underwear. She also put on two pairs of stockings and wash leather insteps to protect her legs against the cold, as well as 'muffetees' which she knitted for her wrists.[8] Not surprisingly she, like other members of the household, suffered from colds and laryngitis, which she dosed with a 'low' diet of tea and bread and butter combined with various laxatives, ranging from blue pills to the more powerful calomel. She even applied leeches to her toes as a cure for chilblains.[9]

Not until 1831 did Lady Elizabeth's father-in-law present them with their own property – the Motcombe estate in Dorset – and two more years elapsed before they moved in. The estate was officially made over to them in 1835 and from then on they spent more and more time at Motcombe 'where the cosy independence of their family life was in such agreeable contrast with the constraints of living as Lord and Lady Westminster's guests in the chilly splendours of Eaton'.[10]

But while one of a wife's duties was to make herself congenial to her husband's family if she wished her marriage to succeed, another still more important requirement was her need to minister to her husband's wants and oversee the welfare of their children. This 'cult of domesticity' applied even in the upper ranks of society where servants were employed to carry out the menial tasks involved in day-to-day household affairs. A wife's 'greatest claim on her husband is by her submission,' asserted *Etiquette for Ladies* in 1900. 'Self-sacrifice is the truest womanly virtue, and above all in a wife; not, as some do, by ostentatiously making martyrs of themselves, but in this loving, unobtrusive adaptation of herself to her husband's tastes and wishes.'[11] In the anonymous author's opinion the fact that women had 'far greater powers of adaptation' than men made their responsibilities in this direction all the greater. And should an estrangement occur between them, it was she who bore the greater blame for it. That was especially true should she be tempted to sever by divorce 'those ties God has declared shall never, but for one cause, be broken'.[12] It was in this context that the attributes of passivity, piety, gentleness and patience were seen as the true feminine virtues.

Needless to say many women failed to live up to this ideal. Henry Polderoy's frivolous and sociable wife, Carlotta, was bored and irritated with her home-loving, dull husband. 'Englishmen were worse than Turks,' she raged, 'and expected their wives to be as docile as cows.' In the end she ran away with another man and obtained a divorce. But few discontented wives went as far as that. Marie Tasburgh retired to a separate part of the house and declined 'all communication with her husband', and a similar solution to marital problems was adopted by Lord and Lady Howard.[13]

Other women, like the strong-willed Lady Selborne, were contemptuous of extreme female docility. Shortly before she married in 1883 she firmly informed her fiancé, who was a Liberal party supporter, that she would not abandon her allegiance to the Conservatives, as had been suggested by one of his sisters. It was essential that he should be '*quite* free from error on the subject. Nothing is sure but death and taxes, but of all the improbable eventualities that is one of the most unlikely.'[14] In a similar vein, over a quarter of a century later, she complained to her daughter that 'one of women's leading faults' was that they would not 'say what they think, & one of the results of this course of conduct … is that they cease to think at all'.[15] Such a negative approach to life had little appeal to her.

These robust attitudes towards female independence became more widely accepted at the end of the Victorian era, as there was a gradual opening up of educational opportunities for women in all ranks of society and as the pressure for the vote increased their interest in political questions. As Lady Fanny Clermont declared crisply, 'I aim at growing a soul in spite of being a wife, a mother and a hostess.'[16]

But in the earlier years of the century, it was seen as a wife's duty to obey her husband and to accept his judgement at all times in the conduct of family life. This is made clear in the journals of Lady Catherine Boileau, wife of the squire of Ketteringham, Norfolk and daughter of the 1st Earl of Minto. In November 1835, she wrote a list of questions for self-examination each evening:

> Have I been dutiful and affectionate in my manner, as well as in my feelings, towards my dear husband this day?
> Have I listened to him when speaking to me, with *attention*, with a desire to understand his meaning, with a readiness to enter into his views, to agree with his opinions?
> Have I submitted with a *cheerful humility* when he has thought right to reprove me for or point out any of my faults?
> Have I tried in *everything* to consult his wishes?

There is much more in a similar key, and it is clear that she tried to abide by these principles even though periodically she was unable to prevent herself disputing with him when he treated the children too severely. Her eldest daughter later compared her efforts in that direction to a peahen protecting its chicks. Perhaps not surprisingly, she was often ill and depressed – something which her frequent pregnancies doubtless aggravated; she was eventually to have nine children. Occasionally she resorted to tears and hysteria, the 'legendary armour of Victorian wives', in order to get her way. But in the main she 'tried to keep herself modest, and meek', even when criticised for extravagance in running the household, or inefficiency in its management. She submitted her household accounts to her husband for his scrutiny, a practice which Victorian ladies widely followed.[17] This remained her approach until her death in 1862.

Even Lady Charlotte Guest recognised that she must keep her strong opinions in check when dealing with her husband. On one occasion she expressed satisfaction that she had quietly accepted his sudden decision to remove the family earlier than arranged to their seaside home at Sully near Cardiff. 'I did not contradict him, which … I am always sorry to do, and I was subsequently very grateful for it.'[18]

Yet if, in most marriages, a wife's submission to her husband was taken as the desired model, the warm affection which frequently existed between them ensured that for the majority, the wheels of matrimony ran comparatively smoothly, with neither imposing intolerable burdens on the other. Some men, like John Arkwright, shared Ruskin's view 'that women were superior to men in their power for good and evil', and they looked to a wife to act as their guide in moral matters. Arkwright saw his future wife's influence as his 'sweet hope'.[19]

Outside the sphere of personal relations, one of the principal anxieties for most new wives was the running of the home itself. For the splendour, comfort and efficiency of this demonstrated the owner's own standing in the world. Mrs Beeton compared the mistress of a household to the commander of an army. 'Her spirit will be seen through the whole establishment; and just in proportion as she performs her duties intelligently and thoroughly, so will her domestics follow in her path.'[20] Organisational problems were made more difficult when families had more than one country seat or when they migrated to London for the Season. In November 1878, the newly married Lord and Lady Carrington moved from Wycombe Abbey in Buckinghamshire to Barleythorpe, their home in Rutland, for the hunting season. They reached Barleythorpe on 3 November, and four days later Cecilia noted that she had 'stayed at home the whole day arranging things as the heavy baggage arrived last night & the rest of the servants'. The next morning was devoted to reorganising the rooms. The couple returned to Wycombe the following April, and shortly after moved to London for the Season. Here Cecilia, who was already pregnant with her first child, spent time arranging 'the downstairs rooms a little differently'. Soon after she suffered a miscarriage.[21]

The removal of households with their large numbers of servants and vast quantities of luggage was no easy matter, even when the detailed work involved was undertaken by the housekeeper and butler or, in larger establishments, by the steward. Lord John Russell's family was described as 'an army on the march', and Georgiana Sitwell remembered that when her family moved from their Derbyshire home, Renishaw, to the Highlands for the shooting season they were accompanied by a vast array of heavy baggage:

> The day of our start, our excitement ... reached its height. The servants packed all night; my mother often till two in the morning ... At length, ... our caravan drew up. It consisted of three carriages with post-horses, a closed chariot, a britschka, and a phaeton, the last usually occupied by my father and mother.[22]

Later in the century, with the spread of the railway network, such migrations became easier, with some of the wealthiest families hiring their own railway carriages for the purpose.[23]

To add to a new wife's difficulties in coping with these complex manoeuvres was the fact that few of them had had much experience in managing domestic affairs before they married. Florence Nightingale, who, ironically, remained a spinster, was one of the exceptions. She was given responsibility for the still-room, the pantry, and the linen-room by her mother in the 1840s, when she was in her mid-twenties. 'I am up to my chin in linen, glass and china,' she told a friend in December 1846, 'and I am very fond of housekeeping. In this too highly educated, too-little-active age, it is at least a practical application of our theories to something – and yet in the middle of my lists ... I cannot help asking in my head, "Can reasonable people want all this?"' In the still-room, she supervised the making of preserves, and earlier in that same year noted proudly that after a hard day's work she was 'surveying fifty-six jam pots with the eye of an artist'.[24]

Another daughter involved in household affairs from an early age was Maggie Wyndham, who took over some of her mother's domestic responsibilities in 1898, when Lady Leconfield was in Ireland nursing one of her sons, who was seriously ill. Her letters to her mother discuss such questions as selecting carpet for the servants' hall, purchasing fruit and flour for Christmas cake, and similar minor matters.[25]

But the majority of brides learnt to run their households by hard experience, perhaps reinforced by advice from parents or married sisters and friends. 'Housekeeping looks alarming when I see the bills,' wrote Lady Amberley to her sister, Maude, just over four months after her wedding. 'Would you ask Mamma what the book is she gave Rosalind on Domestic Economy & order it for me.'[26]

In the case of Mary Elizabeth Lucy of Charlecote Park, it was her father who gave detailed instructions soon after her marriage:

> As you are now a steady housewife remember what I told you respecting all orders at shops. Never allow anyone to give or accept an order that is not in writing, let you or your housekeeper do this and do you inspect her books every week and settle them every month. You will then have full command of your household. For the wages Mr Lucy gives, you ought to have a first class gardener who will produce for you plenty of fruit and have it sent up to you in London where it will be extravagantly dear.[27]

In this social rank it was not customary for wives to perform domestic chores, unless they wished to do so themselves. One who did was Lady Elizabeth Shiffner of Coombe Place in Hamsey, Sussex. She not only assumed responsibility for the sale of produce from the home farm but kept notebooks with recipes for cowslip wine, sloe gin, plum cake, furniture and metal polish, as well as a whole range of medical remedies including 'cures' for cholera, dropsy, neuralgia and chilblains. She kept careful records of the eggs, milk, cream, butter, poultry, pigs and cows produced, and even entered cheese and butter-making competitions. In 1891 she won a prize of 10s for her cream cheese. Some of the cash secured from retail sales of eggs, milk, rabbits, etc., she retained for her own use. In 1893 she obtained between £10 and £11 from this source (out of a total personal income of £274 17s 9d in that year).[28] Like some other country-house ladies she also kept detailed inventories of the linen and china used at her home.

Occasionally, as with Lady Stanhope or the strong-minded Lady Sackville, still greater responsibilities might be assumed. Lady Stanhope combined efficient management of her large household at Chevening, Kent, with the duties of an estate steward, when her husband was away from home. In 1878, for example, 'she reassured him that the farm stock book was in order, the list of leases prepared, the new brick machine operating efficiently and the dairy wall cemented'. Lady Sackville was even more ambitious. In the 1890s she initiated a programme of modernisation at Knole, installing electricity, central-heating and bathrooms. According to her grandson, when she discovered that her decisions on these matters went unchallenged by her husband, she started slowly to take over the management of the estate and its finances. 'When money was short it was she who speculated successfully on the Stock Exchange, she who opened in London a shop called Spealls for the sale of lamp-shades and stationery which became highly lucrative.'[29]

But these women were exceptional. Most wives confined their domestic concerns to supervision of the indoor servants, including the hiring and firing of senior staff, and daily interviews with the housekeeper and the cook to arrange for the reception of guests and the drawing up of menus. They also attended to the household accounts and the ordering of fresh supplies.

The number of servants kept varied with the means and size of the family and the scale of the house in which they lived. Normally gentry families would aim to keep at least eight indoor domestics, but in the most prestigious aristocratic establishments there might be forty or fifty. Lady Leconfield had thirty-two indoor servants at Petworth in the late 1870s and thirty-one in 1891.[30] At Longleat the Marchioness of Bath recollected a staff of forty-three before the First World War (including two lady's maids and a first footman whose prime duty it was to attend to the wants of the mistress of the household). And at Blenheim, Consuelo, wife of the 9th Duke of Marlborough, inherited a household staff of well over twenty in the mid-1890s, even before a nursery was established. They included six housemaids, five laundresses, and a staff of four in the kitchen, under the temperamental direction of a French chef. Frequent disputes broke out between him and the housekeeper over the preparation of breakfast trays, and it was Consuelo's task to smooth the various ruffled feathers.[31]

Staff sizes began to be reduced in many landed families from the 1870s, as agricultural depression led to reduced incomes. At Cranmer Hall, Norfolk, low and remitted rents and the losses of the Home Farm caused the Joneses to close the laundry, dismiss the footman and after him the groom, and not to replace the third gardener when he retired. Partly on economic grounds, Mrs Jones acted as governess to her children – an innovation they regarded with mixed feelings. 'Lessons were delightful when my mother wore a summer frock … But if the brown frock, or some other dress giving warning of a depression over Iceland, was being worn, there would be, more likely than not, tears over the *participe* passé.'[32]

But even the direction of smaller households could prove daunting to some wives. 'I have, I think, undertaken more than I can accomplish,' wrote Louisa Yorke gloomily, about a month after returning from her honeymoon. 'The management of this huge house with six female & three male servants is "no joke".' Just over a fortnight later, she recounted further woes: 'I am having great trouble with the numerous servants. Some are too noisy, some too grand, some find the work too much. I wonder if I shall ever be quite settled.' As the daughter of an impoverished Anglican clergyman, Louisa's problems of adjustment to her new status were likely to be greater than those faced by girls brought up in a country house. In September 1902, after more than four months of married life, she was still encountering staff opposition. 'I interviewed Mr Hughes the Agent. I had rather an awful time … at the accounts. He would not show me the books of the Estate & household expenditure. I insisted and consulted a lawyer on the subject who told me I had a right to see them … I must have the accounts done differently.' But her attempts to economise in the running of the household continued to meet with disappointments, and on 11 November, ill in hospital after an operation and already pregnant with her first child, she was still complaining of 'the trouble of the servants at Erddig. It is sad to contemplate. The new Housekeeper, Mrs Osmond is to leave at once. She will do no work except arrange flowers!'[33]

Over the following months some of the difficulties were resolved, but they never entirely disappeared. Indeed, the peculation of Mrs Penketh, who was cook-housekeeper at Erddig for five years, eventually led to an embarrassing and unpleasant court case in 1907. According to Louisa she had robbed the family of £500, but the legal proceedings were a galling experience. The housekeeper's counsel not only cast aspersions on her competence as a manager but upon her way of life. 'All the evidence was against the prisoner,' she wrote angrily, 'also the Judge, but the Welsh Jury said she was not guilty. Mr Artemus Jones was most rude and only got off the prisoner by abusing us and saying we were "Idlers on the pathway of life". The whole affair is scandalous.'[34] Her anger was doubtless reinforced by the fact that she and her husband were chronically short of cash. In February 1904, she was even reduced to mending holes in the saloon carpet by hand. Two years later she discussed with Mr Capper, the new agent, the desirability of selling the cows and sheep from the home farm and buying in milk and meat as needed. In 1904, there were proposals to sell land in order to finance the building of houses, so as to make the estate 'smaller & more profitable'.[35] But none of this really eased their financial plight.

Servant problems also affected Lucy Arkwright at Hampton Court, Hertfordshire. On one occasion she reported a 'domestic riot' when the housemaid confronted the housekeeper 'in my presence … I have made Jane eat her words about the Beer on Sat[urda]y, & given her a piece of my mind.'[36]

Even the sweet-tempered Lucy Cavendish was not exempt, despite the fact that she had been used to country-house life from birth and had acted as hostess for her father for several years before her marriage. Less than a month after moving into her new London home she lamented that she was 'beginning upon troubles I was experienced enough to foresee when I was preparing myself for a new chapter of household cares: viz. failures. The kitchen-maid turns out sick and incapable; the upper-housemaid pert, fine, and lazy. Woe is me!'[37] Later there was the 'miserable catastrophe' of a housekeeper who drank and a series of lady's maids who quarrelled with fellow servants. 'My life feels shortened by these things,' she observed ruefully, after the encounter with her housekeeper.[38]

Nevertheless, there were inconsiderate employers, too. The only time Margaret Thomas saw one mistress was when the lady summoned her to dismiss her.[39] And the autocratic Lady Londesborough would not even allow the servants to look at one another in her presence. 'My grandmother Londesborough,' wrote Edith Sitwell, 'never spoke to any of the servants excepting the butler, Martin and the old housekeeper, Mrs Selby.'[40] Some mistresses also found blaming the servants for real or imagined faults a convenient way of relieving frustrations built up in other areas of family life, or a welcome means of imposing their will on another human being who could not easily answer back.

But if the 'servant question' caused anxieties to some wives, many found keeping their household accounts an even greater problem. In the early 1840s Mrs Sarah Ellis had written, tongue in cheek, of the need for a 'law ... allowing no woman to marry until she had become an economist, thoroughly acquainted with the necessary expenses of a respectable mode of living'.[41] Her advice fell on deaf ears. Certainly Lucy Cavendish found her first efforts in that direction highly disconcerting. 'Did my house-books for the first time,' she wrote on 16 May 1865, a week after moving into her new home. 'They came to a heavy total, but I trust that is only the start.' Just over a month later she was driving round London 'paying some of the monster bills incident to setting up house. We much fear the total of the furnishing, including linen, crockery, and kitchen apparatus, will be quite £3,000.' A few days later she gloomily discovered that in the two months she and her husband had been in residence they had spent £121 on housekeeping. 'This I *must* cut down!' Not until September was a happier note struck: 'I meditated over money matters, for once, with agreeable results.'[42] At a time when many labouring families were expected to subsist on less than £50 a *year* it is clear that she had cause for concern.

The strong-willed Lady Charlotte Guest also wearied of these mundane domestic duties. 'I toil and strive to controul [sic] all the servants and dependants until really my life is rather that of a steward than a lady,' she complained. She drew up her accounts monthly, and found it a wearying task. 'I feel now that I have completely sunk into the mere drudge,' she wrote on one occasion, when the governess was also ill; 'to look after servants and check expenses and writing accounts, or to supervise tutors and governesses'. Sometimes she spent whole days on the accounts, while 'childbirth was usually preceded by an extra flurry of activity,' her biographers note. 'She finished posting the books at 8.30 one evening and Blanche arrived at 10.30 the next morning.'[43] She also wrote business letters for her husband and sorted correspondence connected with the ironworks.[44]

But many women were less competent. Catherine Gladstone admitted to 'studying Lady Lyttelton's book of instruction regarding household accounts and taking a 'leaf out of it', soon after she married. But a decade later she was still appealing to her husband for help: 'You tidy old thing, can you tell me without inconvenience what money I have had out?'[45] Lady Fanny Russell, too, found difficulty in balancing the books and was often overcharged. She depended on her father, Lord Minto, to provide her with honest servants from his estate.[46]

Where there was extensive entertaining to be arranged, fresh worries arose. Lady Frederick Cavendish admitted to anxiety when she held her first dinner party:

I fussed and fidgeted a good deal all day ... ; arranged flowers, mused over the bill of fare, contemplated the table, displayed china ... All went very well; but I began with a good fit of nervousness, which, however, I craftily concealed.[47]

Lady de Rothschild shared these feelings:

> Today we have our first grand dinner party – our first great bore. I am nervous and fidgety. What trouble we take, what expense we go to for the so called pleasures of society! ... I, who am so anti-luxurious in tastes and habits am made to appear fond of show and glitter ... I must try to bear it patiently and then the gilded walls may be of some use and read me a lesson of humility and patience.[48]

The organising of country-house parties, which in the early and middle years of the nineteenth century could extend over a week or more, required still greater social skills. In the 1890s, Consuelo, Duchess of Marlborough, remembered twenty-five to thirty guests assembling for weekend parties at Blenheim Palace, each bringing a valet or lady's maid. The Marlboroughs came down from London on Saturday mornings, ready to receive their guests in the afternoon. Consuelo made a round of the rooms, to ensure that all was in order. Menus had to be approved and the chef's complaints about the deficiencies of his underlings listened to sympathetically. Hours were spent placing the guests for the 'three ceremonial meals they would partake with us, for the rules of precedence were then strictly adhered to, not only in seating arrangements but also for the procession in to dinner ... There was ... a considerable amount of purely mechanical work ... dealing with correspondence, answering invitations, writing the dinner cards and other instructions which [appeared] necessary to ensure the smooth progression of social amenities.' Not surprisingly, at the end of her first London Season she was so tired that on going to the seaside to recuperate, she slept for twenty-four hours without waking.[49]

Inexperienced hostesses might also consult friends and relatives on the finer points of etiquette. Early in 1902 May Harcourt asked her step-mother-in-law for advice on addressing invitation cards for a party she and 'Loulou' were to hold. 'Would you put "Lord & Lady Chesterfield" or "The Earl & Countess of Chesterfield"? Please send me a line saying "Full Title" or "Not Full Title" & I will quite understand. I am so sorry to bother you but I ... should like to know which of the two is right.'[50] In similar vein, the newly married Elinor Glyn was advised by the Countess of Warwick as to whom she should invite to her home: 'Army or naval officers, diplomats or clergymen might be invited to lunch or dinner ... Doctors and solicitors might be invited to garden parties, though never ... to lunch or dinner.'[51]

Small wonder that to Lady Cynthia Asquith any woman who ran 'a large and hospitable country house' had an arduous task, despite the help she received from servants:

> The châtelaines I knew seemed so very seldom free really to live to enjoy the passing moment. They were too distractingly preoccupied by plans for the future. Indeed, what with the cares of family, household and tenants; incessant village duties; the trickiness of parochial politics and the perpetual coming and going of guests, they seldom had a disengaged hour in which to read, let alone follow any pursuit of their own.[52]

One such busy hostess was her own mother, the hospitable Lady Elcho (later the Countess of Wemyss). Each morning she sat up in bed surrounded by sheets of paper scribbled all over with 'tangled plans for the day'. 'Whilst Mamma organised the transport, sleeping and seating arrangements for those visitors already within her gates a large fraction of her mind would be simultaneously engaged in planning ahead exactly how her next week's party should be occupied during every hour of their stay.'[53]

It was in the face of these pressures that Louisa Yorke, enjoying a lull in visits and entertaining in August 1902, wrote happily in her diary, 'Philip & I who are quite alone now … feel like school children having a perpetual holiday.'[54] But the respite was short-lived and there was a note of weariness in her comment in mid-October 1909 that they had 'already had ninety guests this year so I think we have had our share'.[55]

In return for carrying out such duties, most ladies enjoyed the privilege of having their slightest wants attended to by servants. The Marchioness of Bath, looking back to the late nineteenth century, referred to the 'protected and cosseted lives' led by her ancestors.[56] While Lady Cynthia Asquith remembered nostalgically the 'cheerful willing atmosphere in which nothing seemed too much trouble' for the armies of highly trained housemaids.[57]

Intertwined with their responsibilities as wives, however, many women fulfilled those of a mother. At that time motherhood was not considered a prime occupation for upper-class women. Their roles and duties as companions to their husbands, mistresses of large households, dispensers of charity, and participants in Society were all deemed more important.[58] In addition, few landed ladies had had practical experience of baby-care, unless they had been conscientious older sisters in large families. Lady Clodagh Anson, youngest child of the 5th Marquess of Waterford, frankly admitted that she had not the faintest idea of how to bring up her children, never having seen a small baby 'until I had one myself'. When a prospective nanny asked 'what food we gave the baby ... I could not remember, but said I thought she had a little limewater, as I had seen a large bottle with "Limewater" written on it in the nursery'. The nanny, needless to say, 'had a very poor opinion of my motherly instinct'.[59]

But none of this prevented such women from having children. Indeed, if their husband owned an estate it was regarded as their duty to produce a son and heir as quickly as possible. Hence, especially in the first half of the nineteenth century, most landed families were large. Contraception was frowned upon as irreligious and immoral and, in any case, there were no reliable birth control methods available before the vulcanisation of rubber in 1843. Even then condoms were long identified with prostitution and were thus not quite 'decent'.[60]

Nonetheless a few couples did accept the need for family limitation. They included the Stanleys of Alderley, although in their case the conversion was belated. Lady Henrietta Stanley had already had ten children when she became pregnant again, and her husband wrote reproachfully, 'This last misfortune is indeed most grievous ... What can you have been doing to account for so juvenile a proceeding?' That put all responsibility firmly on his wife and it was doubtless with relief that she was able to inform him shortly after, that a 'hot bath, a tremendous walk & a great dose have succeeded' in bringing about an abortion; 'but it is a warning'.[61]

Likewise in 1923 the feminist Lady Constance Lytton claimed that birth control had been practised in her family and among their numerous friends 'for generations'. But before the 1870s it would appear that such a hard-headed approach to contraception was unusual. Hence, the period 1760–1850 probably represented the era of greatest fertility in the history of the English nobility. One study of fifty aristocratic wives has concluded that during these years it was common for such women to marry at twenty-one, to have about eight children, and to give birth to the last child when aged thirty-nine.[62] Almost half had their first child within a year of marriage, and many spent a large part of their early married life pregnant, or recovering from childbirth. This included suffering the miseries of early morning sickness during the first weeks of each pregnancy at a time when they were coping with the responsibilities of managing a household and organising the entertainment of guests.

Lady Charlotte Guest was one wife who conformed to this pattern. She had ten children in thirteen years, as well as at least one miscarriage. There were only eleven months between the birth of the first and second child, and in four other cases the gaps were only twelve and thirteen months.[63] Although her confinements, with the exception of the last, were uneventful, she was often quite ill during the pregnancy. But she did not allow this to hamper her, and continued to lead an active social life, as well as helping her husband in his business.

Mary Elizabeth Lucy, whose first child was born about nine months after her marriage, was even presented at Court when she was five months pregnant. A few days later she described a ball she attended with her husband and sister, and the following week she gave two dinner parties.[64]

May Harcourt, who also became pregnant on her honeymoon, was another young wife who led an active social life during her pregnancies. She only withdrew from public view for the last month or so before her confinement. In June 1908, for example, about three months before the birth of her son, she told her stepmother-in-law that she and Loulou were spending the weekend with friends. 'They asked us for Ascot as usual but Loulou can't get away & I am not presentable enough for a Race Course! … I shall get out of the Garden party if I can as I think it a boring & certainly tiring entertainment!'[65] In a previous pregnancy, about six years earlier, she had decided to 'withdraw from the world of country house visiting' about three months before the expected date of birth. Like many other ladies in landed society, particularly in the late Victorian and Edwardian period, she always moved up to London for the confinement itself.

But not all wives coped with their pregnancies as easily as did May Harcourt. And even those who did would probably have agreed with Queen Victoria when she warned her newly married daughter of the hazards which lay ahead:

> If you have hereafter (as I had constantly for the first two years of my marriage) – aches – and sufferings and miseries and plagues – which you must struggle against – and enjoyments etc. to give up – constant precautions to take, you will feel the yoke of a married woman! … one feels so pinned down – one's wings clipped – in fact, at the best (and few were or are better than I was) only half oneself.[66]

Later when her daughter ventured to point to the pride 'of giving life to an immortal soul', the Queen firmly replied that that was 'very fine … but I own I cannot enter into that: I think much more of our being like a cow or a dog at such moments; when our poor nature becomes so very animal and unecstatic.' Her rejection of women's sufferings in labour led her to be an early pioneer in the use of chloroform as an anaesthetic in childbirth. She used this for her eighth and ninth deliveries in 1853 and 1857 and thereby made it 'respectable' for other women to follow suit. But even that was no easy option. Frances

Brooke, who gave birth to her first baby in September 1882, after a painful labour of seven hours, had chloroform, but although this eased the pain it caused violent sickness to add to her misery when the delivery itself was over.[67]

Another who experienced the burdens of childbearing in early married life was Cecilia Carrington. She suffered a miscarriage in the spring of 1879, less than a year after marriage, and then became pregnant once more in the summer of that year. But a miscarriage again threatened and by the middle of August she was confined to the sofa and a wheelchair. Later she drove herself about in a donkey cart, but during the greater part of her pregnancy she led the life of an invalid. Her daughter, Marjorie, was born on 4 April 1880, and she then enjoyed a brief return to normal social life before again becoming pregnant in the summer of that year. Once more, she was forced into semi-invalidism, before her second daughter was born the following March.[68] In later pregnancies she was more fortunate, but the stress imposed on a young, newly married woman by this kind of experience must have been enormous.

Cecilia, nevertheless, appears to have accepted her pregnancies philosophically, and to have rejoiced greatly when in April 1895 she at last gave birth to a son, after five daughters. 'A boy born at eleven today,' she wrote triumphantly in her diary. 'Many kind telegrams from the dear family & others. C. & I overjoyed.'[69] Sadly he was to be killed in the First World War, aged twenty.

Consuelo Marlborough, too, appreciated the importance of producing an heir. Her insensitive husband made clear to his young wife that he regarded her as 'a link in the chain' of family succession: 'to produce the next link in the chain was, I knew, my most immediate duty'.[70] She succeeded in that, with two sons produced in the first three years of married life.

But not all newly-weds accepted her view. It was in these circumstances that eugenicists in the closing years of the nineteenth century complained of the way in which upper-class women were limiting the size of their families. Some medical men in the 1880s labelled contraception the 'American sin', and the practice was condemned on religious and moral grounds, much as it had been earlier in the century.

As regards the moral aspects, it was argued that women were postponing a family or curbing its size merely to enjoy the frivolities and pleasures of Society. T. H. S. Escott referred in 1880 to the 'increasing laxity' of marital relations and the way in which women used the 'five 'o'clock tea', picnics, and garden parties as a discreet excuse for meeting admirers, without causing gossip.[71] American brides were considered particularly guilty of artificially limiting family size, and some credence was given to the accusation by the fact that one in four of all transatlantic peerage marriages between 1870 and 1914 were childless. But a closer investigation suggests that in certain cases at least this was because of the age of the women concerned rather than any use of contraception.[72] Nevertheless, that did not prevent alarmists from predicting the 'virtual extinction' of certain landed families within 'a matter of a few generations'.[73]

Although the eugenicists' more dramatic claims about the effects of family limitation proved groundless, there is evidence that by the end of the Victorian era younger brides were questioning the merits of unrestricted fertility. In December 1906 Molly Trevelyan, the future chatelaine of Wallington in Northumberland, and her sister-in-law, Janet, debated the value of the condom as a form of contraception. Each had given birth to a child in both 1905 and 1906 and Janet anxiously reported the comment of the maternity nurse on the need to 'beware of *little coats* [i.e. condoms]. *They bust!* She has had ever so many babies thr' them, whereas the other things have never failed.' As yet she had not 'in the least settled how' to have 'fun' with her husband while avoiding further unwanted pregnancies. In the event, her third child was born in March 1909 and Molly's appeared in the previous May, so whatever techniques they had employed had clearly been of limited reliability.

Maud Yorke, Lady Leconfield's second daughter, likewise admitted shortly after her marriage that it was 'rather a bore beginning [a child] so soon, & it will be a great bore all through the hot summer, but it cannot be helped & I shall not mind so much if it is a boy'. She was particularly annoyed because a family acquaintance had guessed her condition. 'I cannot bear its being announced & talked over, people will find out all too soon.'[74] A few days later she referred, in another letter to her mother, to the way in which Lady Leconfield herself had borne nine children in twenty years. 'I feel quite *appalled* at the amount of experience you have had! How perfectly *dreadful* it must have been, you can hardly ever have been without it!'[75]

But Lady Leconfield appears to have been made of stern stuff. On 4 October 1877, shortly before the birth of her fourth son, she gave her eldest daughter her customary morning lessons. Her only concession to her imminent confinement was not to go into luncheon, 'telling the children that my head ached. George [her eldest son] said to [the nanny] in the evening that when Mother had one of these bad headaches a little brother or sister generally came, & she then told him that one was expected.' The following day, when her children came to see the new baby, her second son looked at it gloomily and declared firmly, 'I have had quite enough of new babies.'[76] He was five at the time.

All the women considered so far survived the rigours of frequent pregnancies successfully, and most were able to breastfeed their children themselves. Lady Charlotte Guest was one who could not and had to employ a wet nurse; Lady Elizabeth Grosvenor chose not to do so; and Cecilia Carrington seems to have fed her first child in part at least on asses' milk. Margaret, Countess of Jersey, convinced both herself and her daughters that none of them would be able to nurse their children successfully. And Lady Clodagh Anson, who was born in 1879, claimed that nobody 'dreamt of nursing their babies when I was young, and I don't fancy they did in my Mother's time either; certainly she never did'.[77]

Nonetheless from the middle of the nineteenth century it was increasingly accepted that except in cases of a mother's serious illness or physical inability to feed her child, wet nurses should not be employed. Bottle-fed babies became more common in the 1880s and 1890s, when some of the hazards of unsterilised feeding bottles had been eliminated, but many country-house wives accepted the value of breastfeeding. Certainly Lady Salisbury made clear to one unfortunate daughter in-law her opposition to the employment of a wet nurse, even when she was ill:

> I am *very* sorry you have agreed to [this] old fashioned folly … you will find the expense enormous especially in rooms and food … Don't be the least afraid but turn off the wet nurse at once and have the same milk from Hatfield that Alice's baby thrives on.[78]

Other women continued to breastfeed their babies while they pursued an active social life. According to Rosalind Howard's daughter, her mother took pride in doing this, even if it meant 'traipsing' the babies around 'most unsuitably, Mary being fed whilst sightseeing in Italian churches and picture galleries. Michael was hastily fed in the back passages of election meetings and then sent home many miles in an open dogcart at night, whilst she returned to the platform.'[79] Lady Frances Horner shared this down-to-earth approach and nursed her daughter, Cicely, when out on picnics, 'sitting on a heap of stones by the roadside'.[80]

The successful cases examined thus far, were, however, sadly balanced by a trickle of other instances where miscarriage or a difficult birth proved fatal to the mother, perhaps because of the onset of puerperal fever or because the strain of too many pregnancies caused heart disease. This was true of Mary Lyttelton, Lucy's mother. She bore twelve children in less than eighteen years of married life, as well as undergoing at least one miscarriage. She called these regular pregnancies her 'yearly penance' and eventually died in 1857, aged forty-four, from heart failure. Her death occurred about six months after the birth of the twelfth child, and her daughter's diary makes clear that she never recovered fully from that confinement.[81] In the years that followed, Lucy noted many similar victims of childbirth, as on 11 December 1866, when she recorded the death of Lady Fortescue 'in her confinement, leaving thirteen children, the eldest only eighteen', or in September 1871, when she lamented the loss of the young Duchess of St Albans from fever about a fortnight after her third confinement.

May Harcourt's correspondence is littered with similar misfortunes, like 'the dreadful tragedy of Lady Isabel Wilson's death' in the autumn of 1905. 'Her baby was born dead last Monday at seven months & she died Thursday morning.' Then there was Lady Rachel Dudley, who had almost died as a result of her pregnancy on the journey down from Scotland. 'I hope she will manage to get through with it this time without some catastrophe,' May told her stepmother-in-law. 'I must say I think her pluck is wonderful. I am sure I wouldn't face it again if I had been as near dying as she was when she had the last still born Baby. She expects to be laid up about the same time as I am, the end of March.'[82] A few months earlier she had contrasted the sad fate of 'poor little Mrs Berkeley Levett', who had had 'a stillborn boy, with the Duchess of Leeds, who had had 'a son at last! I should think she had given up all hopes by now.'[83] The duchess had been married for twenty years when this much-wanted heir appeared and she had already borne four daughters – hence May's comment. Then there was Lady Curzon, who died of heart failure and dropsy in 1906, aged thirty-six. Two years before she had been seriously ill with peritonitis and phlebitis shortly after a miscarriage, and had never fully recovered her health thereafter.[84]

Many of these women spent nearly two decades of their lives in child-bearing and rearing, with the attendant risks of death or serious illness. Small wonder that Maggie Acland, pregnant after only three months of marriage, should confess sadly to her sister-in-law her secret fear that she would not survive the confinement: 'I … think that perhaps I may never see the dear old Home again.'[85] Some, like Harriet, Duchess of Sutherland, made informal wills before the expected date of birth; Harriet was 'so terrified of dying … that she wrote out detailed instructions for her family before several confinements'. Even the hard-headed Lady Selborne warned her only daughter, Mabel, never to 'struggle against it' if she felt 'seedy' during her pregnancy. 'Lie in bed for breakfast, & take life as easy as you can. Not only is it very bad for you to make efforts, but it is very bad for the baby also.' She anxiously inquired whether her daughter had made arrangements for a monthly nurse to attend at the confinement, and advised her to contact agencies in London who could send her 'several to see, so you can choose one you like'.[86] On this occasion all went well and Mabel gave birth to a daughter. But in the summer of 1914 she had to go to Germany for treatment for a range of medical problems, including 'the digestive machinery not working properly'. These had arisen from 'the troubles which followed on her miscarriage'.[87]

Lady Selborne was also insistent that her eldest son's wife should take precautions when she became pregnant for the first time.

> The great point to remember is that a miscarriage with a first baby ... often [results] in a great difficulty of having any others ... Anyhow it is almost sure to ruin one's health for three or four years ... The great danger is over fatigue, & at first it is difficult for a young woman to realise that what would not have tired her at all two months ago, will tire her desperately now ... That is where the young husband is apt to be a danger. He is inclined to think this very sudden change is a fancy of feminine nerves, especially as women usually do become irritable & nervous & otherwise unreasonable when they are pregnant.[88]

Sometimes over-frequent pregnancies led to chronic invalidism, as with Lady Boileau. Even the energetic Rosalind, Countess of Carlisle claimed to have damaged her heart by bearing eleven children in twenty years. However, her daughter cast doubts on the validity of this and it may be that she, like some other wives, used illness as a way of avoiding sexual relations which might have resulted in further unwanted pregnancies. Certainly Rosalind and her husband became estranged in the 1880s, partly over political disagreements as well as other matters. She later used her alleged ill health as an excuse for demanding an immense amount of personal service from her children.[89] Perhaps significantly she also carried prudery to excess: 'my mother was quite unbalanced where sex was concerned,' wrote her daughter. 'Even the mention of the word was an indecency.'[90]

Fortunately, most mothers enjoyed more harmonious relations with their offspring than did the Countess of Carlisle. And although much of the day-to-day routine of their upbringing was entrusted to nursery staff and governesses, many women enjoyed playing with their children or taking them out. Louisa Yorke, whose first baby was born in the summer of 1903, noted proudly that on 10 July it had been taken for its second carriage drive. As they passed through the nearby town of Wrexham the schoolchildren shouted, 'Here comes Squire Yorke's baby,' much to the amusement of the nurse and of Louisa herself. A few days later she reported happily that she spent 'most of [her] time in the nursery &

write all my letters there. It is so sweet & fascinating to have a little son to play with.'[91]

Consuelo, Duchess of Marlborough, likewise considered 6 p.m. the 'best part of the day' because then she and her two sons went to the nursery, 'where a bath and supper awaited them; then they said their prayers as I tucked them into bed'. During the day, if she were free 'of more serious duties' she would take them for drives in an electric car. 'They learned to wield a cricket bat and also how to box. In the evenings, dressed in velvet suits, they came down to tea and I read to them or we played games.'[92]

Lady Leconfield also shared in the children's amusements, including skating in the winter, going for walks, reading to them in the drawing-room, and watching their plays and tableaux.[93] Another proud mother was Ettie Grenfell of Taplow Court, Buckinghamshire. She was heiress to an immense fortune, and combined an active social life with enthusiastic involvement in her children's pastimes. In *Pages From a Family Journal*, which was subsequently privately printed, and circulated among her friends, she not only recorded many of their childish sayings, but described a succession of parties, pantomimes and outings, as well as family holidays in Scotland and Normandy and visits to relatives and friends, to the zoo, 'and once to a biscuit factory' Then there were games of hide-and-seek and 'deer-hunt' at Taplow itself, in which both parents joined.[94] According to this account the five Grenfell children, living in a massive house surrounded by 3,000 acres of land and enjoying the attentions of twenty-seven servants, had an immensely privileged and happy childhood. Yet the truth was that despite Ettie's interest in, and affection for, her children, they always had to compete for attention with her activities as a hostess and socialite. As her biographer points out, 'one of Ettie's sons was permanently scarred by his inability to come to terms with her emotional demands. Another grew up a rough, tough, overbearing bully. At least one of her daughters was positively intimidated by her ruthlessly successful mother.'[95] This suggests that even in apparently calm and secure country-house families, there were hidden tensions and darker shadows to disturb the surface harmony.

One of the darkest of those gloomier aspects was the continuing high level of child illness and death. Even at the end of the nineteenth century in the most favoured rural counties, about one baby in ten was likely to die before it reached the end of its first year, and in the early years of the century the position in many counties had been a good deal more serious.[96] Within that overall picture there were, of course, class differences and youngsters born in the upper ranks of society fared far better than their humbler counterparts. But even in country-house society many mothers had to face the loss of one or two children.

This was true of Lady Elizabeth Grosvenor at Eaton. Much to her disappointment, her first two children were girls, but then in 1823 to her great joy a son and heir arrived. His birth was celebrated in nearby Chester by the roasting of an ox, but the child unfortunately remained weak and sickly. After nine months he died and her mother-in-law noted that although Lady Elizabeth was 'exerting all her fortitude, she [was] suffering greatly from the loss'.[97] Her gloom was compounded when the next child proved to be a third daughter rather than the heir she was seeking. Not until October 1825 did she at last bear another son, the future 1st Duke of Westminster.[98] Later in January 1839, she was to suffer a second loss when one of her daughters, twelve-year-old Evelyn, became ill with typhus fever. She and her husband took turns to sit up at night with the girl, but after a fortnight she died.[99]

Some bereaved mothers, like Mary Elizabeth Lucy, sought consolation for the loss of children in religion. Mary Elizabeth was to lose two sons within two years. The first to die, four-year-old Herbert, 'faded away like a broken flower'. As she admitted she 'strove hard to say, "God's will be done", but it was agony to feel that the object of my care for the four short years of his life was past all the help or need of it; a cold weight presses on my heart and the fountain of grief is awakened from its inmost source'. Herbert had died on 3 August 1839: seventeen days later another son, Edmund, was born. But as the months passed neither Mary Elizabeth nor her husband could recover their spirits after Herbert's death, and they decided to take their children on an extended Continental tour. The outward journey proved uncomfortable, and when they reached Lyons the baby became ill. They decided to continue on to Turin, where they hoped to obtain efficient medical help. But as they crossed the Alps the baby died. 'Eleven long hours did I travel with his dear lifeless body in my lap ere we reached Turin … Never, never can I forget that night of anguish,' Mrs Lucy wrote.

Over the next fifteen years, Mary Elizabeth lost two more children. Her eldest son, William Fulke, died at the age of twenty-three in 1848 and her fourth son, Reginald Aymer, about twenty. To compound the misery of that time, her husband also died in 1845, at the comparatively early age of fifty-six. She was thus left a widow at forty-two with a family of six children, two of them still under the age of ten.[100]

In a period when adult mortality rates were relatively high, a number of other women shared Mrs Lucy's misfortunes. Some, like Lady Glynne, responded to the premature loss of a husband by spending most of their time with friends and relatives.[101] Although she continued to take an interest in the family's estate at Hawarden, Lady Glynne and her children only resided there for about three months each year, usually in the summer. Other widows followed the example of Lady Dalmeny and remarried after the lapse of an appropriate period of time. And many like Mary Elizabeth Lucy herself, reacted by assuming control of household and estate until their eldest son could take over.

But the death of a husband meant more than the loss of a well-loved companion. The sense of physical deprivation experienced was expressed very clearly by the newly widowed Queen Victoria: 'What a dreadful going to bed! What a contrast to that tender lover's love! All alone!'[102] Most widows also experienced a loss of status as well, for in nineteenth-century England, a woman's standing was linked to that of her husband. When he died that link was shattered and with it went much of her social identity. If the heir were married, or when he did marry, his mother was often relegated to a secondary role within the household – despite the legendary influence of the dowager in some families. Often, as with Lady Leconfield, it meant removal to a smaller residence, perhaps in London, or to a dower house elsewhere on the estate. Even the autocratic Lady Londesborough had to face this unpalatable fact when her husband died. 'Not only did the old lady lose [him],' recalled her grandson,

but … nearly all her belongings, being obliged to pursue hereafter the dolorous manner of life decreed by tradition for an English dowager; not only were horses and carriages and grooms and gardens and houses and jewels and plate, and, indeed, the whole luxurious decoration of life by which she had been so long surrounded, snatched from her at a single grab, but she also forfeited … the love of the majority of those who had pretended to be her friends. She felt, I apprehended, peculiarly desolate, though as a rule she would not admit it.

But, as he drily admitted, she also 'continued to terrify and override those near and dear to her who came within her range'.[103]

A few widows, like Frances Anne, Dowager Duchess of Londonderry and, for a time, Lady Charlotte Guest, were able to run estates and even business undertakings with efficiency and determination. But they were the exceptions. For most women, widowhood meant a withdrawing from the world, as epitomised by the reaction of Queen Victoria herself. It also involved the performing of certain very clear rituals, including the donning of appropriate garb. For the first year after a husband's death they were expected to wear black clothes covered with crepe, no ornaments and a widow's cap with a veil. Second mourning lasted for the next twelve months and comprised black with less crepe, without a cap and jet ornaments only. 'The third year was half-mourning when grey or mauve could be added for colour. Some widows chose to remain in mourning for the rest of their lives.'[104]

Although this elaborate cult of mourning reached a peak in the 1870s, after which some of its effects were modified, a distinct ritual continued to be observed up to the First World War. Hence a *Manual of Etiquette* (*c.* 1908) advised friends of the bereaved to leave cards of 'kind inquiry' about a week after the funeral. The family would then respond by sending cards thanking them for the inquiries. Only when these cards had been exchanged was it proper for friends to call.[105] There is more in a similar vein.

In reality, reactions to bereavement varied from individual to individual. Despite her distress at the loss of her husband, Mary Elizabeth Lucy refused to let grief overshadow the lives of her children. As a great-granddaughter-in-law notes, she reacted to the situation in typically robust fashion by modifying her mourning 'in a way that would have been thought shocking a decade earlier and turned her full attention towards the needs and well-being of her children'.[106] Lady Dalmeny, too, displayed a firm sense of the practical when in August 1854, less than four years after her husband's death, she married the elderly but wealthy Lord Harry Vane, later the 4th Duke of Cleveland. This ended all her financial worries and enabled her to re-enter society as a brilliant if sometimes formidable hostess.[107]

But for Lucy Cavendish, the murder of her husband by Fenians in Phoenix Park, Dublin, in May 1882 was a blow from which she never fully recovered. She lived on for another forty-three years, and for much of the time kept a brave face to the world. Only occasionally did she reveal to close relatives her true feelings, as when she wrote to a sister-in-law of the 'sad disheartenment and blank underneath everything', which was 'such a great cross, such a weary load to bear'. In a letter to her youngest brother, she admitted to 'having reached the end of my life with a sort of stupefied feeling … The social delights, the absorbing political life, and all the fun of shooting-seasons, lawn-tennis, riding, is gone by and shut off from me, and I am stranded on an awful quiet shore in the loneliness that none of the dear loving hearts that … help and bless me can ever approach into.'[108]

These feelings of isolation were shared by many widows. Yet, like Lucy Cavendish herself, they often reacted by involving themselves in charitable or religious activities, as well as in visits to an extended network of relatives. Lucy Cavendish never allowed herself to indulge in the 'luxury of woe' but exerted herself to take an interest in what went on around her. That was a code of conduct applicable to most widowed ladies of her class, once the immediate period of mourning was at an end. 'Excessive tears and lamentations were only indulged by the lower classes,' was how Alice Buchan put it.[109]

5

The Role of 'Lady Bountiful'

Finstock. It is our pleasing duty once more to record the generosity of Mrs Oliver ... now residing at Lee Place, Charlbury, who with that kindly feeling ... which has been so often manifested by her in the endeavour to soften and improve some of the stern realities of life, by offers of love and human tenderness, caused ... many a cottage hearth to wear a happier smile, by the distribution of four fat sheep, with accompaniments of blankets, sheets, flannels, bread, tea, beer, and money amongst the inhabitants of this village.

Jackson's Oxford Journal, 9 January 1875.

Alongside their duties and responsibilities as mistresses of large households, country-house wives and daughters were expected to play the role of 'Lady Bountiful' in the wider community. That meant giving assistance to the old, the sick, and other members of the 'deserving' poor and thereby acting as a 'golden bridge' between the elite families who wielded power in the Victorian countryside and the cottagers, who were their subordinates. Many, like Lady Lufton in Anthony Trollope's novel *Framley Parsonage*, were genuinely concerned to promote the welfare of 'their' villagers. Of Lady Lufton, Trollope wrote,

She liked cheerful, quiet, well-to-do people, who loved their Church, their country, and their Queen, and who were not too anxious to make a noise in the world. She desired ... that all the old women should have warm flannel petticoats, that the working men should be saved from rheumatism by healthy food and dry houses, that they should all be obedient to their pastors and masters – temporal as well as spiritual.[1]

As will be seen, she had many real life counterparts.

In Chapter 2 it was shown that youngsters started to carry out their 'Lady Bountiful' duties at a very early age. Hence Mary Elizabeth Lucy was quite a small child in Wales when she began to make baby clothes and flannel petticoats for the villagers. Her governess also encouraged her to give at least a third of her pocket money to the poor, instead of spending it on trifles for herself.[2] Lady Leconfield's diaries reveal that when she visited poor families at Petworth she frequently took the children with her, as on 6 January 1891: 'after luncheon carried toys with the girls, Hughie & Mademoiselle to the Steers (North St), Curtises, & Newmans'. Two days later she and her eldest daughter, aged twenty, spent the evening sending out circulars 'inviting the neighbours to join in a work guild for providing clothing for school children in the distressed parts of Ireland, each member to send one garment by Feb. 1st'.[3] The Leconfields were extensive landowners in Ireland and this doubtless inspired the appeal. On 3 February Lady Leconfield noted triumphantly that she had despatched five boxes of clothes.

It was in these circumstances that one adolescent girl admitted that when her father inherited an estate in 1893 she 'undertook the duties that generally fall to a squire's daughter: played the organ in church, trained the choir, and taught in the Sunday School, not because I had any qualifications for teaching spiritual truths, but because it was expected that one of us should do it'.[4]

The same was true of newly married wives, who were required to assume the duties traditionally associated with their husband's family. Consequently, their patronage of and presence upon committees and boards, and their presentation of prizes at village schools were as much a tribute to their rank – and sense of duty – as to their philanthropic interest. The Duchess of Marlborough tartly remarked that 'opening bazaars and giving away prizes with a few appropriate words could be successfully done by a moron'. But she recognised that at a time when titled ladies had a great deal of star appeal, it was her duty to attend agricultural and horticultural shows, address mothers' meetings, and even watch cricket matches, although, as an American, she had little appreciation of that game's finer points.[5]

The Duchess of Beaufort continued to perform similar tasks throughout her long married life. 'Everybody in Bristol and round about asked Granny to open their bazaars for them,' remembered Lady Clodagh Anson:

And Susan [her sister] and I used to trail behind at these functions, carrying all the babies' woolly boots and tea-cosies that the stallholders insisted on her buying. Granny put these in a special cupboard ... and they did not emerge again until she was asked for contributions to the next one. They made a continuous round from one bazaar to another, which was just as well, as they were no use for anything else.[6]

However, around her home, the Duchess's largesse was more carefully targeted. According to her granddaughter, she preferred 'living quietly at Badminton and going to see all the poor people in the village' to visiting London for the Season. 'She had baskets with china jars in them, and used to put rice puddings, remains of chicken mince, or any little tasty bit left over from luncheon in these, and take them to any old people about the place.'[7]

When the role of 'Lady Bountiful' was carried through sympathetically, it created warm bonds between donor and recipient which made acceptable the patriarchal social system it was designed to bolster. Indeed the failure of a country-house wife or daughter to perform these expected duties could give rise to resentment on the part of cottagers who liked to be able to boast to less favoured neighbours that they had received a visit from 'her ladyship'.[8] But it had a wider function too, not only by demonstrating the donor's superior status and the recipient's dependence, but because it could be used to reward those who displayed suitable deference and to penalise those who displayed unwelcome signs of independence. Cottagers could also be encouraged to be sober, pious, hard-working, frugal, and self-reliant by joining the coal and clothing clubs or friendly societies which their patrons promoted for their benefit.

Lady de Rothschild was one benefactor anxious to achieve these wider social objectives. When she arrived at Aston Clinton in 1853 she recalled the comment of a friend that 'there was no greater evil in the country than a *Lady Bountiful*; ... let me not be carried away therefore by the indolent luxury of giving, but try and do real good at our little Aston Clinton'.[9] That remained her aim as she and her daughters went around the village. Constance, aged fifteen, recorded with satisfaction that her mother was 'not proud and allows us to go about among the farmers and people, how much happier we are than if we kept exclusively and carefully to ourselves'.[10] Even in old age Lady de Rothschild still went visiting in her brougham, calling on families and taking jellies to the invalids reported to her by the village nurse. But it was probably through the educational schemes which she and her daughters promoted that they made the most important contribution to the welfare of the people of Aston Clinton.

Elsewhere steps were taken to improve the employment prospects of younger villagers, especially the girls, by providing training for domestic service, or by seeking posts for suitable candidates in the households of friends. Lucy Arkwright regularly found places for school-leavers from the estate and village, while Cecilia Ridley in Northumberland commented of the local school that it would 'be a great pleasure if the girls [became] clean and respectable and [made] good useful servants afterwards'.[11] Mrs Henley of Waterperry, Oxfordshire, also made a virtue of training young parishioners for 'gentlemen's service'. In the mid-nineteenth century five of her thirteen servants had been born in the village and a sixth – a page boy – had grown up there. 'It is such a good thing for them to get out into nice places and I hope they will all do well,' she wrote to a friend in 1851.[12] At about that time she supplied Lady Dashwood of West Wycombe Park, Buckinghamshire, with both a kitchen maid and a page, and one of her friends jokingly remarked, 'Waterperry seems to supply different houses with servants, for Mrs John has got a housemaid from there – I think at last it will be in the geographical dictionaries as a place famous for its servants.'[13]

Anne Sturges Bourne of Eling, Hampshire, was still more ambitious. She financed a servants' training school in her own house, and in 1853 described rather enviously a visit to a similar institution provided by the Duchess of Sutherland. She had 'a school of forty girls boarded & lodged – who besides their own house work learn in her laundry, & she gets them places – very well for a fine lady. But I wd. not have forty girls if I could – & I think the only reason mine have done well wh[ich] always surprises me, is that they are few & like a family & can be studied individually.'[14]

Similar schemes were instituted by Sarah, Countess of Jersey at Middleton Stoney and by the Countess of Macclesfield at Tetsworth, also in Oxfordshire. Lady Macclesfield lived at nearby Shirburn Castle and opened her school in 1865. It catered for about a dozen girls and had its own premises, under the direction of a matron. The pupils were expected to remain between one and three years, according to their age and proficiency, and during their time there they learnt not only cookery, housework and dressmaking but how to become expert laundresses. This last was their principal occupation, with washing sent from Shirburn Castle as well as from other large households in the neighbourhood. When they left to go to service, Lady Macclesfield provided each of them with an outfit of clothes, and while they were in training the 'ladies at Shirburn Castle [gave] them religious instruction' on Sundays.[15]

Other patrons, such as Lady Brooke and Mrs Eglantyne Jebb, provided instruction in craft work. Lady Brooke opened a needlework school at Easton Lodge in 1890 and within a year pupils had become so proficient that they were chosen to work on the trousseau of Princess May (the future Queen Mary), who had just become engaged to the Prince of Wales' elder son. Later she opened a showroom in Bond Street where the girls' work was displayed and orders taken. Although her own inept management prevented the scheme from becoming a success, it did broaden the employment prospects of some girls in that part of Essex.[16]

Mrs Jebb's plans were a good deal wider. She founded a Home Arts and Industries movement to introduce woodcarving, basketwork, chair caning, and other skills into the homes of country people around her husband's estate at the Lyth, Shropshire. This grew into a national organisation and by the mid-1880s had won the interest and support of the Princess of Wales among others.[17]

If these charitable endeavours were to achieve their desired objective of strengthening villagers' support for the paternalistic system of parish government then in operation in rural districts, they had to win the respect of those assisted. In 1894 the newly married Violet Cecil noted that when her mother-in-law distributed gifts to cottagers, employees and servants at Christmas, she always handed them over 'personally with a word to each … and an enquiry after relatives or any sick people'. Hence 'the people at Hatfield had great admiration mixed with awe for Lady Salisbury. Her robust and forthright style suited them and she gave them the sort of advice and help they understood.'[18] But she had her idiosyncrasies. According to Violet, if the cottagers were ill she would collect

all the medicine bottles of her large family – all that were not actually marked 'poison' – would put the contents into bottles with an equal quantity of Lord Salisbury's best port wine, and would distribute these to the old women in the parish, who always declared that 'her Ladyship's medicine did them more good than the Doctor's'.[19]

Lady Katherine Gathorne-Hardy, daughter of the 1st Earl of Cranbrook, was another benefactor held in high esteem. When she died in 1911 tribute was paid to the 'constant and loving help' she had given to the local girls and young women. This had been 'a continual inspiration in their lives' and she had entered 'into all their joys and sorrows'. When increasing ill-health prevented her from keeping in active touch with them, 'the sight of her as she drove through the village would cheer and strengthen many a heart. "Lady Katherine always gives us a smile as she drives past," one of her girls … said; "and it seems to make the day brighter."'[20]

A number of women offered practical aid as well, like Isobel Gurney, who was a 'splendid nurse giving instructions, ordering homoeopathic medicines, arranging comforts or applying poultices'. While at Hawarden, Mary Gladstone taught at the local night school, although with limited success. 'Loathed … night school having to take two uproarious classes (teachers failing) in dif. stages of ignorance,' she wrote on one occasion.[21] Then there was Lady Midleton who established a class at Peper Harow, her husband's Surrey estate, to teach illiterate labourers to read and write, and herself gave the instruction twice weekly.[22] A daughter also taught in the ordinary village school on one day each week.

Another enthusiast was the Duchess of Bedford. She had long been interested in nursing and when her husband succeeded to the title in the 1890s she decided to open a small cottage hospital at Woburn. It began work in 1898, and she herself took a course of lectures at the London Hospital in order to qualify as a nurse and theatre sister and, in due course, as a radiologist and radiographer. According to her grandson the 'establishment was gradually expanded over the years and became a model of its kind. It must have cost my grandfather a fortune.' Such women as she were following in the tradition of earlier country-house ladies like Jane Shaw Stewart, Mary Stanley and Florence Nightingale herself, who had all nursed in the Crimean War during the 1850s. In 1861, Jane Shaw Stewart, the daughter of a Scottish landowner, was, indeed, to inaugurate the female nursing service in the British Army, although her relations with her military superiors were often stormy.[23]

Less ambitious philanthropists could follow the example of Lady Knightley of Fawsley Park who, among a multiplicity of other charitable activities, took a course of ambulance lectures with a friend. At the end they were examined. 'It was partly paper, partly *viva voce*, and two or three bandages to be done. I hope we are through.'[24] Later she began nursing lectures for mothers living near her Northamptonshire home, and at her death in 1913 she left £1,000 (more than a quarter of her net personal estate) to Northampton Hospital to endow a bed in memory of her husband.[25]

In another instance, Miss Eliza Wedgewood of the Cotswold village of Stanton engaged a dentist, at her own expense, to come regularly to examine and treat the teeth of all the children. The dentist conducted his consultations in her sitting-room. Despite all the painful associations with her house, the deep affection in which she was held by local youngsters was not undermined.[26]

At the end of the nineteenth century, agricultural depression caused some landed families, like the Horners of Mells and the Wilkeses of

Elmdon, to let their homes and to move to a smaller property within the village. The new tenants then often took over some of the duties of the lady of the manor. At Mells, for example, the manor house was rented by a Mrs Cookson, and she soon 'entered into the life of the village with enthusiasm, helping with children's tea parties and annual prize-givings, alongside members of the Horner family'.[27] At Elmdon, the Baileys not only presented the village with a reading room, but Lady Bailey (like the squire) visited the school and gave the children presents. However, the historian of Elmdon comments, there 'is ... no reason to believe that the presence of the Baileys lessened the squire's authority in the eyes of the village'.[28] Nevertheless, in some communities these rival sources of influence could create tensions in the upper echelons of society.

Not all ladies carried through their philanthropic duties with sympathy and sensitivity either. The author and social reformer, the Revd Charles Kingsley, fiercely condemned those who treated 'the poor as *things*':

A lady can go into a poor cottage, lay down the law to the inhabitants, reprove them for sins to which she has never been tempted; tell them how to set things right ... She can give them a tract, as she might a pill; and then a shilling, as something sweet after the medicine; ... clubs, societies, alms, lending libraries are but dead machinery ... needful, perhaps, but ... dead and useless lumber, without humanity; without the smile of the lip, the light of the eye, the tenderness of the voice, which makes the poor woman feel that a soul is speaking to her soul ... that she is not merely a *thing* to be improved, but a sister to be made conscious of the divine bond of her sisterhood.[29]

Sadly his comments all too often fell on deaf ears, as in the case of 'old Lady Hawkins', who would tour the village, giving advice to the cottagers and while there 'she'd ... pull the pot lids off to see what they was cooking'.[30] Then there was Lady Wilbraham, daughter of the Earl of Fortescue, who on most Saturdays drove round the cottages on her husband's estate in a pony carriage, dispensing 'various gifts such as red flannel, soup, puddings, etc. and the basket nearly always contained a bottle of castor oil which was frequently administered, to the consternation of the recipients'.[31] Still more autocratic was Susan Sitwell, who ordered that the hair of the children attending her school should be cut, while Lady Wenlock sought to expel from the village any girl whose conduct or church attendance she considered unsatisfactory.[32]

Even an enthusiastic social reformer like Miss Jessie Boucherett, the younger daughter of a Lincolnshire squire from Willingham, despite her close identification 'with every movement connected with women's work and the improvement of their legal position', nonetheless took a firm line with families on the Willingham estate. 'No sink or other communication with drains ought to exist in labourers' houses,' she firmly declared. 'The inhabitants have not intelligence enough to keep such things in order.' Yet on a wider basis, in 1859, she jointly founded the Society for Promoting the Employment of Women, which sought to broaden the job opportunities of educated females. She was also a founder and early editor of the *Englishwoman's Review*, a journal which publicised the society's schemes. She even instituted special classes in London to prepare girls for commercial careers.[33] But in her home community her attitude towards the lower orders differed little from that of less enlightened country-house ladies.

It was in these circumstances that the Countess of Warwick remembered that although her mother and stepfather generously dispensed charitable gifts to the poor, it was 'always a goodness of extreme condescension. On matters of faith, politics, education and hygiene, they were convinced that those who served had no right to an opinion … A measure of serfdom prevailed … in the surroundings of every country house I ever visited.'[34]

Sometimes this meant that cottagers who did not display the expected outward signs of gratitude and submissiveness would be reproved. At Great Missenden in Buckinghamshire the autocratic Misses Carrington, who lived at the Abbey, gave much help to local people but when they drove through the village they expected the women to come to their cottage doors in clean aprons to curtsey as they passed. On one occasion when two women in the street neglected to respond as required they were asked sharply 'whether their knees were stiff'. A similar feudal spirit prevailed at Mells. Lady Frances Horner remembered that although her in-laws set up clothing clubs and provided soup and beef for the cottagers, they expected them to consult them 'as to what names their children were called by …; smoking was not tolerated in the reading-room; … men and women were not allowed to sit together in church!' Even the state of the cottages was unsatisfactory, and when Frances pleaded for 'sound roofs and dry walls' this was dismissed as 'a counsel of perfection'.[35]

Nor were the children exempt from this type of social control. A little girl, born at Pakenham, Suffolk, in 1891, the fourteenth of fifteen children of an agricultural labourer, remembered that on one occasion when she was scrubbing the doorstep, 'Lady Thornhill from the Lodge came along. Of course, I should have got up, stood to attention and curtsied. I didn't, but just kept on with my job. Lady Thornhill had to walk around my feet.'[36] The girl was reprimanded by her mother for not showing more 'respect to [her] betters', and the next day she was caned at school for her neglect, because 'her Ladyship reported me to the Head Master'. But she remained unrepentant: 'I ... resolved never ... to curtsey to Lady Thornhill again under any circumstances.' It is significant that this incident took place in the early twentieth century, when such ideas of social subordination were under question. Nevertheless, few cottagers would have cared to risk arousing the wrath of the 'powers that be' by such overt defiance. Instead they paid lip service to the rules and conditions laid down by their patrons, while ignoring them where they could.

Typical of the small deceits practised was the reaction of Hertfordshire villagers to Lady Ebury and her two middle-aged daughters from nearby Moor Park. Whenever they saw the ladies approaching they hastened to set out the family Bible on the kitchen table and to open their windows because they knew that religious principles and the benefits of fresh air were two virtues their visitors were anxious to promote. Lady Ebury even founded a society to teach people to sleep with open windows.[37] In this way the cottagers maintained good relations with the family and qualified themselves for any gifts which might be on offer.

Most labouring households undoubtedly welcomed the casual charity which was bestowed, be it blankets in winter, extra food at Christmas, or clothing for the children. On the eve of the First World War the Cholmondeleys in Cheshire were distributing over 1,700 lb of beef and almost £30 worth of flour each Christmas to tenants, pensioners, employees and sundry other people living in eight villages around Cholmondeley Castle.[38] Most households received 10 lb of beef each. Again, at Longleat, a sick woman obtained over a period of two months 'medicines', 'a cheese, grapes, beef tea, puddings, mutton, half pint of gin, and one and a half bottles of port', while the charitable account book kept by the Le Strange family of West Norfolk reveals that during the second half of the nineteenth century about a dozen presents were made each month to widows, infirm old people, and mothers during confinement. Bottles of porter, mutton, and tea were supplied, while the sick were given basins of broth or rice puddings, 'and the budgets of those with large families were eased by presents of broth, meat, or tea'.[39] In these cases the aid was a valuable supplement to the recipient's normal diet.

Even trivial treats were welcomed, especially by the children – like the Band of Hope celebration organised in 1898 by the Birchall sisters of Bowden, Gloucestershire, with prize-giving, games and tea.[40] At Hamsey, Sussex, Lady Shiffner's accounts show minor outlays on sweets for the school feast, an outing for the choir to Seaford, and a pantomime for the choir boys, among other things.[41]

In the case of the most important aristocratic families it was not possible for even an enthusiastic 'Lady Bountiful' to be on hand all the year. Many, like the Countesses of Warwick and Jersey, migrated between their different estates or spent weeks in London for the Season or on lengthy tours of the Continent. However, these absences often occurred during the summer, when charitable aid was less necessary than in the colder months. In any case, it was common for instructions to be given to the housekeeper or estate steward to continue charitable aid to villagers during the family's absence.

Greater difficulties were likely to arise where the owner was permanently non-resident and responsibility for running the estate was given to an agent. This was the case at East Burnham, Buckinghamshire, where by tradition the poor had been allowed to cut turf from the common for firing. The estate was owned by the dowager Lady Grenville and in the early 1850s her steward took action to prevent cottagers claiming their former allowance of turf. At the same time their houses were allowed to fall into disrepair and their water supply became inadequate. According to a sympathetic inhabitant, the poor 'were left without anybody to care for them, except an occasional visit from the curate, all trembling at the nod of "the steward"'.[42] She herself tried to see the steward to persuade him to change his attitude, but without success. As she bitterly concluded, 'There is at present no help for such a state of things. But a time must and will come, as society becomes more exigent as to "rights" and "duties", when owners of real property shall be brought under some kind of legislative control ... if English landlords will not arouse themselves to a more conscientious discharge of their social obligations.'[43] She was writing in the late 1850s. Sadly almost forty years were to elapse before parish and rural, district councils were elected to provide some of that machinery she was demanding to remedy the deficiencies in rural housing and water supplies.

Nevertheless, even where charitable aid was generously bestowed by landed families, the benefits derived were not confined to the recipients alone. Particularly for unmarried ladies, who lacked the status and the responsibilities which went with running a household, charity offered an outlet for their energies and abilities. In this way they secured

> opportunities for independent action and unfettered power over the lives of others ... Their competence in counselling, teaching, planning, organising, and public speaking gave them greater

Two unobtrusive country-house ladies on a summer afternoon, *c.* 1910. (The author)

Guests at a dinner party, *c.* 1900. (The author)

Above left: Louisa Yorke with her elder son, Simon, in August 1905. (Clwyd Record Office)
Above right: Frances Maynard at the time of her marriage to Lord Brooke in April 1881. In the 1890s she became a member of the Prince of Wales's 'inner circle' and was, for a time, reputedly his mistress. (From Frances, Countess of Warwick, *Life's Ebb and Flow*, 1929)

Above left: Madame de Falbe with a pony carriage outside Luton Hoo, Bedfordshire, in the 1880s. In April 1872 she married her second husband, John Gerard Lee of Luton Hoo. At his death in 1875, he left her all his money as well as Luton Hoo for her lifetime. In December 1883, she married for a third time, the groom being Christian de Falbe, Danish ambassador to the Court of St James. (Luton Museum and Art Gallery)
Above right: A lady leaving her London town house duly attended by footmen, *c.* 1902. (The author)

In the conservatory at Luton Hoo on 8 November 1886. The statuesque lady standing on the back row, second from the right, is the Duchess of Teck, mother of the future Queen Mary, who is seated immediately in front of her mother. It was here that Prince Albert Victor (Eddy) proposed to Princess Mary of Teck early in December 1891. About a month later he was taken ill and died at Sandringham in January 1892. In July 1893 Princess Mary married his younger brother, Prince George. (Luton Museum and Art Gallery)

Above: Members of the Curtis family of Alton, Hampshire, taking tea in the garden in the mid-1860s. (Hampshire County Museums Service)
Right: Ladies paying an afternoon call during the London Season, *c*. 1900. This was part of the 'status theatre' which formed an integral part of the social life of all Victorian country-house ladies. (The author)
Below: The importance of 'making a match' is mocked in this *Punch* cartoon. (1875)

A POTENTIAL SON-IN-LAW.

Anxious Mother of Many Daughters. "PAPA DEAR, DO GET MRS. LYON HUNTER TO INTRODUCE YOU TO HIS HIGHNESS; YOU MIGHT THEN ASK HIM TO CALL, YOU KNOW."
Papa Dear. "WHAT FOR?"
Anxious Mother. "WELL, MY LOVE,—YOU KNOW THE CUSTOM OF HIS COUNTRY!—HE MIGHT TAKE A FANCY TO SEVERAL OF THE GIRLS AT ONCE!"

Members of the Wilder family driving out in a pony cart at Sulham House, Berkshire, *c.* 1910. Such conveyances could be used for pleasure or for making charitable excursions. The Wilders were the principle landowners in Sulham for more than 300 years. (Mrs I. Moon) (Museum of English Rural Life, Reading)

A FACT FROM THE NURSERY.

Nurse. "MY GOODNESS GRACIOUS, MISS CHARLOTTE, YOU MUSTN'T PLAY WITH THOSE SCISSORS!"
Miss Charlotte. "I'M NOT PLAYING WITH 'EM, NURSE DEAR—I'M CUTTING 'TTLE BRUDDER'S NAILS!"

Often the nurse or nanny was largely responsible for bringing up country-house children. As this 1856 *Punch* cartoon suggests, the task was not always easy.

The Wrey children at Sulham House, Berkshire, *c.* 1897. The little girl is obviously very proud of her bicycle, while her brother brandishes a tennis racquet. (Mrs I. Moon) (Museum of English Rural Life, Reading)

Above left: Charlotte May Hippisley (b. 1835), daughter of a landed family from Sparsholt, Berkshire, *c.* 1850. Her careful pose suggests that she was very conscious of her elaborate dress. (Chris Howell Collection, Museum of English Rural Life, University of Reading)
Above right: A children's party, *c.* 1900. (The author)

Members of the Wilder family having tea on the beach at Villers-sur-Mer, Normandy, August 1909. (Mrs I. Moon) (Museum of English Rural Life, Reading)

THE CHILD OF THE PERIOD.

Visitor at Country House. "BY THE BYE, YOU DIDN'T KNOW WHO I WAS THIS MORNING, MARGUERITE!"
Small Daughter of the House. "NO; WHO WERE YOU?"

Not all the girls conformed to the desired image of a polite, obedient child, as *Punch* slyly suggests. (1885)

THE SILENT HOUR!

WHEN SHALL YOU COME HOME, MUMMY DARLING?"
"NOT TILL THE MIDDLE OF THE NIGHT, MY LOVE!"
"NOT TILL THE MIDDLE OF THE NIGHT—WHEN THE CLOCK STRIKE NOTHING?"

Left: Many socialite mothers thankfully left their children in the care of a nanny while they went out to an evening engagement. (*Punch*, 1876)

Above: Presentation at Court was the symbol of a girl's entry into adult Society. This drawing-room was conducted by King Edward VII and Queen Alexandra in 1903. (The author)

A peaceful summer picnic in 1889. (Mrs I. Moon) (Museum of English Rural Life, Reading)

Above left: Portrait of Lucy Lyttelton in 1864, the year in which she married Lord Frederick Cavendish, a younger son of the Duke of Devonshire. Lucy was the second daughter of the 4th Lord Lyttelton and his first wife, Mary. (The author)

Above right: Driving home after a round of afternoon calls during the London Season, *c.* 1902. (The author)

AT THE ACADEMY.

Young Lady (indignant). "NOW, I TOLD YOU, PAPA, THIS WASN'T THE FASHIONABLE HOUR. WE'LL HAVE NOTHING BUT THESE HORRID P:CTURES TO LOOK AT UNTIL THE PEOPLE COME!"

Visiting exhibitions at the Royal Academy was part of the London social scene, although as *Punch* suggests, not all the visitors were interested in the paintings! (1871)

A fashionable wedding at St Paul's, Knightsbridge, *c.* 1902. (The author)

A PRACTICAL MEMENTO.

Sir James. "AND WERE YOU IN ROME?"   *American Lady.* "I GUESS NOT." (*To her Daughter.*) "SAY, BELLA, DID WE VISIT ROME?"
Fair Daughter. "WHY, MA, CERT'NLY! DON'T YOU REMEMBER? IT WAS IN ROME WE BOUGHT THE LISLE-THREAD STOCKINGS!"

[*American Lady is convinced.*

At the end of the nineteenth century the influx of wealthy American ladies caused resentment among some English aristocrats during the Season. They retaliated by mocking the alleged brashness and lack of culture of the 'invaders'. (*Punch,* 1890)

Gertie Millar (1879–1952) in the early 1900s. She was the daughter of a Bradford mill-worker and became a 'Gaiety Girl' in 1901. During the early 1900s she had a lengthy affair with the 2nd Duke of Westminster. After the death of her husband, Lionel Monckton, she married the 2nd Earl of Dudley in 1924. She was the most popular musical comedy star of her day. (The author)

Tea in Kensington Gardens during the London Season, *c.* 1902. (The author)

Lady Brooke with her in-laws at Warwick Castle during the mid-1880s. Her relations with them were not always easy. (From Frances, Countess of Warwick, *Life's Ebb and Flow*, 1929)

Managing a large domestic staff could be a taxing responsibility for any country-house lady. Servants employed by Mrs Noble of Park Place, Remenham Hill, Berkshire in 1903. (Oxfordshire County Libraries)

Above: Domestic staff at Erddig, near
Wrexham, in 1912. Seated in the centre
of the front row is Miss Brown, the
housekeeper, who came to the Yorkes
in 1907 and retired at Christmas 1914.
She restored calm and efficiency to the
household, after the criminal dishonesty of
her predecessor. On her left is the butler and
on her right the gardener; the cook is seated
next to the gardener. (Clwyd Record Office)
Right: Blenheim Palace in 1900, when
Consuelo, Duchess of Marlborough was
châtelaine. The photograph shows the first
stateroom, with tapestries on the walls
and a portrait of Consuelo herself over the
mantelpiece. (Oxfordshire County Libraries)
Below right: The servants' hall, with its
hierarchy of domestic staff, *c.* 1900. (The
author)

Above left: The Wilder family driving out in their Humber car, *c.* 1910. In the early twentieth century the chauffeur came increasingly to take over the duties of the coachman as motor cars superseded horse-drawn carriages in many landed households. (Mrs I. Moon) (Museum of English Rural Life, Reading)

Above right: Lavinia Talbot (née Lyttelton) a younger sister of Lucy Lyttelton, *c.* 1875. She eventually had five children but, like many Victorian ladies, was reluctant to publicise her pregnancies before it became strictly necessary. Hence early in 1875 she expressed a strong disinclination to discuss the fact that she was possibly expecting a baby, 'as it is on the cards it will go off in ginger beer', that is it would prove a false alarm or she would have a miscarriage. (The author)

Celebrating the birth of a son and heir. A tree being planted in the park at Erddig in honour of Simon Yorke's christening on 5 August 1903. He is being held by his mother, Louisa and his father, Philip, stands by her side holding the tree. (Clwyd Record Office)

OUR VILLAGE.

Village Dame (describing various aches and pains). "MY THROAT 'E DID GO TICKLE, TICKLE, TICKLE, TILL I SES, 'I MUST BE AGOIN' TO BE ILL.' SO I 'OLDS UN TIGHT WI' MY 'AND, BUT *THAT* DIDN'T DO NO GOOD; THEN I PUTS MY OLD STOCKING ROUND UN, BUT *THAT* DIDN'T DO NO GOOD. SO IN THE MARNIN' I TALKED IT OVER WITH MRS. GILES NEXT DOOR, AND WE THOUGHT AS WE'D SEND OVER TO THE 'WHITE 'ORSE' FOR THREEPENNORTH O' GIN, 'COS I SES, 'PRAPS IT MAY DO I GOOD, AN' PRAPS IT MAYN'T. BUT EVEN IF IT DON'T,' I SES, 'YOU CAN'T TAKE IT WHEN YOU BE DEAD.'"

Listening to the woes of the cottagers was one of the duties of a 'Lady Bountiful'. (*Punch*, 1905)

WOODSTOCK.

·TREAT AT BLENHEIM PALACE.—On New Year's Day the Duchess of Marlborough gave her annual treat to the aged poor of Woodstock and Bladon, about 130 availing themselves of the kind invitation. Tea was provided at four o'clock in the Audit Room, and an excellent repast was partaken of by the assembled guests, who did ample justice to the good things provided for them. The Duchess of Marlborough, and the Ladies Churchill, together with some distinguished visitors, attended on the assembled guests, and assisted in dispensing the creature comforts. Her Grace, addressing the company present, expressed her gratification at again offering them a welcome, and heartily wished them all "a happy new year." A splendid Christmas Tree, well laden with suitable gifts, prepared by the Ladies Churchill, was exhibited in the laundry; every one present received something from it, and a very happy evening was spent.

WORKHOUSE TREAT.—On Thursday, Dec. 28, the aged and infirm inmates of the workhouse, together with the children, were bountifully supplied with tea, plum cake, oranges, sweets, &c., the cost of which was defrayed by private subscription, through the instrumentality of Mr. and Mrs. Otway. Several pieces were sung, and a pleasant evening was spent.

Above left: A report of the kind of casual charity with which ladies of the manor were often associated, from *Jackson's Oxford Journal*, 6 January 1872.
Above right: Ladies attending a charity bazaar in London, *c.* 1902. Such events were part of the wider social scene, rather than purely philanthropic ventures. (The author)

Ladies presiding at a fête in Chipping Norton, Oxfordshire, in aid of the National Children's Homes, *c.* 1910. (The author)

A FELLOW-FEELING.

District Visitor. "I've just had a letter from my son Reggie, saying he has won a Scholarship. I can't tell you how delighted I am. I——"
Rustic Party. "I can understand yer feelings, Mum. I felt just the same when our Pig won a Medal at the Agricultural Show!"

By the early 1900s, rural deference was in slow retreat, as agricultural labourers again began to form trade unions (to match earlier efforts in the 1870s), and as tenant farmers formed their own National Farmers' Union which excluded landowners. That subtle change of mood is indicated in this *Punch* cartoon of 1904.

self-confidence and self-esteem ... They gained a sense of usefulness and worth.[44]

Florence Nightingale was not the only spinster who found compensation for the frustrations of an uninteresting social round and confining family-life in care of the poor and sick.[45] The same was true of Eliza Wedgwood of Stanton Court. Until the death of her domineering mother in 1908 she had virtually no independent existence. The one release for her pent-up energy lay in her concern for the villagers' welfare and her determination to promote their interests. When necessary she drew on her own limited finances in order to ensure the success of a particular scheme and according to her friend, Lady Cynthia Asquith, this small community

> was truly said to be her 'family', so intimate a personal concern did she make the welfare of its every son and daughter ... I often stayed ... [with her] for weeks at a time and I can't remember a single hour in which a knock on that blue front door ... did not announce that some villager had come to seek Eliza's help. Any thing might be wanted – a bottle of medicine, a letter to a hospital, a lift along the road, the use of the village hall, or a so-called 'loan' of money. Often the appeal would be merely for advice or for sympathy.[46]

Elsewhere there were ladies of the manor who combined philanthropic activity with strong religious convictions. When Millicent, Marchioness of Stafford, moved to Tittesor Castle, Staffordshire, shortly after her marriage in 1884 she made it her business to hold weekly Bible meetings for the miners employed at her father-in-law's coal mine near Longton. At Hanchurch, on the edge of the family's Trentham Park estate, she endeavoured to get the villagers to attend religious meetings in the schoolroom. But there was practical assistance as well, with a holiday home for children established in the Potteries, together with a Potteries' Cripples Guild. Around her husband's Scottish estate, her plans were still more ambitious. At Golspie, the village near Dunrobin Castle, she gave packets of tea to the women and twists of tobacco to the men when she visited the cottages. Soon after her husband succeeded as Duke of Sutherland in 1892, she persuaded him to build a gasworks in Golspie and install gas lighting in his tenants' houses, as well as financing the construction of a Fishermen's Rest there. She also sent a number of widows to London to train as midwives and played a leading role in reviving the local home-spun woollen industry. The Scottish Home Industries scheme was one of her favourite projects.[47]

It was with this mixture of the religious and the secular in mind that Lady Clifton claimed that if it was 'only for the good it may do to ourselves we ought to go about among the poor people, and take an interest in talking to them, not only about their body's but their soul's welfare'. While to the newly married Lady Knightley, it was essential that she concentrated 'more than ever [upon] all the helps our Church suggests', in case she should be too easily 'carried away by the luxurious house & habits I have dropped into'.[48] Soon she began to institute various charitable ventures around Fawsley Park and just over six years later, in the spring of 1876, was meditating anxiously whether she had begun too many things: 'looking back … the singing [i.e. the church choir] goes on fairly … the libraries are all right as far as I have anything to do with them; the district visiting served its turn for two or three years while Mr Scratton was without a curate. I do my share languidly. Coal Club I started but can do little to help – my Sunday Class is in suspense.'[49]

Lucy Cavendish, engaged in charitable work in London, similarly linked her philanthropic activities to her own strong religious faith. In February 1870 she rejoiced that she had given some second-hand clothing to a poor dressmaker, for shortly after the woman returned to tell her that she 'had got work the very day after' she received the clothes. 'Such a contrast, in the decent clothes and with a bright face, to the poor, ragged, starving tramp who tottered into the room on Tuesday, crying helplessly and yet giving me the impression of respectability. I keep thanking God over and over for letting me do this.'[50] On other occasions Lady Frederick Cavendish visited inmates at the workhouse at St George's in the East, as well as helping to establish a convalescent home for men. In February 1867 she presided 'at a poor people's dinner just set going in this parish'. Through all these ventures Lucy's own gentle good humour shone through, but equally clear was her failure to question the reasons behind the poverty she so deplored. Like other philanthropic ladies of her day, she sought to alleviate the symptoms of distress rather than to eradicate its cause, or question the need for its existence.

But for many women, charitable activities were merely an antidote to the irritations and limitations of their daily lives. This was true of Florence Nightingale and Eliza Wedgwood, as we have seen, but it also applied to married women, especially those, like the former Constance de Rothschild, who were childless. Constance was highly intelligent and studious, and shortly after her marriage to Cyril Flower in November 1877 it is clear that despite her affection for him, she found his companionship lacking in intellectual stimulus. Much of his time during the autumn, winter and early spring of each year was devoted to hunting and shooting, pursuits in which she took small interest. Hence, just over a year after her marriage, she wrote gloomily in her diary, 'Felt miserable, ill, read nearly all day, what shd. I do without my books.' About a week later came the note that 'Cyril hunted ... I ... rode, drove, grumbled and cried. But I cheered up when I went back to my books: "Consider, consider where unto you are born, ye were not made to live like brutes, but to follow virtue and knowledge."'[51]

It was against this background, therefore, that Constance turned to her charitable interests with renewed vigour. By the beginning of 1880 she was engaged not merely in cottage visiting but in teaching at the village school, conducting a girls' sewing class on one afternoon a week, giving weekly lectures to local pupil teachers on Shakespeare's plays, and visiting the workhouse in nearby Aylesbury. She took her work with the pupil teachers especially seriously, making careful preparations for each lesson and rejoicing when a session went well, as on 7 February, 1880: 'gave the teachers an excellent lesson on Richard III, spoke to them very seriously about their *calling*. Hope & Pray my words took effect.'[52] She also turned her attention to the temperance cause, and began to go around the village seeking recruits. By 9 February, she was able to admit 'fifty members to the Church Temperance [Society]', and shortly after spent a busy afternoon in connection with a new coffee house which had been opened in the village. For her, these charitable initiatives offered an opportunity to exercise her organising abilities and intelligence in a way which was absent from other aspects of her life. She had become a very different being from the woman that had written mopishly a year earlier that she found 'nothing half so delightful as intellectual conversation'.[53]

Rosalind, Countess of Carlisle, shared Constance Flower's interest in the temperance issue, and in January 1883 wrote triumphantly to her mother of the success she was having around her husband's Cumberland estate:

Our mission week was very interesting 300 more people pledged themselves ... The Society is now over 1,300 strong ... I have taken a small public house on a seven years lease to make into a working man's free and easy coffee house.[54]

Over the years she and her husband closed eight licensed premises on their estates, and replaced them with over fifteen reading rooms. The Cumberland estate became, indeed, a prohibition area. Nevertheless, as her biographer points out, her actions were not merely negative and suppressive. She did much to promote education in the area, and to encourage co-operative societies. She also improved housing standards, and from 1888 began to arrange country holidays for children from Leeds and Bradford on the Castle Howard estate in

Yorkshire. The youngsters were 'distributed into cottages in some seventeen villages round Castle Howard'.[55] During the same decade she arranged country holidays at Castle Howard for women from nearby industrial towns, and organised school treats and children's Christmas parties over a period of forty years.

Similar enthusiasm for these broader charitable causes was displayed by Lady Knightley of Fawsley Park. She had been born in April 1842 and was thus in her late twenties when in October 1869 she married Sir Rainald Knightley, a well-to-do Northamptonshire squire twenty-three years her senior. Sir Rainald was a long-serving Conservative Member of Parliament and at first she felt confined by the narrow bounds within which her married life seemed to run.[56] But, like Constance Flower, Louisa Knightley soon found an outlet for her organising skills in a variety of philanthropic endeavours. These were not merely restricted to Fawsley and its environs but covered nationwide social reforms, including schemes for

the improvement of housing and domestic economy, for the spread of education, thrift, and temperance, for village clubs and Reading Unions, model dwellings and penny banks ... Above all, the condition of women and girls in every rank of life was the object of her keenest interest. She was one of the founders of the Girls' Friendly Society and of the Working Ladies' Guild, and afterwards took an active part in the work of Imperial emigration ... In 1901 she was elected the first President of the South African Colonisation Society, and in 1908 ... [became] President of the British Women's Emigration Association ... Lady Knightley was also a member of the National Union of Women Workers, and took a leading part in its Congresses and Conferences ... Her interest in hospitals and ambulance work was ... keen ... An ardent churchwoman herself, she was always ready to help the bishops and clergy in building schools and churches, and constantly visited Northampton to lay foundation stones and open bazaars and fêtes in aid of Church extension in this populous town. After taking a prominent part in the struggle to preserve religion in [elementary] schools, she became a member of the Northamptonshire Education Committee ... No one was a greater lady in Northamptonshire or was more careful of the welfare of the tenants and labourers on the Fawsley estate than Lady Knightley, both during her husband's lifetime and when his death left her the sole mistress of this beautiful home ... It was no easy task to disarm Sir Rainauld's opposition to his wife's appearance on public platforms and to the expenditure of her time and strength on objects for which he cared not a straw.[57]

So runs one biographical account, and there is a good deal more in a similar vein. In fact, the brain reels at the breadth of her interests. Perhaps not surprisingly, from time to time she lamented that her 'thoughtlessness' in taking on so much had caused annoyance to her husband. 'When shall I learn to be less selfish! – I am so pleased with myself too when I do anything for others and how little it is after all!'[58]

Of all the schemes with which Louisa Knightley was associated, perhaps the one closest to her heart was the Girls' Friendly Society. This was an Anglican organisation established in the early 1870s by another country-house wife, Mrs Townsend of Honington Hall, Warwickshire. She had first become interested in the welfare of young women when living at Shedfield Lodge, Hampshire. There she had constructed a sewing class for local girls, and while they worked away busily she had read aloud to them.[59] From this small beginning she began to plan a national organisation to train young working- and lower middle-class girls in religious principles and domestic duties, and to imbue them with a concern for sexual purity, 'dutifulness to parents, and faithfulness to employers'.[60]

The society was launched at Lambeth Palace in May 1874, at a meeting of leading Anglican ladies, including the wife of the Archbishop of Canterbury. Central to its structure 'was the semi-maternal relationship between the upper-class and Anglican "associate" and the working girl "member"; the third of its "central rules" required members to be unmarried and to bear "a virtuous character"'. Over the years its scope was extended to include employment registries, homes, reading rooms, and journals, all designed to assist girls to find work or entertainment for their leisure hours, as well as a refuge when they were out of employment. It was the first Anglican organisation to be run by lay women, and prominent among its leaders were 'ladies of the manor'. By 1899 it had 1,345 branches in England and Wales. Membership reached a peak in 1913, when there were 39,926 associates and 197,493 members.[61] Such figures naturally exclude the many girls who had once been members and had imbibed the society's principles before leaving to be married. In that sense they underestimate the size of GFS influence among the nation's female population.

The society's religious objectives and associated moral precepts appealed strongly to Lady Knightley. She had already held mothers' meetings and had joined various other religious societies when a friend sent her details of the GFS in February 1876. As she noted in her diary, this seemed to be 'the thing which I have so long wanted'. A month later she met some friends in Daventry to discuss the formation of a local branch and on 5 April reported with satisfaction

that fourteen ladies had come to Fawsley 'to talk about the GFS …
I trust the "Daventry Rural Deanery Branch" is fairly organised, &
most earnestly do I pray that by God's blessing it may prove a living
working organisation which may really help the girls to keep out of
mischief'.[62] Shortly after she visited the neighbouring village of Badby
and called on 'the mistresses and mothers of the girls whom I hope to
enlist for GFS. My mind is quite full of it.' The next day she enlisted her
first recruits – four of her own maids. This was followed on 17 April
(Easter Monday) by a tea meeting at Badby at which seventeen girls
joined. 'There are sure to be many disappointments,' she wrote, 'but I
can't help being pleased at having succeeded so far.'

From this modest beginning Lady Knightley became involved in
the national leadership of the new organisation and by 1878 was
commenting happily that a meeting of its branch secretaries was
now so large that they were obliged to assemble in a public hall. The
following year she made her debut as a public speaker, when she
addressed a GFS meeting in Northampton. Her husband went with
her, even though he had little sympathy with the organisation, which
he dubbed the 'Great Fuss Society'. But he was proud of her success as
a speaker and administrator. 'Rainald said my voice shook very much
at first,' she noted after this first venture, 'but when I got to reading, I
did not so much mind … The Lecture Hall was about half full, chiefly
of Parsons & Parsonesses, but they seemed interested & I do hope it
will give the Society a push, & I shall be rewarded for the mental terrors
I went through.'[63] The only occasion her husband vetoed her activities
was in 1882, when he refused to allow her to become GFS president
– despite a personal appeal to him from the founder, Mrs Townsend.
Perhaps he considered such a prominent role unbecoming for a lady of
her rank. In any event, Lady Knightley accepted the decision without
question, noting meekly that '*my* path is clear'. Nevertheless it did not
dim her interest in the society's work, and during the 1880s she became
particularly involved in its newly established emigration committee.[64]

Another keen GFS associate was Lady Katherine Gathorne-Hardy of
Hemsted Park, Kent. She, too, gathered around her a band of young
supporters and continued to keep in touch with them even when
they left the district. Her influence was said to have been the means
of helping them 'onward, upward, and Heavenward. "We should
have been very different but for Lady Katherine," many of them have
said.'[65] Lady Frances Lloyd was a third enthusiast. When she died in
1886, it was stated that she had served as GFS diocesan president for St
Asaph. 'Nothing can exceed the grief of the poor who lived around her
home,' declared the society's journal, *Friendly Leaves*, in an obituary:
'One poor woman said … the day after the funeral, 'Oh, … I could

always open my heart to her. What shall I do now?'"[66]

As these accounts suggest, alongside its prime function of promoting the spiritual and material welfare of its young members and extolling the virtues of family life, the GFS was concerned to ameliorate class differences. Although it repudiated the idea of party politics, in reality it largely reflected the values of late Victorian Conservatism, including its 'timidity on social questions, its exploitation of deferential attitudes and recreational tastes widespread among the poor, its enthusiasm for empire, pageantry and monarchy'.[67] To its leaders, radicalism and socialism were divisive elements which would undermine the benefits of 'moral effort, traditional values and personal benevolence'. The flavour of the relationships it sought to promote is indicated in a report of the annual celebrations of the Shere, Abinger and Holmbury branch held at Tanhurst by 'kind invitation' of the Dowager Marchioness of Hertford. About nineteen associates and eighty-seven members assembled. Various 'delightful amusements were provided' and guests enjoyed a glorious view over the surrounding countryside. Before tea the members were called together and some of them were presented with cards denoting seven years' satisfactory membership of the society:

> Tea on the lawn followed, and then Lady Hertford gave the girls an excellent address especially dwelling upon their privilege as GFS Members of helping one another in various ways, even giving words of warning and advice when needed. At the conclusion of the address all joined in singing, 'True friends', 'Rule Britannia', and 'God save the Queen', followed by three cheers for the Queen and three cheers for the kind hostess ... Soon after the carriages came and took the whole party down to Abinger Church, where a bright and hearty service, with an appropriate and useful sermon ... brought the happy day to a close.[68]

Such gatherings enabled public-spirited ladies to display the splendour of their mansions and grounds while, to some degree, justifying the possession of these desirable assets by claiming to promote the welfare of less fortunate sisters. For, as Queen Victoria herself had written in 1867, 'the fences which hedge in rank, will not be possible to be maintained unless they are justified by character and merit'.[69] The GFS was one organisation which aimed, in part at least, to do just that. But another, still more important reform movement which sought to meet these criteria was the district nursing service, and it is to that we must now turn.

Concern for the health and welfare of the poor had long been a feature of female philanthropy, as this chapter has already indicated.

Action might range from attendance at fund-raising events for local hospitals and convalescent homes to the provision of personal nursing care. Florence Nightingale was not alone when in the early 1840s she supplied medicines, food, bedding, clothes and her own nursing skills to sick cottagers living at Lea Hurst in Derbyshire.[70] Years later, when she had won fame for her efforts to 'professionalise' nursing, she remembered the problems faced by those labouring families during childbirth and sickness. Hence in 1861 she began a scheme to train midwives for work in villages. Under it, suitable women would be sent to the school she had opened in an annexe at King's College Hospital in London. They would remain for about six months and would then return to their home parishes. Significantly a number of landowners' wives seized this opportunity to improve nursing facilities in their own area by sponsoring suitable local candidates. One early recruit was Ellen Ward, who was sent by Lady Dartmouth. After training she was to be paid an annual salary of £25 by her patron, as well as receiving furnished lodgings, fuel, candles and some food. Ellen was not to obtain 'extra payment from anyone she may nurse, but in the event of employment from the Farmers or those above the very poor the payment for such service [was] to form a fund for defraying expense of medicine as provided for the poor'.[71]

Unfortunately, despite the success of the training, persistent outbreaks of puerperal fever in the school's wards (which Miss Nightingale attributed to their too close proximity to the hospital's post-mortem theatre) led to its closure on 1867. Nearly two decades then elapsed before any worthwhile schemes were drawn up to provide domiciliary nursing care for the rural poor.

In the interim, individual ladies continued to make provisions for cottage nursing on an *ad hoc* basis within their own communities. One of the best known was Lady Georgina Vernon of Hanbury, Worcestershire. Not only did she recruit a private nurse for the parish but she regularly accompanied the woman on visits to patients on the estate. Much of the nurse's time was taken up with midwifery, but the diary she kept between 1867 and 1875 shows that she also rendered simple medical aid, such as poulticing and bandaging, as well as laying out the dead. Medicines such as quinine, linseed, cod-liver oil and 'ointment' were distributed, doubtless at Lady Georgina's expense, and were supplemented by stimulants like gin, brandy and port, as well as various items of food. From time to time, she supplied blankets, clothing, and admission tickets to the local infirmary.[72]

In urban areas, domiciliary nursing among the poor had, meanwhile, been growing rapidly, following the employment of the first district nurse in Liverpool in 1859. But in the countryside no comparable initiative was taken until the 1880s, when three major schemes were launched.

The first came in 1883 when Miss Bertha Broadwood established the Holt-Ockley system of cottage nursing around her home parish, Ockley. It was run on provident lines, with subscribers entitled to the services of a nurse when sick. The nurses were recruited from women of the 'village class', whom Miss Broadwood sent on short training courses in maternity and district nursing to a special centre at Plaistow in London. When they returned home much of the help they gave was of a domestic rather than a clinical nature. Miss Broadwood was determined that her nurses should not challenge the pre-eminence of the medical profession in their dealings with the sick poor. Instead they were merely to serve as lowly helpers, working under the direction of local doctors. 'The cottage nurse is one of the humblest of the great army of nurses that are fighting ... the three D's – dirt, drink ... and disease,' she declared in 1909. By that date her organisation had 137 branches in England and Wales as well as forty other branches which were unaffiliated, and employed a nursing staff of about 800.[73]

A year after Miss Broadwood introduced her scheme, Mrs Elizabeth Malleson of Dixton Manor, Gloucestershire, took a similar step, although in her case she decided to employ a nurse who was already trained. When she had first come to Gloucestershire from London at the beginning of the 1880s, she had been appalled at the neglect of cottage wives during their confinements. The low calibre of many of the untrained midwives employed aggravated the situation at a time when many labouring families could not afford the services of a doctor. Often, the midwives combined their nursing duties with field work or other manual labour. It was in these circumstances that in 1884 Mrs Malleson recruited a nurse and midwife for the village of Gotherington. At first the women were reluctant to use her services, but soon her willingness to attend patients in all weathers and her 'kindly, energetic, devoted' character won them over.[74]

Like Miss Broadwood, Mrs Malleson wished to extend her organisation beyond her immediate locality. To this end she pressed for the formation of 'an Association remote from medical aid', and invited any ladies interested in such an initiative to contact her. A number did, particularly from Gloucestershire and Worcestershire. They included a neighbour, Lady Lucy Hicks-Beach, wife of the Chancellor of the Exchequer, who lived at Winchcombe. By 1890 Mrs Malleson and Lady Hicks-Beach had gained sufficient support among the landed classes to permit the formation of a Rural Nursing Association to promote the employment 'of trained Midwives and Nurses in Country Districts, in co-operation with existing Nursing Organisations'. Mrs Malleson became its honorary secretary.[75]

Yet, despite the importance of these activities, the main impetus for the creation of a comprehensive district nursing service came in 1887, when Queen Victoria agreed to devote £70,000 given by the women of England for her Golden Jubilee to this cause. Two years later Queen Victoria's Jubilee Institute for Nurses was incorporated. Its value lay not merely in the wide scale of its operations but in its emphasis on the importance of training for all 'Queen's nurses'. A distinctive uniform had to be worn and the professional standing of the nurses was underlined by the requirement that they be provided with a home of their own by the district associations which employed them. A minimum salary of £30 a year was suggested.

As the influence of the Queen's Institute spread, a number of independently established nursing societies became affiliated to it, including Mrs Malleson's Rural Nursing Association, which in 1891 became its Rural District Branch. Among an impressive list of aristocratic vice-presidents in that year it could boast two duchesses (of Rutland and Westminster) as well as eight countesses.[76]

Elsewhere the publicity given to the Queen's Institute further increased awareness of the needs of the poor among country-house wives and daughters and encouraged them to promote district nursing associations. In Hampshire, where a County Association was formed in 1891, it gained the active support of the Countess of Selborne and the Marchioness of Winchester, among others. In Somerset, where the County Association became affiliated to the Queen's Institute in 1903, it had as its president the Countess of Cork and Orrery. There are numerous other examples, although many lady patrons operated on a far smaller scale. This applied to the Boxgrove and Westhampnett Association established in 1893 by Lady Caroline Gordon Lennox, elder daughter of the 6th Duke of Richmond. Lady Caroline personally financed the venture, which came under the Queen's Institute's supervision in 1898. The nurse employed was accommodated in furnished rooms in an estate cottage and was cared for by one of the Gordon Lennoxes' old family retainers. She was also supplied with a bicycle to enable her to go on her rounds, although the number of cases she dealt with was small, totalling only around thirty a year in the late 1890s.[77]

A similar situation applied at Appleby and Bongate in Westmorland, where the secretary of the Association was Lady Hothfield of Appleby Castle. She started her scheme in January 1895 and not only provided the nurse's salary and uniform allowance but accommodated her in the castle lodge, with the lodge-keeper as her landlady. The nurse's washing was done at the castle laundry and it is clear that her professional duties were carried out under Lady Hothfield's watchful eye.[78]

As this example perhaps indicates, the district nurse's position in such cases could be one of some delicacy. On the one hand she was expected to maintain her professional integrity at all times; on the other she had to submit to the close supervision of a local patron. Not surprisingly, a large number of the nurses found this, and the loneliness of their position, too difficult and they left. During these early years there was a high turnover among district nurses in many country areas.[79] Among the ladies who took their responsibilities in connection with the nursing schemes very seriously was the Countess of Selborne. The issue which aroused her particular concern was the passage of the 1902 Midwives Act. This set up a new Central Midwives Board to oversee the midwifery profession and to organise relevant qualifying examinations. From 1905 only women certified under the act could use the title of midwife, and from 1910 it was to be illegal for any woman 'habitually and for gain' to attend mothers in childbirth, unless she were certified or were working under the direction of a qualified medical practitioner. In a letter to the Central Board, Lady Selborne pointed out that given the limited number of certified midwives available, numerous country districts would be left without maternity aid of any kind. 'We are impressed with the danger of trying to go too quickly,' she declared, on behalf of the Hampshire County Association, adding sourly that although the qualifying examination might appear 'an easy one to educated men, [it] is terrifying to a comparatively uneducated woman, and for some time to come, County Midwives must be recruited among women who have only had an elementary education'. She suggested an easing of the examination to allow such women to pass, providing they met appropriate criteria in regard to the practical side of their work:

> We think that ... safety to the women attended is more likely to be attained by a Midwife who is thoroughly and practically instructed in cleanliness, and the dangers of blood poisoning and infection, than by one who can answer medical questions in an examination paper.

Yet by 1910, if no changes were made to the regulations, country districts would face 'a dearth of Midwives which [would] be most serious. It [would] inevitably end in [a] neighbour giving the necessary assistance, ostensibly not for money, which [would] really be a return to a lower standard than that which at present obtains.'[80]

Although no official concessions were made in response to Lady Selborne's appeal, in practice, following representations from the local authorities, the regulations were relaxed in 1910. A further five hundred uncertified women were to be entered on the register as qualified practitioners, providing they were recommended as efficient by county midwifery inspectors.[81]

The growth of the district nursing service was, then, one important way in which the philanthropic activities of country-house ladies contributed to the welfare of the wider rural community. Through the initiative of women like Miss Broadhead, Mrs Malleson and Lady Hicks-Beach there was a general raising of standards of medical care in villages. In particular, fewer cottage wives were dependent during their confinements on the uncertain aid of a neighbour or the variable ministrations of unqualified 'handywomen'. In this connection it is significant that when May Harcourt (herself then pregnant) decided to set up a nursing scheme at Nuneham Courtenay, she gave as her reason for so doing the dreadful conditions which applied locally in maternity cases. 'There is *absolutely* nobody to look after a woman in her confinement. The last old woman who attended to these mothers having died some five years ago.'[82] Similar feelings of concern undoubtedly prompted the intervention of other ladies of the manor, who became involved in this work in the late Victorian and Edwardian years.

6

Leisure & Pleasure

Country life was much the same in most country houses ... Most ladies played whist, consequences, and the piano. If they were young and active, they also played lawn tennis and rounders. If they were tall and graceful, they shot with bows and arrows. Whatever their figures, they took part in charades and private theatricals. They did not do all this primarily for love of the things themselves, but because to do them was part of the duty of entertaining ... Sketching was ... [an] accepted 'object' for a country walk, for these leisured ladies did not satisfy their artistic tastes only by visiting the Royal Academy.

Edith Olivier, *Four Victorian Ladies of Wiltshire* (1945), 10 and 14.

Like a vast spider's web with filaments invisible yet tougher than the toughest steel ... these relationships spread and multiplied, throwing, through marriages, a network of fine glittering strands over the whole of the British Isles, enclosing Society in its seemingly imperishable web.

Alice Buchan, *A Scrap Screen* (1979), 92.

The 'accomplishments' which formed so essential a part of the education of the daughters of landed families were, in many respects, an invaluable preparation for their leisure hours in adult life. At a time when their social circle was limited to family members and an interlocking network of friends and acquaintances from a similar background to their own, the opportunities for the exercise of individual initiative were strictly limited. Indeed, in the case of younger, unmarried girls (as we saw in Chapter 3) even their contacts with members of the opposite sex were carefully supervised by chaperons. As Lady Cynthia Asquith wryly recalled of the Edwardian era, to be seen 'at a theatre, a picture gallery, a restaurant or in a hansom cab alone with a young man was tantamount to announcing your engagement to him, or openly advertising that you had decided to throw your cap over the windmill'.[1]

Hence most ladies spent much of their leisure time engaged upon embroidery, sketching, reading and practising the piano, perhaps supplemented by a superficial study of French, German or Italian. Girls learned 'to paint a little, sing a little, and play the piano well enough to accompany a drawing-room ballad with suitable embellishments'. At Lord Cottesloe's home, Edith Brodrick joined a small family choir 'culled from the musical members of the large cousinhood gathered [there] ... we got up to all sorts of motettes, glees and duets for female voices, the results being considered sufficiently successful to warrant the giving of a concert'.[2]

From the mid-nineteenth century a few ladies, like Georgie Mildmay and Lady Lucy Bridgeman, a daughter of the 2nd Earl of Bradford, took up the new art of photography. Unfortunately Lucy died in her early twenties, when her dress accidentally caught fire as she was reading in her family home, Weston Park. But surviving prints suggest her work was highly skilled.[3]

Letter writing was another major female pursuit, with news exchanged about the health and welfare of family members, the conduct of servants, the doings of mutual acquaintances, possible holiday destinations, and even the contents of a recently heard sermon. Thus Alethea Adeane, granddaughter of Lady Stanley, wrote to her Aunt Lucy to explain that her mother, despite indifferent health, had been forced to stay in London for an extra day 'to look for a housemaid'. In a later letter she added that the previous maid had been dismissed 'on account of being engaged to the butler which Mama does not allow. We should have been more sorry to lose her had she gone before we went to London and even as it is we are grieved to lose anyone who has been with us so long as three yrs.'[4] It was doubtless this kind of correspondence that Lili Cartwright of Aynhoe Park had in mind when she commented sourly in her diary on 25 January 1835 that 'there was nothing of note today. Sunday passed like all Sundays in writing letters in the morning and in being bored in the evening.'[5]

A few women followed the examples of Constance de Rothschild, Millicent, Duchess of Sutherland, and Vita Sackville-West and turned their literary skills to fiction writing. On 8 March 1874, Constance occupied herself with 'letters persistently the whole morning until

... [her] eyes ached'. The next day, after practising on the piano, she settled down to write a story about Nell Gwynne. 'Wrote with real pleasure', this absorbed most of her attention for the next few days: 'Delight in my quiet happy life,' she noted in her diary.[6] The Duchess of Sutherland's first novel, *One Hour and the Next*, was published in 1899. It was written with Millicent's characteristic exuberance, but its artificial dialogue and improbable plot led to poor reviews. However, she was undeterred and in the next few years published several other works, including a restrained and well-argued chapter, 'On the Dangerous Processes in the Potting Industry', which she contributed to Harold Owen's *The Staffordshire Potter* (1901).

In the case of Vita Sackville-West, her early scribblings were eventually to lead to a successful career as an author. In 1907, when only fifteen, she wrote triumphantly that she was about 'to restore the fortunes of the family', since she had that morning received £1 for a poem which had appeared in the *Onlooker*. But she also admitted ruefully that her mother had scolded her 'because she said I wrote too much, and Dada told her he did not approve of my writing ... Mother does not know how much I love writing.'[7] According to her son, between 1906 and 1910, Vita wrote eight full-length novels (one of them in French) as well as five plays. Many were based upon episodes in the lives of members of the Sackville family or in the history of her beloved family home, Knole. (Later, Vita was also to gain considerable notoriety on account of her lesbian relationship with Violet Trefusis, who as Violet Keppel had been a friend from childhood.)[8]

Two other girls who turned their talents to commercial purposes were Rosamund and Matilda Talbot of Lacock Abbey, Wiltshire. Their father, William Fox Talbot, was a pioneer of modern photography and they used their abilities as watercolour artists to maintain a convalescent home in the village, devoting the proceeds from the sale of their paintings to that cause. In later life they spent much time abroad in search of suitable subjects for their work, and Rosamund eventually died at San Remo in the early 1900s.[9]

In a different sphere, Julian, Lady Radnor, was an accomplished singer who gave public recitals and also formed a 'Ladies' String Band' and a 'Ladies' Chorus', which gave annual concerts for fifteen years. However, in 1896, five years after her marriage and shortly after the birth of her third child, her doctor told her she must choose between her musical career and her domestic and county duties, as she lacked the strength for both. 'Needless to say, as we were then living at Longford Castle, the latter was obviously the right choice,' commented a member of the family.[10]

But for most women, such accomplishments were pursued purely for personal pleasure or as a way of passing the time. At Eaton in the 1830s, Lady Elizabeth Grosvenor's day followed a regular pattern, with breakfast at 10 a.m., lunch at 2 p.m., and dinner at 7 p.m. During the day there were walks in the garden with the children, drives in the carriage with her mother-in-law to pay calls on neighbours, and riding about the estate or to local meets of the hounds. In the evenings and when the weather was bad she 'devoted her time to embroidery, reading, and letter-writing'. House-parties brought variety to the routine, especially during the long, dull winter months, although not all of the guests were welcome. Lady Elizabeth particularly disliked the all-too-frequent appearance of the elderly Miss Luxmoores, daughters of a bishop, and on one occasion complained to her mother that 'those vile harpies the Miss Luxmoores – vulgar and detestable in every way – arrived yesterday'. That morning they had gone to inspect one of the local schools, where she expected them to 'punish, exhort, examine and condemn the miserable children and frightened schoolmaster and mistresses'.[11] She avoided them where she could by going for long walks or spending as much time as possible in her own room.

Fortunately most of the Eaton guests were more congenial and although in the daytime she and her lady visitors spent many hours walking in the garden, going for drives, or sitting at their needlework in time-honoured fashion, the evenings were enlivened with cards (usually whist or commerce), billiards, games and charades. Lady Elizabeth thoroughly enjoyed these diversions. 'A delightful evening of battledor [sic] and shuttlecock in the Library,' she reported on one occasion; 'dancing country dances and polonnaises and playing round games till 1 in the morning – had great fun' on another. But her greatest delight was to play charades, which became popular in country houses from the mid-1820s.[12]

Half a century later, another country house lady – Cecilia Harbord of Gunton, Norfolk – was spending hot days at the end of July 1877 in the garden, sitting under the lime trees with her sister, Alice. Here she did her needlework, 'read & drew some lovely pictures of Alice in her big hat … & her Japanese umbrella'. In the late afternoon, as it grew cooler, the sisters drove themselves in a pony cart to visit villagers or to shop in nearby Cromer. They also had tremendous games of lawn tennis.[13] A few days later they entertained Lady de Rothschild and her elder daughter, who had driven over from Cromer. 'We took them over the gardens & gave them tea.' There is so much more in a similar vein.

The situation had not changed much by the Edwardian era. Lady Cynthia Asquith recalled the simple amusements with which she and her friends beguiled the hours, including reading aloud, whereby one of the party read while the rest of them diligently plied their needles. Sometimes Shakespeare's plays would be read in parts, or poetry learnt by heart. Many girls kept 'commonplace books' – 'large albums … into which in laboured script we reverently wrote out our best loved poems'.[14] As in Lady Elizabeth Grosvenor's day these various indoor occupations were supplemented by games. At the end of the nineteenth century, whist and commerce had largely given way to bridge, although Lady Cynthia herself was reluctant to play this 'unless press-ganged by three other players'. For bridge was taken so seriously by addicts, including the Prince of Wales (later Edward VII), that inexperienced or unskilful players were afraid to join in, especially when gambling was involved and considerable sums were at stake.

'I need not tell you Bridge is the order of the day,' wrote May Harcourt to her step-mother-in-law of a house party at Mymms Park in December 1904, 'poor Susie has had awful luck & is a heavy loser. This is so unfortunate but of course if one plays cards for money one must run those risks.'[15] In the autumn of the following year, she referred to 'acrimonious' games of bridge at another house party of which she was a member. The prim Louisa Yorke at Erddig disapproved of it entirely, considering it to be a 'most … dissipated game'.[16] Only a few women were able to match the tact and humour of Mrs George Keppel, who when reproached by Edward VII for muddling her cards, wittily excused herself by claiming she could not 'tell a King from a Knave'.[17] The story was given particular point because she was the last (and the most discreet) of Edward's long line of close female companions.

Other popular pastimes included what Lady Cynthia Asquith vaguely called 'the occult', that is table-turning and planchette. But her greatest delight was to visit the theatre. Despite her limited means, there was 'never any boggling over theatre tickets'.[18]

In less affluent circles, such as those of the Yorkes of Erddig or the Shiffners of Coombe Place, Hamsey, far simpler entertainments were enjoyed. Thus in the period 8–17 March 1904, Mrs Yorke attended a play at the Wrexham theatre (which she disapprovingly dismissed as 'so vulgar, to suit the Wrexham taste that Philip [her husband] & I had to come out early'); a lantern lecture, which her husband gave to members of the Church Army in Wrexham; a concert and organ recital at the nearby small town of Rhos; a University Extension Lecture on the Brontës; and a play performed by schoolchildren in Wrexham.[19] When all else failed there were musical evenings at home, in which friends frequently joined. The Yorkes never visited London for the Season, although they did pay prolonged visits to friends and relatives.

Lady Elizabeth Shiffner and her daughters also found most of their entertainment locally, notably in nearby Lewes and in Brighton as well as in neighbouring villages. The girls were enthusiastic sportswomen, with the second daughter riding frequently to hounds, and the two youngest ones playing a good deal of women's cricket and lawn tennis during the summer. On 3 August 1887, for example, Lady Elizabeth and her daughters went to a circus at Lewes'; the following day they attended a 'Married & Single Ladies' Cricket' match and the day after that while two of the girls played lawn tennis, she went to dine with friends. Later there was a garden party at the home of a friend and a visit to Tunbridge Wells Show.[20] Most of the year was spent at Coombe Place, although there were occasional holidays in Devon and the Isle of Wight and brief visits to the homes of relatives and friends. The Shiffners rarely went to London and when they did it was for business and shopping rather than purely for pleasure.

Elsewhere, as with Louisa Knightley in Northamptonshire, arranging a concert for the villagers could become an excuse for county families to exercise their theatrical talents. In January 1889, Lady Knightley and her house party went 'down to Badby and did a little entertainment for the reading room in Hare's barn'. To her delight the audience proved so 'thoroughly cheery' and receptive that 'it quite warmed one up':

Rainald & I read Sir Peter & Lady Teazle … Mary & Charlie did a 'Candle' Lecture & then we acted a charade – Mistake – made up from scenes from Pickwick wh. nobody guessed & everybody enjoyed. Harry Knightley as the fat boy was quite excellent & Juliet [her niece] also very good. Then we sang a parody on John Peel & … they cheered & sang 'He's a jolly good fellow' for Rainald & 'She's a jolly good lady' for me!!! and were so genial & friendly it did one's heart good.[21]

So successful was the performance that the following day they decided to repeat it at Fawsley for the benefit of the servants. Unfortunately they proved a less enthusiastic audience, although Lady Knightley thought that, in general, they had enjoyed it.

However, not all women welcomed these trivial pursuits. 'People talk nowadays of the peace and restfulness in those days,' wrote Lady Clodagh Anson in the 1950s, 'but there is nothing restful in having no interest to take you out of yourself. Certainly everybody "rested" up in their rooms, but as they had done nothing all day it was a mystery how they became tired, unless it was through complete boredom, which is always very exhausting.'[22] After the death in the 1890s of Lady Clodagh's parents, the 5th Marquess and Marchioness of Waterford, she and her sister would sometimes go to the theatre with their paid companion or a woman friend, or would make up little parties to dine at Ranelagh and wander about the grounds afterwards. But these excursions were frowned upon by their elders who were 'astonished and shocked' that they should go to a theatre 'without a man to escort them,' so 'we lay low about going if we thought it would upset them'.[23]

Other, more serious-minded girls railed against the intellectual sterility of such a regime. In the 1840s and 1850s Florence Nightingale complained of girls 'singing Schubert … reading the *Review*, and … embroidering' under the complacent eye of their family.[24] 'The family uses people, *not* for what they are, nor for what they are intended to be, but for what it wants them for – its own uses … If it wants someone to sit in the drawing-room, *that* someone is supplied by the family … This system dooms some minds to incurable infancy, others to silent misery.'[25]

Perhaps fortunately, most women accepted the limitations placed on their lives and activities with more philosophy than did Florence and Lady Clodagh. In any case, in some families the girls were encouraged to express their opinions freely and to read widely in their fathers' libraries. This was true of the Marquess of Salisbury's daughters. The Cecil children learned from an early age to 'participate in incessant family debates on philosophy, metaphysics, politics, and every other subject except religion'.[26] It is clear from the letters of his elder daughter, Maud, later the Countess of Selborne, that these qualities of intellectual toughness were retained and developed in later life. Of her debating skills within the family, one sister-in-law drily observed that it was 'so difficult to be always stemming a torrent!'[27]

Many wives and daughters also found happiness in the practice of their religion. Among them was Lady Knightley, who on 7 November 1880, in a typical comment, noted that she had 'had the great privilege of receiving the Holy Communion … I was very *much* rejoiced to see all the eight maids.'[28] Then there was Lady Sitwell and her daughter, Florence, whom the young Edith Sitwell cruelly labelled 'Lambeth Palace lounge-lizards' because of their strong Anglican piety. Lady Sitwell welcomed a steady stream of clergymen to her home. In her granddaughter's unflattering opinion, the house positively swarmed with curates and others, who were a 'particularly smooth and particularly uncultured lot'.[29] Needless to say, her disapproval influenced Lady Sitwell not one whit.

Occasionally, as with Mary Elizabeth Lucy, an interest in ecclesiastical affairs could lead to schemes for the restoration or rebuilding of local churches. In Mrs Lucy's case the original Charlecote Church was demolished in 1849 and its replacement was conceived, planned and wholly paid for by her. She laid the foundation stone in April 1850 and in the months that followed the work on the new structure absorbed her 'more and more … as I watched my ideas daily taking shape'.[30] She also planned much of the restoration and development of the north wing of the house itself during the mid-1850s.

But while these activities provided outlets for some women's ideas and energies, it was less easy to avoid the feuds and tensions which arose when family members were forced to spend so much time in one another's company. This was especially true of the winter months, when outdoor pursuits were likely to be restricted, and houses were very cold. At Moor Park, the home of Lord and Lady Ebury, their sons' wives huddled together in one another's fire-lit bedrooms, rather than brave the draughts downstairs, according to a member of the family.[31] Unheated passages struck an icy chill, and the 'moment you were outside the orbit of the fire … your feet became as cold as stones'.[32] Nor was this all. As Lady Tweedsmuir declared, although in a 'quiet country life' there were days of regular routine and peace, this was not an unalloyed blessing:

> It led to the magnifying of trifles, and to an intensely personal attitude to life. People quarrelled easily, became heated by little things, foibles were magnified, and the machinery of a house which could work so well and harmoniously, jarred and creaked; men and women, instead of trying to improve their characters, often cherished their failings … Families were a little like tribes, and to enter into the house of one of these clans was formidable to the young and shy.[33]

Hence at Hesleyside, the newly married Barbara Charlton was shocked at the coarse table manners of her in-laws, and learnt to eat her own food with downcast eyes. Her relations with her strong-minded, unpredictable mother-in-law were difficult, and were compounded when the elder Mrs Charlton hired an incompetent monthly nurse from the neighbourhood for Barbara's first confinement. The result was that she 'did not recover from the effects of [her] mother-in-law's egregious folly for almost the whole of two years'.[34]

Even Lady Randolph Churchill, although she avoided the unfortunate experiences of Barbara Charlton, found at Blenheim Palace extremely dull when the family was there alone:

> Everything went on with the regularity of clockwork. So assiduously did I practice my piano, read, or paint, that I began to imagine myself back in the schoolroom. In the morning an hour or more was devoted to the reading of newspapers, which was a necessity if one wanted to show an intelligent interest in the questions of the day, for at dinner conversation invariably turned on politics. In the afternoon a drive

to pay a visit to some neighbour or a walk in the gardens would help to while away some part of the day. After dinner, which was a rather solemn full-dress affair, we all repaired to what was called the Vandyke room. There one might read one's book or play for love a mild game of whist. Many a glance would be cast at the clock, which sometimes would be surreptitiously advanced a quarter of an hour by some sleepy member of the family. No one dared suggest bed until the sacred hour of eleven had struck. Then we would all troop out into a small anteroom, and, lighting our candles, each in turn would kiss the Duke and Duchess and depart to our own rooms.[35]

She also remembered that although her father-in-law, the 7th Duke, was 'extremely kind' and courteous, the duchess was something of a tyrant, who 'ruled Blenheim and nearly all those in it with a firm hand. At the rustle of her silk dress the household trembled.'[36]

In these circumstances, prolonged visits to friends or attendance at hunt balls or similar events could be welcome diversions. Violet Cecil much appreciated staying with the Horners at Mells Park when her husband, Lord Edward Cecil, was abroad and she found 'the intensive Cecil life at Hatfield overwhelmed me'. 'Mells in my early married life was a haven,' she wrote, where with her hostess she could walk, sketch and arrange excursions, as well as engage in congenial conversation. Lady Horner was 'a good thinker as well as a brilliant talker'.[37]

On a more frivolous note the usually serious Constance Weld much enjoyed her stay with the Pagets of Park Home, Wimborne, early in January 1874. Shuttlecock and battledore, dancing and a 'riotous round game' were part of the entertainment and when she and her sister left for home on 10 January it was with much regret. Ten days later, her father invited a shooting party to Lulworth, and the two sisters spent the evenings in games, dancing and playing cards. Then on 28 January, they persuaded their brother, Shireburn, to escort them to a ball in Weymouth:

We accordingly dined at seven, left here [Lulworth] at 8.30 & arrived at the Royal Hotel at 10.30. We didn't find it so long after all, it was a lovely moonlight night ... but I don't think we will ever do it again. I enjoyed the ball muchly – we left a little before three o'clock ... we got [home] at five thirty.[38]

After this flurry of excitement, Constance's normally uneventful routine was resumed, with walks, reading, practising the piano, and some German translation, as well as regular attendance at church or family prayers.

Of the various outdoor pursuits in which the ladies engaged, walking and gardening were undoubtedly the most popular, although some wives, like Lady Horner and Lady Knightley, also helped their husbands plan plantations or manage the home farm when this was in hand.[39] During the summer months, archery and croquet had their devotees, with the latter game growing in popularity from the 1860s. One enthusiast was Lady Knightley, and her diaries record innumerable contests with friends and relatives at Fawsley, as on 12 April 1870, when she had 'another great fight' with her brother-in-law. A few days later she played croquet the whole day and found it 'very enjoyable'. It was perhaps appropriate that in August of that year the Knightleys' 'first big party for the neighbours' took the form of an invitation to 'every lady we could think of for miles round to come to croquet from four to seven – wh. they did to the extent of about 100 – we had a band & gave them refreshments in the old Hall & it all went off very well'.[40]

Boating was favoured by certain of the younger women and there were some, like Lady Londonderry, Lady Ormonde, and Lady Gerard who owned and sailed their own small yachts. 'In spite of the fact that not even their oilskins could prevent their being soaked to the skin,' wrote the Countess of Warwick, 'it seemed to me that they enjoyed themselves far more than those of us who merely looked on.'[41]

At the end of the century bicycling was taken up on an increasing scale, and the Marchioness of Londonderry, writing many years later, considered that this and lawn tennis had contributed more to the freedom and health of women in late Victorian England than almost any other development. 'The fact is that sportswomen of … fifty years ago, had to be very strenuous, exceptional creatures,' she wrote in the late 1930s, 'as in everything they did they were hampered by their clothes and petty conventions … Before the advent of lawn tennis, badminton was played in garments which would have been impossible even in a restricted game of lawn tennis.'[42]

As bicycles grew in popularity, it was common for women to take their machines to country house parties in order to make expeditions. 'We carried our ardour so far that some of us insisted on cleaning [them] ourselves,' remembered Lady Horner, 'and [we] would not let them be touched by the rude and ignorant hands of the footmen of the houses where we stayed.'[43] However, her enthusiasm was not shared by her sisters-in-law at Mells, who considered it vulgar. 'I think it was the fact of riding astride on the bicycle that they found shocking,' she recalled drily.

Riding was another common female recreation, especially in fine weather, although in the early Victorian years it was not yet regarded as entirely proper for girls to go hunting. 'I hope you will *never* allow your daughters to "meet ye hounds",' wrote Lady Neville to her sister-in-law, Lady Glynne; 'it would indeed grieve me most sadly to hear that they joined in such practices … it lowers women in ye eyes of all and renders them what I am sorry to know many young ladies are-cheap.'[44] But Lady Glynne ignored her strictures and both of her daughters became skilled horsewomen. Later Mary Glynne's daughter, Lucy Lyttelton, was to share this enthusiasm. She described her first day's hunting as 'the most glorious exciting enjoyment I have ever had':

> I saw the fox break away. I heard the music of the hounds, and horns and halloos, I careered along to the sound of scampering hoofs … I flew over two or three fences, too enchanted to have a moment's fright; in short, I galloped for half an hour in all the glory of a capital run.[45]

Lady Brooke, the future Countess of Warwick, was another keen rider, following four of the most fashionable hunts in Leicestershire as well as visiting Ireland to hunt with the Ward and Meath packs. When she and her husband stayed at Warwick Castle with the old Earl of Warwick, she ignored her father-in-law's disapproval of women who hunted and would 'breakfast primly downstairs, before hurrying off to change into hunting costume and slip away to the stable by a side door of the Castle'. Lady Brooke was a dashing horsewoman who 'could always be relied upon to be up with the hounds at the end of a long run'.[46] Her half-sisters, Millicent, Duchess of Sutherland and Lady Angela Forbes, shared her zeal. Indeed, Millicent attended morning prayers with the assembled domestic staff clad in her riding habit, before embarking on a pre-breakfast ride. And Lady Angela, who admitted that life without hunting would be like bread without butter, reputedly agreed to marry James Stewart-Forbes only on the understanding that he gave her his chestnut horse.[47]

By the 1890s, a few women, such as Miss McClintock, were being appointed Masters of Hounds. Of Miss McClintock, who in 1899 became the first Lady Master of a subscription pack, *Country Life* commented that she was 'one of the hardest riders the country [had] ever known'.[48] Another expert horsewoman, the Duchess of Bedford, was, according to her grandson, the first female to ask her London tailor to make her a ride-astride habit, instead of the customary side-saddle costume worn by ladies.[49]

Towards the end of the century a small minority of women began to join in shooting parties on their own account, although this was still considered highly controversial. Even in the early 1900s, Dorothy

Beresford-Peirse of Bedale remembered that although she 'loved shooting … it wasn't the done thing, it was rather done under your hat'.[50] (Fishing, another favourite sport, was considered a more acceptable pastime both for Dorothy and for other women.) Certainly, Lady Randolph Churchill, who could in no way be considered narrow-minded, had to admit that even if there were 'no harm in a woman shooting game, I cannot say I admire it as an accomplishment'. She then described how while in Scotland, she had watched 'a young and charming woman, who was surely not of a bloodthirsty nature, kill two stags in one morning'. The first she shot through the heart, the second was wounded in both forelegs:

> He attempted to gallop down the hill, his poor broken limbs tumbling about him … I shall never forget the sight, or that of the dogs set on him, and the final scene, over which I draw a veil. If these things must be done, how can a woman bring herself to do them?[51]

But for most women, participation in a shooting party meant admiring the prowess of its male members as they killed vast numbers of game, and, from time to time, accompanying them while they did so. Lady Cynthia Asquith, who had little love of shooting parties, described one such occasion at what she labelled 'Seventh Hell Hall'. This had involved standing

> for hours … in sodden woods watching gloomy men kill happy birds … Besides, being bored and disgusted, I don't know what is expected of me. Ought I to talk to my 'Gun', or not? … I suffered agonies of cold – rainbow face, rainbow hands – yet I was expected to stand stock still … I enjoyed the luncheon and talking to the delightful keepers and the dogs … [but] I've got a bad attack of social nausea … The prospect of being nailed to the Merry-Go-Round of another Season makes me feel positively giddy.[52]

Between April or May and the end of July each year, many ladies of the manor spent at least some time in London, where they met their friends and engaged in the excitements and pleasures of the Season, with its balls, dinner parties, exhibitions, concerts, and similar events. Lady Brooke, a member of the Prince of Wales's 'Marlborough House Set', claimed that during these months their special achievement was 'to turn night into day. We would dine late and long, trifle with the Opera for an hour or so, or watch the ballet at the Empire, then "go on" to as many houses as we could crowd in.' As she wryly added, every 'extravagance was held up to the public as a proper expenditure of money – it was good for trade! ... As a class, we did not like brains. As for money, our only understanding of it lay in the spending, not in the making of it.'[53]

It was events such as these which formed the staple of the 'society' columns in such publications as the Radical journal *Truth* and the ultra-conservative *Morning Post*, to say nothing of such specialist magazines as *Lady's Realm* or the *Playgoer and Society Illustrated*. A writer in the former in May 1909 gave an indication of some of the wide spectrum of activities which constituted 'the Season':

> Courts, levées, state dinners and balls, Royal garden parties ... The balls ... include private and semi-private dances and the balls for countless charities. The list of friends ... dinners ... comprises innumerable regimental banquets, Empire Day banquets, political dinners, Derby Day dinners, such as that at which the Duchess of Devonshire entertained Her Majesty and thirty other guests in 1907 and afterwards received a thousand favoured friends, dinners in aid of charities, and private dinners without number. The receptions are divided up into almost as many classes as the dinners, while the *raisons d'être* of the numerous *conversaziones* are almost bewildering in the range of subjects which should, but rarely do, monopolise the conversation. The opera, the theatres, and concerts, sales of work, musical receptions at Mansion House and elsewhere, picture shows, meetings in aid of charities, Congresses, lectures, May Meetings ... exhibitions, the Horse Show ... cricket, croquet, lawn tennis, and other sporting events, bring together great crowds of people interested in these diverse items. The Henley Regatta ... Ascot, the Fourth of June at Eton, Speech Day at Harrow and countless garden parties, are also important items of the Season that assist to occupy the time of those who pursue the giddy round of pleasure.[54]

In the Season of 1865, for example, Lucy Lyttelton attended 'seventeen balls, eight parties, nine dinner-parties, eight private concerts, besides breakfasts of different sorts', among other events.[55]

Not all women, however, shared Lady Brooke's zest for the pleasures of the Season. The young Edith Brodrick, Lord Midleton's daughter, considered the 'late hours and the bad atmosphere' associated with London balls 'made one a wreck next day'. She preferred county assemblies and recalled with satisfaction the 'merry party of young people' who went over from her home, Peper Harow, to Guildford; 'it was a general re-union for hosts of friends'.[56] Even Lady Brooke had to admit that the 'chief folly of those of us who belonged to the Marlborough House Set was to imagine that pleasure and happiness were identical'. She recalled 'many joys ... but we were never able to cling to happiness'.[57]

Hedonistic, philistine, fond of racing, playing cards and gambling, the members of the Prince of Wales's circle took little interest in the arts or in serious conversation. That was left to a small group of late Victorian and Edwardian aristocratic intellectuals who were labelled 'the Souls'. Their wit, style, and good looks made them the focus of attention, as well as the envy, of their contemporaries. They prided themselves on 'their aesthetic sensibility, their unique interpretation of the taste and manners of their time'.[58] Some, like Lady Granby (later the Duchess of Rutland) and Lady Horner, were gifted amateur artists in their own right. Others, like Lady Elcho, Cynthia Asquith's mother, and Ettie Grenfell were valued for having 'elevated hospitality into something close to an art'. Visitors to their homes 'enjoyed a lost perfection of comfort, conversation and cuisine'.[59]

From the 1880s there was also a widening in the scope of London Society to include not merely those whose incomes were derived from land but wealthy businessmen, financiers and the new breed of South African mining millionaires. Many were Jewish in origin and it is possible to detect a note of anti-Semitism in the comments of some of the more established members of Society. Thus in July 1900, Lord Carrington sourly observed that he had dined 'with the Blythwoods. Werner [sic] the S. African Jew Millionaire: and a flashy painted wife dined – The way London Society toadies these S. African German Jews is horrible. They are subsidising half London and the women take their beastly money as greedily as the men'.[60] The Duchess of Buccleuch, likewise, was strongly opposed to 'the vulgarity and ostentation of the smart set' and prided herself on knowing none of them personally. She only 'once entertained a Jew, as a personal favour to Edward VII'. Other high-minded ladies banded themselves into the 'Lambeth Penitents' and unsuccessfully urged the Princess of Wales to join them in bringing about 'the moral improvement of society'; among their number were the Duchess of Leeds, Lady Tavistock, Lady Aberdeen, and Lady Stanhope.[61] Another die-hard who deplored the change which had taken place since her youth was Lady Dorothy Nevill. Then, Society had been 'like a large family' and everyone knew

exactly who everybody else was ... The laws of etiquette, now so lax, were severe in the extreme ... The forties and fifties were aristocratic days, when the future conquerors of Society were still 'without the gate'. The vast increase of railways ... ended all this exclusiveness, and very soon the old social privileges ... were swept aside by the mob of plebeian wealth which surged into the drawing-rooms, the portals of which had up till then been so jealously guarded. Since that time not a few of that mob have themselves obtained titles, and now quite honestly believe they are the old aristocracy of England ... It is, I think, a good deal owing to the preponderance of the commercial element in Society that conversation has sunk to its present dull level of conventional chatter.[62]

But however much Lady Dorothy and her friends might deplore the transformation, it was irreversible. And in accelerating this process at the highest level the Prince of Wales and his 'Marlborough House Set' had played a major part. For the Prince's circle included some of the wealthiest financiers and businessmen of the day.

With the ending of the Season, some families returned to their country homes – perhaps, like Lucy Lyttelton, rejoicing in the 'delicious repose and refreshment' of the 'precious old place ... Can't but be so glad I have fallen back upon dear old Hagley's loving arms.'[63]

Others visited the seaside with their children or embarked on lengthy tours of the Continent. In the 1840s, Lady Dorothy Nevill, daughter of the Earl of Orford, set off for Italy with her parents, brothers, and a cavalcade comprising 'fourgons, family coach, britzka, French cook, gold-laced ... courier, maids, footman, and six saddle-horses, with two grooms'. On the way they spent six weeks in Bruges before settling down in a beautiful old Florentine palace. There they spent the winter, before moving on to Padua and Venice. After this came three months in Rome before they began their return journey via Innsbruck, Nuremberg and Cologne.[64]

The Lucys of Charlecote also set out with a vast quantity of luggage and a staff of servants when they toured the Continent between October 1840 and May 1842. They even took two beds for the children and two baths, as well as a vast array of bed linen, towels, books, tea, arrowroot, and 'everything we fancy we could want'. Italy was the main object of the expedition, and they spent time in Naples, Florence, Milan, Verona, Perugia and Venice. 'I have walked round galleries till my legs ached intolerably and I was ready to *scream* with fatigue,' complained Mary Elizabeth Lucy. 'Dear Mr Lucy is perfectly happy with his sketch book, making drawings of the pavements of varied marble in which his soul delights.' The winter of 1841 was spent in Rome, where Mrs Lucy had mixed feelings about some of the exhibits in the galleries they visited. 'I feel the colour mounting in my cheeks seeing so many undraped figures ... I keep the girls away from such sights as far as possible that they may not have their innocence impaired.'[65]

By the end of the nineteenth century such lengthy European trips were much less common, although a few ladies, like Lady Galloway, who visited New Zealand, and the Countess of Jersey, who went to New Caledonia, seized the opportunity to travel farther afield.[66] More common was the practice of countering the effects of excessive eating and drinking during the London Season by taking a 'cure' at a foreign spa. Homburg, Marienbad, Wiesbaden, Bad Ems and many others all claimed their adherents. May Harcourt, for example, accompanied her mother to Marienbad in 1905, and proudly recorded that she had lost eight pounds as a result of a régime of baths, exercise and diet. 'I rose at 6.15, had my first glass of water in my room, then walked to the spring where I partook of a second glass and walked till 8.30,' she told her step-mother-in-law;

> at 9.45 I had massage for my feet & ankles & eleven o'clock saw me in a Bath … After which straight home & in between blankets for an hour. Then lunch & a certain amount of rest. About 4.30 another walk to get coffee, after which still more exercise, then home. Dinner at eight – *one* dish … & then bed. Throw into the day a certain amount of bridge & you have a pattern of all our days … I enjoyed it enormously, that sort of foreign life always amuses me for a little while.[67]

For those most abstemious in their habits or less concerned with their health and figure, the ending of the Season was marked by a round of country house visits. Adeline de Horsey, later the Countess of Cardigan, recalled that during her youth it was 'an understood thing for people to go to certain houses at certain times, a yearly institution only disturbed by marriages or deaths'. Hence at the end of her 'gay season of 1842' she and her mother went to Cowes, where they spent 'a delightful month':

> Mamma gave a ball for me at the King's house, a former residence of George IV, which we had taken that year … From Cowes we went to stay with the Ailesburys at Savernake, and then to Badminton, where the Beauforts had a large family party …
>
> From Badminton we went on a visit to Lord Forester at Willey Park, Shropshire, where I met Lady Jersey and her daughter, Lady Clementina Villiers.
>
> Lady Jersey was the greatest *grande dame* in London Society, and her house in Berkeley Square was the centre of the Tory party … We usually spent Christmas at Beaudesert, Lord Anglesey's lovely old place … There was no hunting or shooting at Beaudesert, and our amusements were very simple ones. After lunch we walked over Cannock Chase, and those ladies who did not care for walking rode sturdy little ponies, We returned to tea, and after dinner there was music, cards or dancing. We thoroughly enjoyed ourselves and nobody was bored.[68]

For mothers with marriageable daughters, these country-house gatherings provided welcome opportunities for matchmaking, to supplement the opportunities of the London Season. Admittedly with transport improvements in the later Victorian years it became increasingly common to substitute 'week-end' visits for some of these more lengthy stays. But earlier in the century, parties lasting for a week or more were common. Many were associated with sporting events, such as cricket or racing in the summer and fox-hunting and shooting in the winter. Lady Warwick, for example, enjoyed Newmarket, but was scornful of the 'stilted, expensive, extensive and over-elaborate garden parties that made up Ascot, and lasted for four days on end'.[69] More to her taste were the cricket weeks held at Easton Lodge, during which she entertained a large number of visitors. At least two teams were accommodated in the house, a big luncheon tent was erected in the grounds, and county neighbours were invited to see the play.[70] The cricketer H. D. G. Leveson-Gower described what he considered an ideal week of country-house cricket:

> People are asked to stay in the house who are all previously acquainted with one another, thereby removing any stiffness or undue formality. I ... like a hostess to act as mother to the team ... A bevy of nice girls is needed to keep us all civilised, and the merriment is then tremendous ... there is a dance one night. On the others, songs, games, practical jokes, any amount of happy, innocent nonsense, as well as perhaps a flirtation.[71]

At the beginning of the twentieth century, Lady Cynthia Asquith (then Cynthia Charteris) remembered country-house visits arranged in the winter for shooting and hunt ball parties – the former, as we have seen, often being viewed by her with distaste. Much time was spent in changing clothes, according to accepted social ritual, and perhaps also to allow the hosts and guests to enjoy a little privacy in their own rooms, away from the rest of the company. Hence on Sunday morning

> you came down to breakfast ready for church in your 'best dress', made probably of velvet if you could afford it, velveteen if you couldn't. After church you went into tweeds. You always changed again before tea, into a 'tea-gown' if you possessed that special creation; the less affluent wore a summer day-frock. However small your dress allowance a different dinner dress for each night was considered necessary.
>
> Thus a Friday-to-Monday party meant taking your 'Sunday Best', two tweed coats and skirts with appropriate shirts, three evening frocks,

three garments suitable for tea, your 'best hat' – probably a vast affair loaded with feathers, flowers, fruit or corn – a variety of country hats and caps, as likely as not a riding-habit and billycock hat, rows of indoor and outdoor shoes, boots and gaiters, numberless accessories in the way of petticoats shawls, scarves, ornamental combs and wreaths, and a large bag in which to carry your embroidery about the house.[72]

Inevitably this meant travelling with a great deal of luggage – at least one huge trunk, a large hat-box and a substantial dressing-case. At first, Lady Cynthia was afraid that she would be late for dinner, 'a somewhat sacramental affair, half an hour before which the boom of the dressing-gong threw me into a fluster, for ... guests were expected to assemble in the drawing-room some minutes *before* the second gong went'.[73]

Dinner normally comprised seven or eight courses and then, while the men sat over their port, liqueurs, and cigars in the dining-room, the ladies repaired to the drawing-room. The first evening was spent in conversation and playing cards or games. At Stanway, Lady Cynthia's own home, her mother expected the guests to play 'intellectual games, sometimes to the detriment of their digestions even at the dinner-table'. Charades were also popular but so was 'any kind of impromptu tomfoolery', including blind man's buff.[74]

If such parties were to be successful, there must be a congenial mixing of the company and a skilful host and hostess. When Elizabeth Eden, daughter of the 1st Baron Auckland, stayed at Panshangar in the 1830s she found it 'full to the brim of vice and agreeableness, foreigners and roués ... all very pleasant'. By contrast after a visit to Studley Royal, during which she had been ill, she considered her 'illness ... remarkably opportune, inasmuch as ... Studley ... was so uncommonly dull, that the impossibility of dining down was an immense advantage that I had over the rest of society'.[75]

Between 22 November and 13 December 1869, the newly married Lady Knightley embarked on a tour of six country houses, but noticed acidly when she left the first, Weeting in Norfolk, that this has been 'certainly the least agreeable visit I ever paid there'. At Longleat, the fifth stop on the list, she enjoyed seeing over the house and spending time in the Library, with its collection of rare books and manuscripts, but the evenings she found 'slightly dull'. At the end of the trip she concluded that it had 'not been altogether a successful visit – there had been no one to draw one out – & I am anxious to succeed among Rainald's friends, both to please him and myself'.[76] During a later visit, in January 1879, to Orwell Park near Ipswich she summarised her reservations concerning country-house parties:

Four days of a country house ... don't afford much material for a journal. Miss Burrell and I drove on Tuesday to Ipswich to inspect a local exhibition of pictures, one or two nice ... Today we had a long expedition to Playford, a quaint old Elizabethan house with a moat and a ghost story – belonging to Lord Bristol, but chiefly interesting as having once been inhabited by Clarkeson – Wilberforce's coadjutor in putting down the slave trade. The other two days I walked with Lady Jersey, who is always agreeable of course. Lady Cork has kept us alive. Certainly in this party the goodness has been in one place, the pleasantness in another. The Gwyndyrs are doubtless worthy, but most dull. I have spent a good deal of time poking about in the library. A charming one it is ... In the evenings chess and loo have been the order of the day – the latter an old game revived which I have never played before – somewhat too gambling.[77]

Newcomers to country-house life could also be bewildered by the tight network of relatives and friends they encountered. Mrs Humphry Ward, who found herself lionised after the runaway success of her novel, *Robert Elsmere*, in 1888, at first felt somewhat out of place when invited to such parties: 'It is difficult,' she commented, 'for plain literary folk who do not belong to it to get much entertainment out of a circle where everybody is a cousin of everybody else and where the women, at any rate, though pleasant enough, are taken up with "places", jewels and Society with a big S.'[78] Nevertheless, she grew to enjoy the experience and in 1892 she, her husband, and their family moved into Stocks, a modest country house near Aldbury, Hertfordshire. There they held their first ball at Christmas 1892 and their first shooting party two years later.[79]

For those interested in flirtation (and that did not include either Lady Knightley or Mrs Ward), country-house parties offered opportunities for discreet sexual encounters. The novelist, Elinor Glyn, herself the wife of an Essex landowner and a friend of the Countess of Warwick, considered it to be 'quite normal in Society circles for a married woman to have a succession of illicit love affairs, during the intervals of which, if not simultaneously, intimate relations with her husband were resumed'.[80] At Easton Lodge, Lady Warwick would carefully arrange the household routine so as to facilitate 'little attentions pregnant with meaning':

In such houses there was always a tray, on which stood beautifully cleaned silver candlesticks, in the staircase hall, one of which you carried up to your room, even if you did not need it at all. It might be that in lighting it for you your admirer might whisper a suggestion of a rendezvous for the morning; if not, probably on your breakfast tray you would find a note from him given by his valet to your maid, suggesting where and when you might chance to meet him for a walk.[81]

It was this kind of arrangement which shocked the eminently respectable Lord Selborne when in August 1910, he stayed for a time with members of the 'smart set' at Crag Hall, near Macclesfield. With the exception of one couple, it was 'exclusively a party of wives without husbands & husbands without wives, most characteristic of the set'. Although he liked individual members of the group, he admitted that 'the atmosphere … has a decidedly nasty taste to me'. Shortly after, he travelled to Scotland to meet another party, this time from a more traditional landed background. These, he wrote to his wife, were 'immensely' more agreeable 'than the smarties'.[82]

For those interested in pursuing love affairs, the most important consideration was that they should be conducted with circumspection, so as to avoid gossip. Lady Warwick later claimed that what a man or woman

> might feel or do in private was their own affair … our rule was No Scandal! Whenever there was a threat of impending trouble, pressure would be brought to bear, sometimes from the highest quarters, and almost always successfully. We realised that publicity would cause chattering tongues, and as we had no intention of changing our mode of living, we saw to it that five out of every six scandals never reached the outside world.[83]

However, the Countess of Warwick, as Lady Brooke, did not always obey her own injunctions. In the late 1880s she narrowly escaped the social ostracism which followed divorce when her relationship with Lord Charles Beresford was publicised by Lord Charles's resentful wife. According to Lady Brooke, from the beginning of her married life her husband had accepted the 'inevitability of my having a train of admirers. I could not help it … It was all a great game.' On this occasion the 'great game' got out of hand and despite his easy-going nature Lord Brooke seems to have contemplated divorce. In the end, perhaps under pressure from his father or because it was contrary to his social training, he desisted.[84] Subsequently he seems to have accepted with equanimity his wife's intimacy with the Prince of Wales in the 1890s. During the early years of that decade

> the coveted invitation 'to meet the Prince of Wales' went out with almost monotonous regularity … drawing favoured socialites to the famous Easton Lodge house-parties. At the other houses the prince visited, Lord

and Lady Brooke were almost invariably included among the party; and during the racing season Lady Brooke travelled in the Prince's special train and shared the royal box. In the eyes of Society, she had conquered Everest.[85]

For some women, however, these infidelities could lead to disaster, and of none was that more true than of Lady Harriet Mordaunt of Walton Hall, Warwickshire. Lady Harriet was the fourth daughter of Sir Thomas Moncreiffe of that Ilk and she and Sir Charles Mordaunt were married in December 1866, when she was eighteen and he was thirty-two. Within months of the marriage she was committing adultery with a number of partners, including, it was alleged, the Prince of Wales. After two miscarriages, she eventually conceived a child by one of her lovers, Lord Cole, while her husband was on a fishing holiday in Norway. When the little girl was born, Lady Mordaunt feared that she had contracted venereal disease and that this would affect the child's eyesight. Overwhelmed by guilt, she confessed to her husband that she had been unfaithful to him on many occasions and that the child was not his. The next day, he broke open the lock to her desk and discovered a number of incriminating letters, as well as some short notes from the Prince of Wales. Sir Charles immediately left for London and severed all connections with his wife. He issued a writ for divorce soon after and in February 1870 the case came to court. By this time Harriet had had a mental breakdown, and her parents claimed that she had been insane at the time of the alleged confession and had not known what she was saying. The case aroused immense public interest, not least because of the appearance of the Prince of Wales in the witness box to clear himself of the charge of adultery. After several days of legal argument it was decided that Sir Charles's petition had failed because his wife's insanity prevented her from being party to a divorce suit. Five years later, however, the divorce was granted with Lord Cole named as co-respondent. Shortly after, Sir Charles remarried and had several children. Meanwhile, the little girl at the centre of this sad affair grew up, without suffering the blindness her mother had feared, and eventually married into an important aristocratic family. Only her mother lingered on in the shadows, her life destroyed by indiscretions committed before she had reached the age of twenty-one.[86] She died in 1906.

Few married women who were guilty of infidelity were required to pay such a heavy penalty as Lady Harriet. More typical was the situation described in Vita Sackville-West's novel, *The Edwardians*, when the duchess was preparing for a house-party at her country mansion, Chevron:

This question of the disposition of bedrooms always gave the duchess and her fellow-hostesses cause for anxious thought. It was so necessary to be tactful, and at the same time discreet. The professional Lothario would be furious if he found himself in a room surrounded by ladies who were all accompanied by their husbands ... Then there were the recognised lovers to be considered ... So she always planned the rooms carefully.[87]

At Knole, Vita had witnessed these clandestine relationships at first hand, for both her father and mother had taken lovers, with the former having a long-standing connection with Lady Constance Hatch and the latter taking up with 'millionaires and lonely elderly artists'. Among Lady Sackville's conquests were the wealthy Americans, J. Pierpont Morgan and William Waldorf Astor.[88]

Significantly, however, even in families where such affairs were commonplace, every effort was made to maintain the outer trappings of a secure, happy and respectable family life. The number of petitions for divorce or nullity filed in England and Wales did, admittedly, climb steadily in the second half of the nineteenth century, following the passage of the 1857 Matrimonial Causes Act. This made civil divorce available for the first time and both cheapened and simplified the whole procedure. Hence the number of petitions increased from an average of 226 per annum between 1861 and 1865 to 675 per annum between 1896 and 1900.[89] By 1913 it had risen to more than a thousand a year. But comparatively few of these involved members of landed society. (Among the peerage, just over twelve per cent of all marriages of the cohort born between 1875 and 1899 ended in divorce, with most of the divorces taking place after 1900.)[90] For the relatively modest response before the First World War there were several practical reasons. First, for the women concerned divorce meant not only social ostracism but, in many cases, loss of children and of financial security as well. Secondly, if wives wished to divorce their husband they had to prove not only the husband's adultery, but also his desertion or cruelty; a husband, on the other hand, could divorce his wife on grounds of her adultery alone. Female-initiated divorce was thus relatively difficult until the legislation was changed in 1923.[91] It was because the Marquis of Blandford had not merely committed adultery with Lord Aylesford's wife, Edith, but had eloped with her that Lady Blandford was able to divorce him in 1883.[92] Finally, divorce was shunned because it signified a breakdown of the structure of family life on which Victorians and Edwardians placed so much store. Violet Maxse expressed a typical view when she called the separation of her parents when she was five years old 'the greatest misfortune' of her life. Although in her case there was no question of divorce or remarriage – those 'disasters did not come near us' – she felt the family division, 'the separation, the never seeing our parents together, the differing views about our lives they often held, all ... were a terrible burden' for her and her sister and brothers to bear.[93]

Consequently, as Consuelo, Duchess of Marlborough, remembered of the 1890s, 'husbands and wives who could not get on together went their separate ways and in the great houses in which they lived practised a polite observance of the deference each owed the other'.[94] Ironically, in Consuelo's own case, relations with her husband became so difficult that a formal separation was arranged in 1906, and she ruefully recalled the 'excessive' public interest which this aroused. Fortunately for her, friends and relatives rallied round, including her mother-in-law, the divorced Lady Blandford. So although Consuelo was excluded from Court circles, she was able to play a part in the wider London social scene.[95]

More common was the reaction of the Marquis and Marchioness of Londonderry. Theresa Londonderry had become involved in a passionate love affair with Harry Cust, younger brother of Lord Brownlow and a notorious philanderer. Some of her letters fell into the hands of another of Cust's mistresses and she passed them to Lord Londonderry. His reaction was to return them to his wife with a note attached: 'Henceforth we do not speak.'

He was as good as his word, communicating with her always through a third party. Later he became Viceroy in Ireland and held various official positions, while Lady Londonderry herself became a leading political hostess for the Conservative Party. But they always received their guests standing a little apart, and he seemingly never spoke to her.[96] The core of their relationship had been shattered, but they both conspired to preserve its outer shell.

Most women avoided even this penalty. Either they remained virtuous or, if they did stray, they ensured that any relationships they did contract were conducted with sufficient discretion to avoid unwanted public disclosure. When they ended an erring wife (or husband) was welcomed back into the family fold, while any children of the liaison were always reared as the husband's child. This was true, for example, of Lady Elcho's daughter, Mary, whose father was the poet and traveller, Wilfred Scawen Blunt. She was always treated as a member of the family by Lord Elcho. Similarly, Lady Granby had one daughter by Montagu Corry (Lord Rowton), a former secretary to Disraeli, and another by the ubiquitous Harry Cust; both were brought up as part of her husband's family.[97] Such arrangements were considered the least damaging for all concerned. However, it was an unwritten rule that a wife should provide her husband with at least one legitimate male heir before she became seriously involved with anyone else. Those like Lady Harriet Mordaunt who neglected that precaution were condemned for failing to observe a convention which offered protection on the all-important question of property rights and estate inheritance.

7

Politics, Power & Professionalism

Though politics are denied to me still I have got hold of the reins of government in estate matters ... This gives me scope ... I have been more amused and interested than I have been for some time past.

Rosalind Howard, the future Countess of Carlisle, 30 May 1888. Quoted in Charles Roberts, *The Radical Countess* (1962), 136.

During the nineteenth century country-house wives and daughters, like their humbler sisters, had little opportunity for the personal exercise of political power. Not until 1918 were women able either to vote in parliamentary elections or to stand as candidates and ten more years were to elapse before they achieved full electoral equality with men. In the intervening period some progress was, admittedly, made. The 1869 Municipal Franchise Act gave unmarried women ratepayers a vote in council elections – a right which had been lost to females under the 1835 Municipal Corporations Act – and after the passage of the 1870 Elementary Education Act they could also vote and stand for election to the new school boards. Five years later the first female poor-law guardian was elected.[1] Further modest advances came in the 1880s and 1890s, notably with the 1894 Local Government Act, which opened up a wider sphere of political activity to married and single women alike. Soon after the first parish and district council elections were held under its provisions in December of that year, a supporter of female suffrage estimated that 'nearer 2,000 than 1,500 women [were] now actually engaged in great administrative work' on school boards, poor law boards, parish vestries and various parish and district councils.

That compared with less than 220 so engaged in the previous year.[2]

Among them were a number of 'ladies of the manor', who saw membership of such local bodies as an extension of their traditional Lady Bountiful role in caring for the young, the sick and the disadvantaged within their communities. They included Mrs Ames-Lyde, the principal landowner at Thornham, Norfolk, who helped revive the economic life of her village by developing a flourishing wrought-iron industry. 'She travelled the world for new designs, winning gold medals in international exhibitions for her craftsmanship, dying in Shanghai in 1914.'[3] Then there was Mrs Barker, wife of the squire of Sherfield-on-Loddon near Basingstoke. She was concerned to improve sanitary conditions in the village and to secure the efficient distribution of local charities. While a 'polluted well, an overcrowded cottage, a barrier across a footpath' were 'too trivial for men to make a stir about ... an independent woman, knowing that "trifles make the sum of human things" ... will be earnest for frequent meetings,' she declared; 'her cry will ever be ... "never ... stand still till all the good you have the power to do for the poor of your parish is an accomplished fact".'[4] A Devon landowner, Mrs Christie, held similar views. As a member and later chairman of her local school board, she repeatedly dipped into her own pocket to cover educational expenses which the board itself should have met.[5] Even Lady Brooke, who was soon to become an enthusiastic if controversial supporter of Socialism, in December 1894 successfully offered herself for election as a poor law guardian at Warwick, 'in the ... service of the poor'. She emphasised women's special qualifications to oversee the child welfare, 'home-making and nursing carried on by the work-house', and the value of a 'joint and mutual responsibility of man and woman' for the administration of community affairs.[6]

In a few cases, as with Mrs McIlquham of Tewkesbury, these duties were seen as a way of demonstrating women's administrative and political abilities, and were thus a necessary precursor to full female suffrage. She became successively a poor-law guardian, a school board member and a parish and rural district councillor.[7] Mrs McIlquham and other landed ladies who thought like her were particularly incensed when the 1884 Reform Act gave the vote to impoverished male agricultural labourers while they, as property owners, continued to be excluded from this basic political right purely on gender grounds. Mrs McIlquham quoted with approval the comment of a fellow agriculturist that while a woman who farmed 500 acres of land and paid 'the usual contributions to the taxes of the country' had no voice in its government, the labourers she employed had that right.[8]

There was an upsurge of interest among some women in serving as churchwardens. *A Women's Suffrage Calendar for 1895* (1894) noted among the successful candidates in 1894 the Dowager Lady Hindlip in Worcestershire, the Dowager Lady Heathcote in Hampshire and the Dowager Lady Londonderry in North Wales.

But many country-house ladies, no matter what their attitude towards local government, firmly turned their face against the parliamentary franchise. Like Lady Laura Standish in Anthony Trollope's novel *Phineas Finn*, they wished 'to be brought as near to political action as was possible for a woman without surrendering any of the privileges of feminine inaction'. Lady Laura rejoiced when her father became a Cabinet minister but considered the fact that women should even wish to vote at parliamentary elections was 'abominable … the cause of the Rights of Women generally was odious to her'.[9]

Among those who shared this view was Lady Frederick Cavendish. As early as 1867 she had condemned the subject of female suffrage as 'odious and ridiculous' and had expressed alarm that it was beginning 'to be spoken of without laughter, and as if it was an open question. I trust we are not coming to that.'[10] Twenty-two years later she was one of about two thousand women signing an anti-suffrage petition published in *The Nineteenth Century*. This declared that the enfranchisement of females was unnecessary and 'distasteful to the great majority of the women of the country … and mischievous to themselves and to the State'.[11] Their objections were based on the lack of female experience of such questions as foreign and colonial policy or 'grave constitutional change'; in addition, the rough and tumble of national politics was regarded as something essentially 'masculine' and therefore unsuited to women's more delicate sensibilities.[12] Lady Frederick's fellow signatories included five duchesses, two marchionesses, ten countesses, and seven viscountesses. As a pro-suffrage commentator acidly observed they were ladies for whom 'the lines of life [had] fallen in pleasant places'.[13]

Such attitudes persisted into the new century. Louisa Yorke at Erddig probably expressed a typical view when in 1904 she scathingly noted the election of the mayoress of Wrexham as a poor-law guardian: 'I cannot understand a mother with seven children caring for public life.'[14] May Harcourt took much the same line when she confessed her loathing for 'the role of a Public Woman striding on Platforms "saying a few words"'.[15] It was in these circumstances that a Women's Anti-Suffrage League was set up in 1908.

Yet, if women's *direct* political role was circumscribed by traditional 'separate spheres' arguments and by the restrictions of electoral law, *indirectly* they could exercise considerable influence. At a time when political power was concentrated in the hands of a small male elite largely drawn from the upper ranks of landed society (at any rate up to the 1880s), the wives and daughters of such men might offer opinions and advice within the intimacy of the domestic circle. Lady Frances Balfour, a relative of the 3rd Marquess of Salisbury, was one such enthusiast. According to her daughter, Blanche, when she visited Hatfield she had no time for her children: 'Conversation, especially on politics, was to her like brandy to the drunkard ... and in that house she had her fill.'[16] She was also determined that Blanche should share her zeal: 'The multiplication tables might remain a sealed book, but if you had asked me the difference between a Conservative and a Liberal-Unionist, I could have told you by the time I was ten.'

Similarly, even before their marriage, Sir Rainald Knightley found himself debating Irish Church disestablishment with his future wife, while the correspondence between Maud Cecil and her fiancé, the future Earl of Selborne, on the eve of their wedding in October 1883, was largely concerned with the need to improve slum housing.[17] Throughout their marriage Maud was to bombard her husband – and later her eldest son – with advice and opinions on a wide variety of political issues.

This opportunity to exert influence was, however, especially significant for the small coterie of political hostesses who, as in earlier centuries, offered hospitality and congenial company to their chosen party leaders. Their aim was to smooth the process of discussion and debate and avoid damaging squabbles or divisive legislation which would undermine their broader class interests. Despite a widening of the male parliamentary franchise in 1867 and 1884 and the changes which took place within the parties themselves as a consequence, the influence of political hostesses remained an important feature of parliamentary life up to 1914.[18]

Among the most prominent of these hostesses in the half-century before the First World War were the Marchioness of Londonderry, the Duchess of Devonshire, the Countess of Jersey, the Duchess of Buccleuch and the Marchioness of Salisbury for the Conservatives, and Lady Waldegrave, Lady Spencer, Lady Cowper and Lady Fanny Marjoribanks on the Liberal side. In addition, there were those like Millicent, Duchess of Sutherland whose consummate social skills were called upon in a wider political context. According to Millicent's biographer, the Sutherlands' town house, Stafford House, was in demand for a variety of 'diplomatic receptions and other prestigious social occasions. Court and government officials often asked [her] to stage a ball or banquet in honour of foreign royalty or distinguished potentates.'[19]

In return for carrying out this role, some of the women used their influence with ministers to secure preferment for relatives, friends and protégés who, left to themselves, would have been unlikely to make much progress. They might also promote or retard the careers of junior politicians. 'An ambitious young MP might be flattered into loyalty, or suddenly dropped from the guest list for playing the rebel too often.'[20] Austen Chamberlain once claimed that he could gauge the 'state of his own political fortunes by the number of fingers, ranging from two to ten' which Lady Londonderry extended to him when they met, while Winston Churchill benefited from Lady Jeune's influence with the War Office in getting to the Sudan in the 1890s.[21] Sir William Harcourt, too, was aided in his early career in the Liberal Party by the support and encouragement of Lady Waldegrave. She was also a powerful influence in healing the divisions which had afflicted the Liberals in the 1850s. It was an indication of the importance of her contribution that in 1900 (twenty-one years after her death) *The Graphic* could describe her Twickenham home as the 'Mecca towards which the eyes of the ambitious [had] turned with longing looks':

> It was at Strawberry Hill ... that political programmes were discussed and decided upon; that differences were patched up which otherwise might have switched history on to other lines ... It was an especial honour for a young man to be invited to visit Strawberry Hill on a Sunday, for it meant that his elders perceived that he possessed qualities which, if properly cultivated, might be useful to the State or to the party.[22]

Lady Warwick, too, regarded the reception rooms of a successful political hostess as the 'rendezvous of a thousand strivers', and her country house as

> the meeting-place of men who ridiculed or reviled each other in Parliament, yet were on the best of terms when the curtain fell upon the perennial farce. Because she knew everybody who was anybody, she was able to collect under her roof the most diverse interests, and there reconcile them ... [It] can be said that matters of high importance to the State were constantly decided between Liberals and Conservatives in the country houses of England.[23]

Some, like the Duchess of Buccleuch and the Marchioness of Londonderry, were highly selective about those whom they chose to patronise. For the Duchess of Buccleuch, remarked Lady Warwick sourly, Society 'consisted only of those upon whom she permitted herself to smile'. She was even more critical of Theresa Londonderry, calling her 'a born dictator, [who] loved to encounter opposition, so that she might crush it'. Lady Londonderry was tirelessly involved in a wide range of national and local issues before 1914, including Home Rule for Ireland, tariff reform, and the debates over the future of the House of Lords. Throughout she refused to make any concessions to Radical opinion and excluded from her north country home, Wynyard Park, and her Park Lane town house all those who did not share her powerful political prejudices.[24]

Lady Warwick was unlikely to be numbered among that select group once she had embraced socialism in the mid-1890s. As she herself admitted, the most charitable of her friends considered she had taken up this cause only because she had been so spoiled and so bored that she had been looking for a fresh diversion. This was a charge she vehemently denied.[25] Eventually in 1904 she joined the Social Democratic Federation, the most militant of the left-wing groups of her day. She then became something of a political hostess herself, entertaining trade unionists and various Labour supporters both at her town house and at Warwick Castle.[26]

Ironically, however, despite this close involvement in the parliamentary questions of their time, the major political hostesses were among the firmest opponents of the female suffrage movement. In part this was doubtless due to their desire to maintain the existing power structure and their adherence to the 'separate spheres' argument on electoral matters. But they may also have feared losing their own influence if the political world were opened up. In her reminiscences, written in the early 1900s, the anti-suffragist Tory, Lady Dorothy Nevill, quoted approvingly a long poem on 'The Rights of Women', whose sentiments were made very clear in one of the verses:

The RIGHTS of Women, what are they?
The RIGHT to labour, love and pray;
The RIGHT to weep with those that weep,
The RIGHT to wake when others sleep ...[27]

Significantly, when the Women's National Anti-Suffrage League was inaugurated in July 1908, it was chaired by Lady Jersey, one of the most important of the political hostesses. Others similarly active, like Lady Glenconner, Lady Sheffield, Lady Ilchester and Lady Wantage were also among its members, and its backers included many members of high society. Their position enabled them to exert pressure upon younger pro-suffrage women in their midst. Even in the 1970s, Lady Ricardo recalled how as a girl she had dreaded 'going anywhere and meeting people' because she favoured female suffrage. These social pressures intensified on the eve of the First World War as a result of increased suffragette militancy by Mrs Pankhurst and her supporters in the Women's Social and Political Union. According to Lady Ricardo,

> if you went to a dinner party … you were terrified of whom you'd sit next, and you could feel it coming round gradually to them saying 'oh … those *awful* women, did you see that somebody did so-and-so', and you *had* to say that you quite agreed with what they were doing … It was rather a nightmare.[28]

Even those, like Lady Knightley, who had long favoured the suffragist cause, were forced on to the defensive by the activities of the suffragettes. In March 1912, she bitterly attributed the recent defeat of a woman's franchise bill by fourteen votes 'to the mad folly of the militants', as well as to the fact that a 'good many members who never cared for it – were glad of the excuse of the militants to turn round'.[29] Nonetheless a few weeks later she chaired a suffrage meeting at Northampton and expressed confidence that the movement was now too strong to be suppressed. But she was also concerned that the vote should remain in the hands of the propertied classes. 'I shall never cease to regret that the Conservative party did not carry it on a tax-paying basis before universal suffrage came into practical politics.'[30] In a letter to *The Times* written in June 1913, a few months before her death, she declared that although 'suffrage for women' was 'most desirable, and [would] be attained in time … the means adopted by the militants are most reprehensible, and have put back the cause for many years. It can never be right to do wrong that good may come'.[31]

The Countess of Selborne, another suffrage supporter, shared many of these reservations. In her case they were combined with anxiety that the Conservatives should not be seen as opponents of the measure, and thereby allow Liberal rivals to make political capital out of it when enfranchisement took place:

> The thing is going to be incorporated in the Liberal programme pretty soon. Asquith is the only impediment, & he is showing signs of climbing down. The Dissenters have declared in its favour, & Grey & Lloyd George together will carry the party.
>
> It … should be made clear that a large portion of the Conservative party have always been in favour of giving votes to women.[32]

It was to promote that end that in 1908 she and Lady Knightley were involved in setting up the Conservative and Unionist Women's Franchise Association.

Other country-house ladies shared the cautious approach of Adeline, Duchess of Bedford and preferred to stand aside from the debate. When invited to sign a public appeal by the Anti-Suffrage League in 1910, she refused on the ground that this might undermine her wider work for female reforms: 'I have kept apart from public movements because I am under the impression that such slight influence as I am able to exercise on questions that affect women in general might be weakened or impaired were I to take part in matters of controversy.'[33]

Given the dependence of most females in landed society upon their families for sustenance and support, it is not surprising that few chose to join the militant Women's Social and Political Union, since this aroused particular hostility in propertied circles. One who did was Lady Constance Lytton, the daughter of a former viceroy of India. For her, the franchise battle became almost a religious mission; she felt 'the rhythm of the world's soul calling … women to uncramp our powers from the thraldom of long disuse'.[34] Nevertheless she faced strong opposition in the family for her stand. 'Poor Granny [was] in an awful state of distress yesterday,' wrote a sister in 1908, when Constance was a mature spinster of almost forty:

> Hearing Con had gone to the Suffragette meeting in Caxton Hall, and then in the *Daily Mail* it stated that she had taken warm clothes to the prisoners at Bow Street. Poor Mother talked of the disgrace to her name and you would have thought Con had done some real crime. She was quite ill over it and is still very seedy and upset.[35]

But Constance was undeterred. In October 1909 she threw a stone at Lloyd George's car and was arrested. She refused to pay the fine imposed and was sent to prison. There she went on hunger strike. Three doctors examined her and declared that her heart was too weak to permit the forced feeding which other suffragettes had to endure. As a result, she was released after two days. However, she felt her privileged family background had been the cause of this relatively lenient treatment. On future demonstrations she therefore disguised herself as a working woman and when she was arrested after another disturbance she gave a false name. Once more she went on hunger strike and this time her heart condition was not noticed and she was forcibly fed. Release came after several days of sickness and pain when the prison governor realised who she was. From then on her health deteriorated and in May 1912 she suffered a stroke. Although she survived until 1923 she remained an invalid and was never again able to take an active role in the cause.[36]

Most country-house wives and daughters, however, saw their

political role in a far less dramatic light. Perhaps like Lady Carrington and Lady Randolph Churchill, they attended parliamentary debates to hear their husbands speak or they followed political discussions in the press. Many, including Lady Randolph, also accompanied their husbands to political meetings.[37] And, as we saw in Chapter 1, when Lord Randolph was unable (or unwilling) to organise his election campaign at Woodstock in 1885, his wife took this in hand with great success.

Some women followed the example of Lady Fanny Russell, wife of the early Victorian Whig statesman, Lord John Russell, and kept 'politics' at a distance from their domestic life. She had little sympathy with the 'regular hardened lady politicians' who were perpetually preoccupied with party debates and intrigues.[38] Others adopted the same approach as Lady Leconfield, who was a sister of the Liberal Prime Minister, Lord Rosebery. Her husband's family were pillars of the Conservative party and, according to her obituary, when 'views opposed to her own were advanced, she did not argue but took refuge in discreet silence … it was only occasionally, when challenged to do so, that she would express her own with the utmost lucidity and trenchancy'.[39] Likewise Lady Tweedsmuir's mother Caroline Grosvenor, remained 'a silent but convinced Conservative all her life', despite her father's support for the radical wing of the Liberal party.[40] Even Lady Carrington, while maintaining her political interest, nonetheless saw her role increasingly as that of a background figure, listening when her husband rehearsed his parliamentary speeches at home, and then waiting anxiously for his return to discover how they had been received.[41]

For those with relatives in parliament a further opportunity for political activity arose through an involvement in election campaigns. That was particularly true after the 1883 Illegal Practices Act placed a limit upon the amount candidates could spend on electioneering and imposed severe penalties on those found guilty of bribery and corruption. In such circumstances, enthusiastic unpaid female canvassers and election organisers became very valuable. Hence a number of auxiliary political organisations sprang up in the 1880s to cater especially for women. The first, and the most successful, was the Primrose League, formed by the Conservatives in 1883 to revitalise the party. It started to recruit women on an equal basis to men in the following year. Although it adopted much pseudo-medieval flummery, with members known as Knights and Dames and branches as habitations, it proved highly effective in mobilising support and harnessing female electoral effort. By 1910, its mass membership was over two million and it had 2,645 habitations.[42] In 1885 a Ladies' Grand Council was established with the Duchess of Marlborough as its first president, and Lady Salisbury coming in soon after to share that role.

For many ladies the league provided a welcome political outlet. Even those, like Lady Knightley and Lady Randolph Churchill, who were sceptical or amused at its archaic terminology, could see its wider merits. Lady Randolph remembered laughing 'immoderately over the grandiloquent names – the "Knight Harbingers" (or "night refuges", as we dubbed them), ... the Brummagem gaudy badges and ye ancient diplomas printed on vellum'. But she was nonetheless 'determined to do all I could to further its aims'.[43] Lady Knightley felt much the same when she was enrolled as a dame in May 1885: 'It sounds all rubbish – but the objects "the maintenance of Religion, of the Estates of the Realm, & of the ascendancy of the British Empire, are excellent & I can quite believe that the paraphernalia helps to keep Conservatives together; means, in short, an army of unpaid canvassers'.[44] The league encouraged women to combine their existing educational and philanthropic work

> with the challenge of electoral battles ... they could indulge in league activity without losing caste or alienating themselves from male aristocratic society ... No one could mistake a Lady Jersey or a Lady Londonderry for one of the 'New Women' who so antagonized late Victorian males.[45]

As well as helping to canvass during elections (a task we shall consider later), Primrose Leaguers financed various political ventures. In the late 1880s the Ladies' Grand Council alone was spending £500 a year on literature for mass circulation.[46] Between 15 June and 6 August 1886 – a period which included a general election – it was responsible for supplying and distributing over 1.2 million leaflets and posters. By the end of the financial year to May 1888, that had risen to 7 million leaflets per annum. In addition, the ladies took in hand the registration of voters and chased up supporters who had moved away, to make sure they cast their vote in the right direction.[47] During elections they offered their carriages to convey electors to the polling stations and also offered refreshments. When the agricultural trade unionist Joseph Arch lost his NorthWest Norfolk seat in the 1886 general election, his supporters bitterly blamed this on electors being bribed by 'a two-shilling meat tea, provided by Primrose dames and others at sixpence per head'.[48]

However, some Conservative ladies of the old school could be capricious. Lady Dorothy Nevill, a founder-member of the league, ruefully recalled the wife of one of the most prominent Tory leaders who declared she would only lend her carriage to convey voters to the poll if she 'could be fully assured that the Conservative candidate would be successful. "We do not care," said she, "to be associated with failure!"'[49]

On a wider front, the Primrose League provided entertainment for its supporters throughout the year, including concerts, tea parties, outings and the like. As Lady Salisbury briskly observed, although much of this might seem vulgar, it appealed to the masses: 'that is why we have got on so well'.[50]

Meanwhile the women themselves had an opportunity to practice the arts of public speaking and to exercise their organisational skills. In the long run this could only increase their confidence and general political awareness.

The Liberal party responded in 1887 by forming its own Women's Federation. However, with a membership of only 10,000 in 1888 and 60,000 in 1904, it was never able to match the impact of its Conservative counterpart. The situation was further complicated in 1892 when, under the determined pressure of Rosalind, Countess of Carlisle, the Federation adopted a suffragist policy. This led to a membership split which was not healed until 1919. Indeed, in 1902, under Lady Carlisle's guidance, the Federation decided not to endorse electoral candidates who opposed women's suffrage, although it allowed individual members to work for such candidates, should they so wish.[51]

The WLF and the Women's Liberal Unionist Association, which appeared in 1888, both followed the Primrose League in recruiting female help for canvassing, distribution of literature and hunting up of supporters who had moved away. Canvassing, in particular, was regarded as an extension of existing female charitable activity. As Meresia Nevill, an enthusiastic Primrose Leaguer, put it, 'I consider women the best canvassers, in as much as they are used to district visiting. They have the habit of going among the poor, and speaking to [them] and learning their wants.'[52]

Even before these auxiliary political organisations appeared in the mid-1880s a small number of ladies had acted as canvassers. In 1874, for example, Rosalind Howard had campaigned on behalf of her father-in-law. On 8 February she described some of her doings in his East Cumberland constituency, beginning with her attendance at Brampton market:

I canvassed right and left, all the people whom I was introduced to. I was blue [the Liberal colour in that constituency] from head to foot – blue gown, blue chuddah, blue bows, and people were amused at the blue lady. We had a capital meeting at two o'clock ... On Thursday I drove to Warwick Bridge four miles from Carlisle, met the local agent there and had a long day's canvassing from house to house. I was out nearly twelve hours. On Friday I was out from 9 a.m. to 8 p.m. riding most part of the day in a thick cold white mist on the fell sides near Armathwaite. That is a very Liberal district and we met with the most cheering support and gained some waverers … Yesterday I had a tremendous day, I was out fifteen hours with very little to eat, yet I am quite fresh to-day … John Grey and I started riding at nine o'clock and went to Bewcastle parish nine miles off … and were riding from nine in the morning till ten at night long after it was pitch dark … We reached Naworth [her home] at twelve o'clock.[53]

After these formidable exertions she was doubtless gratified when her father-in-law was returned with a majority of 314, polling 2,943 votes to his Conservative opponent's 2,629. In view of Rosalind's determined attitude, it is not surprising that she soon became committed to the cause of female suffrage, though not to that of the suffragettes.[54] In the 1890s she was also elected to two rural district councils under the 1894 Local Government Act. One was in Cumberland, the other in Yorkshire, and both were in the vicinity of the family's estates.

Another keen canvasser was Constance Flower. In 1880 she spent three weeks at work in her husband's Brecon Boroughs constituency before the election on 1 April. She also attended his adoption meeting, but when it was clear she was the only lady present, she modestly concealed herself behind a screen: 'I could hear but was not visible.'[55] Subsequently she addressed a few words to a 'huge meeting' in the Town Hall, but when election day arrived confessed to feeling 'faint, sick with nervousness'. 'Cyril sent for us quite early. I went off in my blue gown accompanied by my faithful Gwen [a local election helper].'[56] As she drove through the crowded street to the inn which served as the Liberal headquarters she felt 'dreadfully alarmed', but then she and Gwen settled down to await the outcome:

People in & out all day long, crowds in front of the windows, all our carriages drawn up in a line taking the people to & from the polling booths. Cyril was enormously cheered and walked about with a mob of people behind him.[57]

At last polling ended and the result was announced. Cyril had won by fifty-nine votes, gaining the seat from the Conservatives.

We danced about as if we were mad … A roaring shrieking crowd assembled under the window & the Inn swarmed with people. Cyril had to get out of the window & to speak from the portico … I went to the open window and when silence was enforced said, 'I must thank you for the good work you have done today ...' Then I returned to the room and talked to some of our supporters.[58]

In none of these cases does it appear that the electioneering contributions of the womenfolk had been decisive in securing the return of the winning candidate. But from the mid-1880s there is evidence that this was changing. That was true of Lady Knightley's role in the general elections of 1885/6, as we shall see.

Louisa Knightley's interest in politics dated back to the 1860s when she and her cousins, Louisa and Jessie Boucherett, had been early supporters of female suffrage. The opportunity for her to put this interest into practical effect, however, came only with the general election of 1885, when her husband's South Northamptonshire seat was threatened by the Liberals. Sir Rainald had been a Conservative MP in the county since 1852, but with the enfranchisement of the agricultural labourers under the 1884 Reform Act there was a possibility that he would be defeated. This was reinforced by his reluctance to make more than token appearances at election meetings, and by his indifferent health.[59] Lady Knightley consequently decided to lend a hand, both for her husband's sake and because she believed that the cause he supported was 'the cause of religion, of liberty, and of prosperity for this country, and *every* class of its inhabitants'.[60] Armed with canvassing literature obtained from Conservative Central Office, she began her campaign in the village of Badby, near to her Fawsley home. There she obtained promises from thirty or more voters, although she admitted there were a few who were immune to her powers of persuasion: 'one Smith for instance whom I hunted out – & who is a reader of the Labourers' Chronicle ... we had a long talk about the land laws – whether with any result I know not. However – so far good – tho' as Rainald says – if Badby were wrong – one might as well throw up the sponge at once.'[61]

During the succeeding weeks she extended her activities to other villages. At Charwelton, for example, 'in spite of having heard about its radicalism,' she thought this was 'a good deal of swagger & ... when it comes to the point, they will vote for the man who has always been kind to them – though perhaps they will not tell each other so'.[62] But after a visit to Farthingstone, another 'doubtful' parish, she was less sanguine, regarding it as '*most* unsatisfactory – the labourers ignorant and prejudiced to a degree – I got barely a dozen votes. If there are many such villages it will be a bad look out.'[63] Nonetheless she remained undaunted and on 26 October, little more than a month before the poll, claimed proudly to have 'arranged for the canvassing of every village' in the constituency.

On the day of the election – 27 November – she drove to Badby with Rainald and saw with satisfaction that it was 'a mass of blue, [the Conservative colour in this constituency] & full of enthusiasm'.[64] But her strong suffragist feelings were also to the fore as she waited outside while her husband voted: 'I ... felt, for the first time personally, the utter anomaly of my not having a vote while Joe Bull has.'[65] The next day this was forgotten, as she and Sir Rainald drove to Towcester where the result was to be announced. 'I was deposited at the Pomfret Arms while R. was at the Town Hall, where the votes were being counted.' In the end he won by sixty-two votes, but that was scarcely the five hundred vote margin for which they had been looking.[66] Nevertheless, at a time when many Conservative candidates were losing their seats in rural constituencies, Sir Rainald had done well to be returned. As Lady Knightley proudly recorded in her diary, he attributed his success to her efforts.[67] But it had been a bruising experience, and he vowed never to contest the seat again. Events were to prove otherwise.

Although the Liberals were returned to power at the election, the issue of Home Rule for Ireland cast a shadow over proceedings from the outset. In the early summer of 1886 the party split over the issue, and a second general election was called. Once again, Lady Knightley took up her campaigning role. By 25 June she was hard at work 'with leaflets in the morning, in the afternoon drove into Daventry, called on all those who went around canvassing with me before'. Four days later, she attended a public meeting on her husband's behalf, saying a few words 'as a message from him. Oh how I long to speak but that I will not do.'[68] Perhaps her reticence was due to a feeling that such self-assertiveness would displease her husband, but whatever the reason the following day her desire to speak got the better of her. At Charwelton she made a few brief remarks at a meeting and noted that it had been 'altogether rather pleasant and interesting' although it was 'very hard work'.[69]

At this election the Liberal party's internal squabbles made the position of Conservative candidates a good deal easier, especially in the rural areas. Sir Rainald was returned once more, and this time with a majority of over three hundred. He never contested the seat again, retiring at the 1892 general election with a peerage, and dying three years later. His wife, meanwhile, continued to pursue her own political interests. In July 1903 she was co-opted as a member of Northamptonshire Education Committee, and her support for the Primrose League and the Conservative Party generally continued unabated.[70]

Lady Knightley's vigorous electioneering in South Northamptonshire was soon being matched by a growing number of women elsewhere.

This became particularly true after about 1900, as females grew more experienced in the political arena. The redoubtable Lady Selborne, for example, was involved in canvassing and in organising meetings around the family estate in Hampshire during 1897. 'The Oakhanger meeting seemed very friendly,' she told her husband.

> Jem [her brother] says all the estate men are right except Vokes ... Fred Bicknell is ... ardent, & helped me in getting up the meeting very much ... I told Major that I thought Carpenter was the best man to canvass Oakhanger ... He was at the meeting with a good deal of beer on board, but full of zeal ... I told Finch [the estate steward] he was to neglect all his other work & go round with Major whenever he wanted him. Finch is liked by the people I think. He is very civil & they all think it is a good thing to keep in with him as he so often can put them on to a job.[71]

In the 1905 election campaign, she 'again gave sensible advice about ... canvassers, floating voters who might be swayed, and the most receptive locations for meetings'. Five years later she assisted her brother, Robert Cecil, who was contesting a Cambridgeshire constituency. She considered he would have done better if he had established a 'decent organisation ... three months ago ... Our people are just buzzing about in most places.'[72] Nevertheless, she did her best.

> I have been working the respectable quiet women all I can ... I have got a little steam on here [in March] but Whittlesea is a most tiresome place. They come to meetings & wear pink bows, but won't work ... My use is to set the local women to work on the men.[73]

In the end, as she had feared, Robert was defeated, but her sister-in-law thanked her for the attempt: 'We should have done nothing with the women without you.'[74]

With her background, it is not surprising that Maud Selborne should be one of the country-house wives most involved in politics. In letters to her husband she freely discussed policies and tactics and judiciously used her contacts, as the daughter of a Prime Minister, to promote the causes she espoused. Her interest in the suffragist campaign led to her becoming president of the Conservative Women's Suffrage Society.[75] In 1911 she was part of a deputation invited by the Liberal Prime Minister H. H. Asquith, to Downing Street. 'I gather that Asquith being frightened of Christabel [Pankhurst], resolved to receive her, but diluted her with every other kind of suffrage society he could think of,' she commented ironically to her husband. 'So a very motley crowd assembled ... Christabel began. She was very extreme & said she would be satisfied with nothing less than equal voting rights for men & women ... I followed her with a speech in favour of the Conciliation Bill [supporting a modified female suffrage] ... Asquith ... volunteered the information that although he was against women's suffrage the large majority of his colleagues were for it.'[76] In the event the granting of votes to women was delayed until the end of the First World War, when Asquith himself had ceased to be Prime Minister.

Molly Trevelyan was another politically active wife. She took part in her first election campaign in January 1906, less than three years after her marriage and when she was still nursing her three-month-old first baby. 'For twelve days in January 1906 she attended three or more meetings daily, usually speaking for about twelve minutes at one or two meetings. The baby was brought by her nurse to various committee rooms, to be fed between meetings.'[77]

Even May Harcourt, despite her deep dislike of public speaking, took over her husband's election campaign in December 1910, when he was too ill to organise it himself. As she told her step-mother-in-law, this not only involved making arrangements and interviewing people but addressing various meetings:

> Two ... each night ... Last night yet another workers' Meeting & then two Public Meetings ... It is simply awful but there is nothing for it but just to set one's teeth & go through with it. They are very lenient but I am much ashamed at my efforts – I cannot imagine why they want a person who can't speak to address them ... I am also doing all the letters for Motor Cars for Polling day ... Everyone is very kind & very keen & I feel will do their best for Loulou in his absence. The Drs. say that had Loulou attempted the campaign he ran the risk of killing himself ... I imagine he is just short of a nervous breakdown.[78]

In the end, she, like Molly Trevelyan, had the satisfaction of seeing her husband safely returned. And despite their initial diffidence, the approach of both women had been very different from that adopted twenty years earlier by the redoubtable Lady Knightley. She, with all her determination and desire to help, had had to debate with herself whether it was appropriate for her to address a public meeting at all. By 1906 it was widely accepted as proper for women to take such initiatives, although, even then, the 'separate spheres' argument had not entirely disappeared. Molly Trevelyan discovered to her disappointment that her husband soon became agitated and angry if she expressed opinions which did not conform with his own.

Above: Lady Knightley of Fawsley Park, Northamptonshire, in the late 1870s. She was involved in a large number of charitable activities both in the villages around her home and on a national scale. To her great regret, she remained childless. (Northamptonshire Record Office)

Above right: A Queen's Institute district nurse in cycling uniform, *c.* 1900. The institute was an important philanthropic venture with which country-house ladies were associated from the late 1880s. (Queen's Nursing Institute, London)

Below right: Mrs Townsend of Honington Hall, Warwickshire, founder of the Girls' Friendly Society. The society began work at the very beginning of 1875. (Girls' Friendly Society)

Left: Leaving Her Majesty's Theatre, London, *c.* 1903. 'Next to a dance, a little party for the play was our most elegant occasion,' wrote Lady Tweedsmuir of her Edwardian youth. (The author)

Below: A leisurely summer afternoon on the lake at Erddig, near Wrexham, in 1909. (Clwyd Record Office)

INGENUOUS!

Jones to his fair Partner, after their opponents have declared "Clubs". "SHALL I PLAY TO 'CLUBS,' PARTNER?"
Fair Partner (who has never played Bridge before). "OH, NO, PLEASE DON'T, MR. JONES. I'VE ONLY GOT TWO LITTLE ONES."

Bridge became a popular leisure activity in high society at the end of the nineteenth century, especially in the Prince of Wales's 'set'. As *Punch* suggests, not all the players were skilful. (1904)

A ladies' archery competition in Regent's Park in 1902 – part of the London Season. (The author)

A summer boating excursion on Conway from Park Place, Remenham Hill, Berkshire, home of Mrs Noble, *c.* 1898. (Oxfordshire County Libraries)

The Curtis family of Alton playing croquet in their garden in 1865. Croquet became a popular country-house game during the 1860s and 1870s. (Hampshire County Museums Service)

Above: A ladies' cycling party at Sulham House, Berkshire, in 1897. (Mrs I. Moon) (Museum of English Rural Life, Reading)
Opposite: The active participation of ladies in shooting-parties was frowned upon before the First World War, as *Punch* mockingly suggests. (1904)

UNNECESSARY QUESTIONS.

Lady (with gun). "AM I HOLDING THE THING RIGHT?"

Left: Spectators at Henley Royal Regatta from Phyllis Court, Henley, *c*. 1910. This was a private club and a popular vantage point for watching the Regatta. (The author)

Centre: Country-house gatherings were an integral part of the social scene for landed families before the First World War. This group at Luton Hoo in the mid-1880s includes, standing on the far left, the mistress of the house, Mme de Falbe, holding an open parasol; on her left is Princess Mary Adelaide, Duchess of Teck, who is linking arms with her son, Prince Adolphus. Sitting slightly to the right of Prince Adolphus is Princess Mary of Teck (the future Queen Mary), holding a parasol. Princess Mary found Luton Hoo an agreeable house where 'one played tennis, went on the lake in a "tricycle boat", [and] "danced vigorously" till one-thirty in the morning'. (Luton Museum and Art Gallery)

Below: Country-house parties offered opportunities for discreet flirtation – as was perhaps the case in this croquet match at Luton Hoo in the 1860s. (Luton Museum and Art Gallery)

Opposite: Gardening was a popular – and highly respectable – leisure activity for many Victorian and Edwardian ladies. One enthusiast, who had an attractive garden in Sussex, emphasised to a young niece the wisdom of keeping 'a garden as a plum for your middle age'. (The author)

The 9th Duke of Marlborough addressing a meeting of the Oxford City and County Branch of the Women's Unionist and Tariff Reform Association at Blenheim Park on 23 July 1908. The association was concerned to end the Government's current free trade policies. In his speech the duke noted this was the first time in Oxfordshire's history that a large-scale political gathering had been arranged by the county's women. About 6,000 people attended the meeting and its associated fête. (Oxfordshire County Libraries)

ATMOSPHERE OF DISTRUST AT A GARDEN PARTY OWING TO RUMOUR THAT A MILITANT IS PRESENT.

The alarm caused in propertied circles by the violent activities of the suffragettes is mocked in this *Punch* cartoon of 1913.

THE ELECTIONS.—BRIBERY AND CORRUPTION.

Lady Canvasser (Yellow!). "WHAT, NOT IF I GIVE YOU A KISS, MR. BULLFINCH?"

(Obdurate Voter (Blue!) does not seem to see it, and is lost to the Liberal party.

Above: In 1866 *Punch* was reflecting widespread public reservations about women taking an active role in political affairs by depicting this lady canvasser as dowdy and unfeminine.

Right: Frances Wolseley (Later Viscountess Wolseley) with Leggett and Funnell, two local men whom she employed in the gardens at her School for Lady Gardeners at Ragged Lands, Glynde, Sussex, *c.* 1911. At the school lady students followed a 'systematic scientific Comprehensive Course of Horticulture', according to the first prospectus, issued in 1905. Bee-keeping and fruit storage were also covered and students were expected to wear a khaki uniform, this being the colour of the local soil! (East Sussex County Library)

Lady students learning to prune at Studley Agricultural College, Warwickshire. The college was promoted by the Countess of Warwick and began work at Reading in 1898. It transferred to Studley Castle in 1903. (Studley College Trust)

Studley Agricultural College students working with chrysanthemums, *c*. 1905, at a time when agriculture and horticulture were being suggested as possible occupations for educated girls. (Studley College Trust)

Left: Bee-keeping skills being imparted to lady students at Studley Agricultural College in 1905. (Studley College Trust)

Right: Lady Hulse of Breamore House, Hampshire. During the First World War she was active in the local Red Cross branch, vice-chairman of the Savings Committee and a member of Queen Mary's Needlework Guild. After the war she built Hulse House in Salisbury as a memorial to her son, who was killed in 1915. It was used principally as a centre for child welfare and for maternity work. (Hampshire County Museums Service)

Room at Coldhayes, Liss, Hampshire, which was converted for use as a hospital in 1914 by its owner, Mrs Hannay. Mrs Hannay's husband had been killed in the Boer War and she became commandant of the wartime hospital. (Hampshire County Museums Service)

The drawing-room at South Warnborough Lodge, Hampshire which was used as a war hospital supply depot from 1915. It was organised by the owner, Mrs Ridley, and was run under her personal supervision and at her expense. It supplied 1,292 gift articles to British combatant troops and 6,479 items to the British sick and wounded in hospital during the war period. (Hampshire County Museums Service)

Resourceful Tommy (after tea and a dull afternoon). "WE'RE SORRY, LADY, WE MUST GO NOW. YER SEE, WE 'AVE TO GET BAC AND 'AVE OUR TEMPERATURES TOOK."

Not all convalescent soldiers welcomed the hospitality they received from well-meaning ladies while they were recovering from their wounds. (*Punch*, 1916)

Reluctantly she confined herself to playing the supportive political role he demanded.

It is also ironic that Lewis Harcourt should have been so dependent on his wife's efforts for his electoral success, since he was one of the most implacable opponents of women's suffrage in the Liberal government.

In bringing about this wider acceptance of the female political role, there is little doubt that women's participation in the various auxiliary organisations, like the Primrose League and the Liberal Federation, and their modest contribution to local government had given them much-needed confidence, as well as electoral experience. In 1919, Lady Astor became the first woman MP to take her seat in the Commons when she contested her husband's old constituency at Plymouth, following his elevation to the peerage. A decade later there were fourteen women MPs – several of them, including the Duchess of Atholl, Lady Iveagh, Lady Cynthia Mosley and Nancy Astor herself, coming from a titled background.[79]

In economic matters, however, the exercise of power by country-house wives and daughters showed far less change compared to the beginning of the Victorian era. Given the continuing operation of the principles of primogeniture and entail, and the financial limitations placed upon most females, very few had a real opportunity to demonstrate their abilities by running an estate or a business on their own account. One of the exceptions was Alice de Rothschild, who inherited her brother's Waddesdon property in Buckinghamshire when she was already a spinster of fifty-one. She immediately resolved to arrange things her own way, looking after every detail of the estate. She visited the gardens, glasshouses, and farm daily, personally managing all departments and not resting until she was satisfied with what she saw. Even when she was away in the south of France during the winter months, Miss de Rothschild rarely allowed Waddesdon to slip from her mind. A flow of instructions, enquiries and exhortations was despatched to her employees. She also took her role as lady of the manor seriously, improving amenities in the village and its environs by the construction of schools, a nursing home and recreational clubs. She became a familiar figure in the surrounding countryside as she drove around in a phaeton.[80]

Rosalind, Countess of Carlisle, likewise seized the opportunity to manage her husband's estates, with his agreement, in 1888. When she assumed control, the property was heavily mortgaged, but these liabilities were cleared in 1889 and 1890 by sales of land from the Morpeth estate. Rosalind then built up the Naworth property in Cumberland, as well as managing about 13,000 acres in Yorkshire around the Castle Howard seat. About a year after she had taken over, she admitted to her husband that her role might be seen as 'a sort of usurpation' of his position, 'and I have a shy apologetic feeling about it. Yet I too want a sphere … some incentive to learn and to achieve – not to flit merely.'[81] The burden of the work was considerable, involving much travelling between the estates. It also required a knowledge of various kinds of farming as well as of housing, building, forestry and colliery management.[82] On one occasion she wrote of the 'bottomless morass of work' connected with the estates but under her supervision their net annual income rose from around £15,000 in 1892–94 to almost £25,000 by 1911–13. However, her lack of professional training led to mistakes, too, and her daughter had reservations about some of her managerial decisions, beliving they had led to 'many serious ill consequences and waste'. Not only did she let farms to tenants because they claimed to be Liberals and teetotallers rather than because they were efficient agriculturalists, but her knowledge of forestry, in particular, was deficient.[83] Yet, despite her weaknesses, there was little doubt about the importance of her administrative role. When it came to estate management, her daughter confessed, 'her authority ran alone and unchecked'.[84]

Still greater responsibilities were taken on by Frances Anne, Dowager Duchess of Londonderry. She controlled the family's collieries around Seaham in County Durham from 1854, after the death of her husband. Benjamin Disraeli, who visited her at Seaham Hall in 1861, described in graphic terms her way of life:

> Our hostess is a remarkable woman … Twenty miles hence she has a palace (Wynyard) in a vast park, with forest rides and antlered deer, and all the splendid accessories of feudal life. But she prefers living in a hall … surrounded by her collieries and her blast furnaces and her railroads and the unceasing telegraphs, with a port hewn out of the solid rock, screw steamers and four thousand pitmen under her control … In the town of Seaham Harbour, a mile off, she has a regular office, a fine stone building with her name and arms in front, and her flag flying above; and here she transacts with innumerable agents, immense business – and I remember her five-and-twenty years ago a mere fine lady; nay, the finest in London! But one must find excitement if one has brains.[85]

It was at her instigation that blast furnaces were constructed near to Seaham Harbour, and throughout her period of control she kept a ruthless grip on the whole enterprise. In one memorandum apparently written to her chief agent in about 1855, she commented sharply,

I observe in the return of Agent's Duties for Seaham Harbour Mr Errington is put down as 'collecting Ground Rents' and 'overlooking fortnight's Pay Bills'.

He has signally failed in both and ought to be discharged for either...[86]

When her first general manager and the first works manager at the blast furnaces sought to cheat her – the former by borrowing money at 2.5 per cent interest and charging her 5 per cent for it – her reaction was swift. Both were dismissed.

In other cases, widows had to oversee estates until their eldest son came of age, as Mary Elizabeth Lucy did at Charlecote Park in the middle of the nineteenth century. The same was true of Lady Airlie, whose husband was killed in the Boer War, and who was left with a family of six children and a 69,000-acre Scottish estate to administer. In spite of its enormous acreage, Cortachy had never been a rich property, for nearly 40,000 acres of it were given over to moorland and forest; 'the farms were small, which meant many boundary fences and dwelling houses to be maintained by the landlord. The shootings were lucrative in certain seasons, but they were a precarious source of income.'[87] Lady Airlie often spent sleepless nights after going through the accounts with the factor, as she struggled to live within her means and to understand financial problems for which she had received no previous preparation. She visited the tenants at least once a year and supervised the running of the home farm and dairy. She also learnt book-keeping, and began her day's labours at 4 a.m. each morning. By the time her maid arrived with tea at 6 a.m. she had dealt with the correspondence and the substantial pile of exercise books she used for her accounts, and was ready to join the children for breakfast.[88]

Lady Sitwell, too, was left a widow with young children and with a ruined estate as well. By a mixture of shrewdness and good management she was able to restore the family fortunes.[89] Mrs Bankes at Kingston Lacy, Dorset, was also to prove a successful administrator of the estate during her son's long minority.[90]

But most women lacked either the will or the means to exercise this kind of authority. Fewer still looked around for a profession or training which would allow them to develop their individual abilities. One who did was Frances Wolseley, the strong-willed only child of Field Marshal Viscount Wolseley. Ever since the age of fifteen Frances had been interested in horticulture and in 1902/3, when in her early thirties, she decided to set up a training school for lady gardeners near her home at the Glynde, Sussex. In 1906 it was formally established, but almost at once her parents showed their disapproval. Such independence was not expected of a dutiful daughter in well-to-do Edwardian society. Lady Wolseley reproached her for leading 'an absolutely selfish & self-centred existence (I cannot call it *life*, there is no life in it)' and of neglecting her family.[91] Years later Frances ruefully remembered that her parents had dismissed the garden as a mere 'cabbage patch, all of which inspired me to surpass their expectations and convert the little place into a rather charming and stately terrace garden. Between 1908 and 1914, I worked very hard at organising the work and the teaching for my students.'[92] In the end she was successful, with thirty students under instruction on the eve of the First World War. In that same year she was given the freedom of the City of London through the Gardeners Company, for founding the Glynde College for Lady Gardeners, as it had now become. But she never overcame her mother's hostility to her action.

Attendance at university aroused similar displeasure in many landed families. When Lady Cynthia Asquith expressed a desire to go to college, the notion was firmly vetoed by her parents:

> For a girl to go to a university was a deviation from the normal almost as wide as taking the veil, or, by a stride in the other direction, going on the stage ... to be associated with a university education would undoubtedly be a scandal it would take many seasons to live down.[93]

Nevertheless, a few girls with greater determination than Lady Cynthia or more amenable parents were able to take the plunge. Among them were the Jebb sisters of the Lyth, Shropshire. The venture was made easier in their case by the fact that their aunt Louisa (always known as Bun) had years before taken a course at the newly founded Newnham College, Cambridge. Bun was a firm believer in higher education for women and a strong ally when her nieces expressed a desire to go to university. The first to show interest was Louisa (Lill), a serious girl with a scientific bent, who wanted to study geology and to learn how to run the home farm. Her aunt considered that the recently established agricultural course at Cambridge would be highly suitable, but her father had distinct reservations. In a letter to his wife in October 1891 he bluntly declared,

> As for Lilly and education, I should say, if a girl were marked with small-pox and had good abilities, if she were [so] short-sighted as to make spectacles a perpetual necessity and had great common sense, if she were to be obliged hereafter to gain her livelihood as a teacher at some sad seminary, then there might be something to be said for Cambridge. Otherwise a ladies' college seems to me only a ladies'

school with all its evils intensified, because the time of life is just the most impressionable and hazardous of any. Another point ... I suppose I should have to give Lilly at least £40 a year ... I have not now forty pence per annum to the good.[94]

Eventually, perhaps under the influence of his strong-minded sister, he relented, and Lill went to Newnham. At the end of her agricultural course she returned to the Lyth to act as bailiff on the home farm, which was now owned by her brother, following the death of their father in 1894. She became an expert dairy farmer and a leading figure in the smallholders' movement. Some years later, after she had married, Lill became a governor of the Agricultural Organisation Society and in 1914 was called in to help mobilise women's land work during the First World War.[95]

Soon after Lill went to Cambridge, her younger sister, Eglantyne, began a three-year history course at Lady Margaret Hall, Oxford, with aunt Bun meeting part of the cost. There she threw herself into the life of the college and made friends with other girls from a similar background to her own, like Lettice Verney. In 1898 after three years, Eglantyne emerged determined to become a qualified elementary school teacher. To this end she spent a year at Stockwell Training College, London, before taking up a post in a school at Marlborough, Wiltshire. But the stress of teaching proved too great and she gave up after little more than a year. Nevertheless, her desire for an independent career was undiminished and eventually she went on to become founder of the Save the Children Fund.[96] She was also an enthusiastic supporter of women's suffrage.

The third sister, Dorothy, also attended Cambridge University, where she read moral science and economics. In 1904 she married Charles Buxton, who was, like herself, from a landed family. Subsequently both she and her husband were involved in Liberal and later Labour Party politics.

Other women, less serious minded than the Jebbs, could follow the example of Lady Cynthia Colville. She combined piano studies at the Royal College of Music with the social round associated with a London Season. At the end of four years she emerged with an ARC certificate as a piano teacher, although she had, of course, no intention of pursuing such a career. Drily she recalled that one of the drawbacks of being both a music student and a debutante was that 'occasionally the times did not quite agree. With a piano in my bedroom I could generally fit in some leisure for practising, but paper work often went to the wall. It became a fairly common experience for me to return from a dance, say, at 2, 3, or 4 a.m. and then sit down for a couple of hours to write a fugue, work at my harmony or struggle with counterpoint.' Nevertheless, she regarded the effort as worthwhile and called her four years at the college a period of 'unadulterated delight'.[97]

Much the same applied to Elizabeth Mary Barnard, who lived at Ham Common and subsequently married Francis Randle Wilbraham of Rode Hall, Cheshire. She regularly attended drawing classes and also visited the National Gallery to copy some of the paintings.[98]

Elsewhere a small minority of women followed the example of Frances Wolseley and took up agriculture or horticulture, perhaps by attending training institutions like Frances' own School for Lady Gardeners, or the Lady Warwick Hostel at Reading. This latter was initiated by the Countess of Warwick in 1898 to work in association with Reading College (later Reading University). It appeared at a time when, as *Country Life* suggested, farming was beginning to be seen as a possible occupation for educated girls. It was intended for the 'daughters of former landowners who [had] lost their money through agricultural depression' or other 'ladies in reduced circumstances' who wished to take up land work.[99] The subjects covered included dairying, horticulture, poultry farming, beekeeping, fruit growing and marketing, and some of the lectures were given by staff at Reading College and from the British Dairy Institute. But in 1902 these links were severed, largely because the college was dissatisfied with the level of training offered. Practical work was undertaken on farms in the area as well as on land attached to the hostel itself. At least one student also brought her own pony, which was accommodated on the premises for a weekly charge of 7s 6d.[100]

During its first six years, the Lady Warwick Hostel trained 146 full-time students, of whom twenty-four were reported in 1904 to have smallholdings of their own (either farms or market gardens), while twelve more were working on home farms or gardens, perhaps attached to parental properties.

Initially the countess had envisaged the scheme as part of a wider plan to establish 'unmarrying women' on agricultural settlements in various parts of this country and in the colonies. The settlements were to comprise six to twenty holdings, each worked by two women, who would share a cottage and run the venture as partners. There would be co-operative buying and selling of the produce and equipment used, as well as a co-operative dairy, and a 'lady warden' to transact each settlement's business. The whole would be run from a central office in London. In the end, this broader plan failed to materialise, but the training scheme had modest success. In 1903 it was relocated at Studley Castle, Warwickshire, where it remained until its closure in 1969.

By this time the students came largely from the professional classes, rather than the 'gentlewomen by birth and education' who had been its original targets. But a few girls from a landed background were still recruited, including Doris Bowes Lyon, first cousin to Queen Elizabeth, the Queen Mother. She died during the influenza epidemic of 1919.[101] In February 1899 the first warden of the Lady Warwick Hostel had emphasised in a letter to Viscountess Cranborne that although the scheme needed the support of women of 'all ranks and classes ... it is our great English Aristocracy ... who can throw in their weight if they will, & lift the whole movement into the realms of Patriotism'.[102] Despite occasional assistance – the Countess of Bective sent chickens to the hostel in 1899 and the Countess of Kilmorry provided some bees – it is clear that significant aristocratic commitment was in short supply.[103] Throughout these years the enterprise remained small in scale.

The same was true of Frances Wolseley's training school. Records show that at Glynde early students were more likely to be the daughters of clergy or middle-class business families than girls from any more elevated social background.[104]

Other bodies offering agricultural training included the Women's Agricultural and Horticultural International Union, founded in 1899, to help women working their own land or who were in salaried horticultural and agricultural posts, and the National Political League, formed in 1911, to find openings for ladies in land work and 'to further other social reforms on a non-party basis'. As a first step, this body began to establish settlements where females could carry on poultry-farming and 'kindred industries' like fruit farming and market gardening.[105]

But none of these ventures appealed to more than a tiny minority of girls from landed families. And of those who did embark upon them, most had to face opposition and scepticism from parents and friends, as Frances Wolseley did. Indeed, even those who supported the initiatives were anxious that the women should not become so involved in the work that they 'unsexed' themselves. 'All ladies should devote a portion of their time to literature or music, or the practice of some other feminine accomplishment calculated to bring relaxation if not pecuniary gain,' wrote one well-wisher.[106]

Not until the First World War did attitudes begin to change, as it at last became accepted that the daughters of the aristocracy and gentry, like their lower-class counterparts, should be free to develop their talents, instead of being confined within an exclusive but cramping social strait-jacket of etiquette and custom.[107] Symptomatic of the general pre-war approach was that of the Duke of Sutherland. When he decided to vacate Trentham Hall in the early 1900s he offered the building to Staffordshire County Council, and the council suggested it might be used as a training college for women teachers. The Duke answered sharply that he would prefer to have it used as an art museum rather than an institution for producing female teachers! What the Duchess thought of this anti-feminist response is not known, but the outcome was that the council refused the offer and Trentham Park was sold in 1911. It was demolished soon after.[108]

8
Epilogue:
The Impact of War, 1914–18

Comforts for both soldiers and sailors were badly needed, and a large party of country neighbours assembled weekly ... to knit the socks and the hood-comforters ... needed for the bitter cold of the North Sea for the Navy.... One of the most touching developments was the way in which country-house after country-house was turned into a War Hospital ... In one, the whole family and any staying guests were relegated by the Hostess Commandant to the attics so that the large guest-chambers and spacious sitting-rooms might be available for the wounded.

The Hon. Mrs E. M. Gell, *Under Three Reigns 1860–1920* (1927), 263–64, on the impact of the First World War in her part of Derbyshire.

In the evening some joyous singing in chorus ... along the road that passes this house. It was the harvesters. It sounded strange as one hears no shouting or laughter anywhere now. Nobody smiles.

Entry in the diary of Lady Laura Ridding of Wonston, Hampshire, 15 August 1914.

When war was declared on 4 August 1914, few landed families appreciated either the scale or the bitter nature of the conflict which lay ahead. Certainly to Dorothy Beresford-Peirse, secure on her parents' large estate at Bedale in North Yorkshire, it all seemed 'rather a distant thing ... it didn't sink in'.[1] This sense of unreality was shared by Lady Laura Ridding, although in her case it was combined with deep foreboding. 'One feels so weak in body,' she wrote in her diary on 10 August. 'The awful horror that hangs over one night & day … The extraordinary experience of being suddenly shorn of the peace in which all our elderly lives have always been wrapped – the safety – the security – the certainty vanishes.'[2] Yet in the days that preceded that fatal declaration there had been few premonitions among the inmates of most country houses that the comfortable world they had known was about to disappear for ever. Admittedly rumours were circulating of the tense situation in central Europe, following the assassination on 28 June of the Archduke Franz Ferdinand, heir-apparent to the crowns of Austria and Hungary. But at Taplow Court, Lady Desborough recalled that members of a house party at the end of July were more 'absorbed in the subject of the Dublin Riots' than in 'the first murmurs about graver causes of anxiety'.[3] In the week that followed she and her family continued on a round of country-house visits.

Likewise at Easton Lodge, Lady Warwick held her customary August bank holiday flower show and fun-fair for the neighbours. One youngster who attended remembered it as a 'warm and sunny day, the villagers were in their Sunday best, and the distinguished visitors down from London were seated under the trees or walking around in pairs, the ladies in great "picture" hats carrying parasols, the gentlemen in white, with panama hats carrying elegant walking sticks.'[4] Yet on that same August Bank Holiday Monday news came through of the threat to Belgian territory from Germany and the mobilisation of the British Army was begun.[5]

Much the same sense of drifting into conflict applied at The Woodhouse, Rowsley, where the young Lady Diana Manners, daughter of the Duke of Rutland, was staying with her brother and some of his friends. As they enjoyed the hot sunshine they played 'the war game, then very much the fashion'. It had been

> elaborated by Winston Churchill into a pastime for strategists and involving hundreds of tin soldiers. As my brother, Bunt Goschen and our adored Ego [Hugo] Charteris lay on their stomachs in a stone courtyard lining up their army corps, they quarrelled more hotly over the campaigns and planning of battles than summit generals were ever to quarrel over war itself.[6]

Charteris (Lord Elcho) was heir to the Wemyss estates in Gloucestershire and Scotland and was Lady Cynthia Asquith's eldest brother. When war was declared he was pursuing a legal career but as a result of his membership of the Gloucestershire Yeomanry, he was called up immediately. On 9 August his mother went to Gloucester Cathedral to watch the soldiers at church parade. As she saw the 'quiet earnest faces' of her son and his troop praying in the ancient cathedral, 'it sank into my heart for the first time that they were going to fight'.[7] Within two years two of her sons were dead. Hugo was killed in Egypt in April 1916, while his younger brother, Yvo, who was still at Eton when the war broke out, died even earlier. He joined up straight from school and went to France on 11 September 1915. He was killed on 17 October, shortly after his nineteenth birthday.

The losses experienced by the Wemyss family were to be matched in many country houses up and down the land, as the hostilities pursued their relentless course. Already by the end of 1914 the dead included six peers, sixteen baronets, ninety-five sons of peers and eighty-two sons of baronets. It was in these circumstances that C. F. G. Masterman claimed emotionally that in the retreat from Mons and the first Battle of Ypres, during 1914–15, the 'flower of the British aristocracy' was destroyed. Lady Curzon shared his feelings. 'Truly,' she wrote, when the war was over, 'England lost the flower of her young men in those terrible days … There was scarcely one of our friends who did not lose a son, a husband, or a brother.'[8] In the event, landed families, with their long-established military traditions, were to suffer more grievously in the war than any other class of society.'[9]

Even those who escaped the disasters of the Western Front or the later Dardanelles Campaign did not necessarily emerge unscathed. At the beginning of October 1914, Lady Selborne had rejoiced that her two younger sons were going to India rather than to any more dangerous theatre of war. 'I certainly find it a better place than France at present,' she told her husband.[10] Yet, by January 1916 the elder boy, Bobby, had been sent on an ill-fated military expedition to Mesopotamia. There he was first reported wounded, and then missing; only after weeks of gnawing fear and uncertainty did it finally transpire that he had died in Turkish captivity. Months later his mother was still mourning her loss:

There is certainly a topsy turveydom in the circumstances that have struck … Bobby to die for a very heathen conception of duty. Mind I don't say it is wrong because it is heathen. It is the primitive virtue, & has to come first I suppose. But Bobby was really a Xtian & I should like to have had him working for Xtianity proper … There are so many men willing to die fighting – so few who can feel active interest in the weak & the oppressed.[11]

Over the years, her sense of the tragic waste of life continued to grow, and in October 1918, less than three weeks before the Armistice, she was lamenting the current 'black look out':

> *The Times* today says we have had a very good day & advanced three miles! At that rate it will take us several weeks to get to Germany. Every day there is an enormous casualty list. Today it is 5,000. I suppose 1,000 of those are killed, perhaps another 500 crippled. That is only the English (sic) Army. You must add the French & American – aye & the German too if you are recognising all the damage that is being done.[12]

Wives and mothers reacted in different ways to their grief. The Hon. John Manners' mother displayed Spartan courage on hearing of the death of her son less than a month after the declaration of war. She proudly declared that if she had six such sons 'she would give them all'.[13] Likewise a mere four days after a memorial service had been held at Stanway for Yvo Charteris, his mother, Lady Wemyss, took out three convalescent soldiers from Winchcombe hospital for a drive through the Cotswolds, followed by tea. The next day she again gave them tea, this time at Stanway, and in the weeks and months that lay ahead she carried out a wide range of war work, seeking to numb her pain by constant activity.[14]

For Ettie Grenfell, Lady Desborough, who lost two sons within two months, during May and July 1915, consolation was found in the compiling and publishing of *Pages From a Family Journal 1888–1915*, which included letters, diary entries and reminiscences of happier days when the family had still been together.[15] Lady Curzon paid tribute to the way the Desboroughs had 'stood the loss of their two brilliant sons as only such characters as theirs would'. But inwardly their lives had been devastated by 'such utter desolation, such extinction of joy, glamour and hope'.[16] Elsewhere, as with Lady Hulse of Breamore House in Hampshire, the loss of a son was commemorated after the war. In her case, the memorial took the form of a welfare clinic in Salisbury known as Hulse House, which was designed to benefit mothers and children in particular.[17]

But not all were able to display such stoicism. Letty Charteris, Lady Diana Manner's sister, was driven almost insane when she learnt of the death of her husband, Hugo. Day and night she lay moaning gently, 'How can I face the long years? ... What does one do?'[18] For Lady Longford, too, confirmation of her husband's death in the Dardanelles came as a bitter blow. She was the mother of six children, the youngest of whom was only eighteen months old, and for nearly a year she was not sure whether her husband had survived as a prisoner or had been killed. Throughout the winter of 1915–16 Lady Longford struggled to find out her husband's fate, clinging to uncertainty as better than accepting the finality of loss. Not until June 1916 did the War Office at last tell her that it must be assumed that he had died in an attack on the heights above Suvla Bay on 21 August 1915.[19]

In all, of the peers and their sons under the age of fifty who served in the war, almost one in five was killed. Although the heavy losses experienced in the first years were not repeated in 1917 and 1918, a steady and inexorable toll continued to be exacted. During those final years six peers and sixty-five peers' sons died as a result of hostilities, twenty-four of them aged twenty-five or less. Among them was the nineteen-year-old 7th Earl of Shannon, as well as at least five others who were only nineteen or twenty when they died. In many cases, as has been pointed out, 'titles, after the war, passed direct from grandfather to grandson, while others – like that of Willy, 1st Baron Desbrough – died out together'.[20]

However, in August 1914 these tragedies lay in the future, and it was in a wave of patriotic enthusiasm that the sons of landed families flocked to the colours. Numbers shared the sense of urgency of Sir Oswald Moseley, the son of a Staffordshire landowning family, that they must join up quickly so as not to miss any of the action. 'Our one great fear,' Mosley said of his generation, 'was that the war would be over before we got there.'[21] Meanwhile, night and day, trains ground along the nation's railway tracks carrying troops, guns and horses to the coast in readiness for embarkation.[22]

Wives and mothers shared in this excitement, carefully hiding any deeper fears they may have had. Lady Tullibardine 'nearly burst with pride' when she learnt that her husband was to mobilise and command the Scottish Horse. And even in the mid-1930s Viscountess Barrington remembered 'the pride and exaltation of fond parents and wives, their willing offering of their sons and husbands, to fight in so great a cause in the early days of the war'.[23] Some intervened to help their menfolk reach the front. Thus Edward Horner considered that 'getting out' was 'the point beside which nothing else matters' and because his North Somerset Yeomanry seemed unlikely to do this, he persuaded his mother to pull strings so that he could secure a commission in the 15th Hussars. He got his wish for an early share in the action and was seriously wounded in the spring of 1915. Two and a half years later he was killed. Lady Horner consequently lost her only surviving son (a younger boy had died in childhood), as well as a son-in-law, and it was with bleak despair that she wrote to her widowed daughter, Katherine, that 'all that is left of our beloveds [is] the vision of a grave in France'.[24]

But the landed elite were not content with offering only their sons to the war effort. They proffered their homes as well. Numerous mansions were converted into hospitals and convalescent homes to cater for military casualties or to act as temporary lodgings for the Belgian refugees who streamed out of their stricken country in 1914. By the end of the year accommodation had been found for about 100,000 of them. In Cumberland, Lady Carlisle provided and equipped some thirty or forty cottages rent free for the refugees, and eventually had about 150 of them in her care.[25]

So great was the enthusiasm of estate owners for the cause that as early as 21 August the *Hexham Weekly News* claimed that the authorities had been literally inundated with offers of houses. At Woburn Abbey, the riding school and indoor tennis court were converted into a 100-bed hospital, and although trained nurses were employed, such duties as those of orderly and stretcher bearer were performed by household servants, gardeners, chauffeurs, and grooms on the estate who were unfit for military service.[26] The Duchess herself, as a trained nurse, took an active part in the venture, often putting in sixteen hours a day on duty. During the time that it was open she never left the hospital for a single night and in the final three years she was responsible not only for all the operating theatre sister's work but the whole of the official correspondence, book-keeping and returns associated with its running.[27]

Lady Selborne's Hampshire home, Blackmoor, was also converted into a hospital, with herself as commandant – although her sister-in-law critically commented that 'in numberless ways the house & management are quite unadaptable to a Hospital. I hope it won't all go smash.' Nevertheless, despite her reservations she helped Lady Selborne and the servants make the house ready, with the china carefully packed away, rugs and carpets rolled up and removed, furniture moved, and new bedsteads for the patients ordered. The drawing-room, dining-room and smoking-room were turned into wards, the hall became the men's living room, and the library served as the nurses' sitting-room. The billiards room became a store.[28] Not until Easter 1919 was the house at last restored to normal domestic use.

Sometimes, as with Dorothy Beresford-Peirse's family, mansions were used for hospitals because they were too large and expensive for the family to run. Dorothy's mother converted Bedale Hall into a twenty-bed convalescent home, staffed by her own Red Cross detachment and with herself as commandant. Lady Beresford-Peirse would not allow her daughter to work there because she thought this would be bad for discipline, but she was permitted to push some of the patients round the garden in a wheelchair or take them out for drives in a pony cart. In 1915, at the age of twenty-one Dorothy moved to Harewood

House, which had also been partially converted into a convalescent hospital, although the Earl of Harewood and his family continued to live in a large portion of it. The earl's daughter, Lady Boyne, was commandant, but the nursing staff were controlled by what Dorothy called 'a perfect fiend of a matron'. Some of the latter's hostility may, however, have been due to the quite widespread suspicion of trained professionals towards the amateurs who were 'playing at nurses', and thereby eroding the status of the skilled practitioners. In any event, it was at Harewood House that Dorothy commenced her nursing career, working in the long picture gallery which had been turned into a ward with about thirty beds.[29]

At Cheveney in Kent, Colonel Borton and his wife, Laura, displayed similar zeal when they applied to convert the local institute into a twelve-bed hospital. Permission was granted and on 24 October 1914, the hospital began work with its first patients – four wounded Belgian soldiers. Laura Borton acted as matron, a post she continued to hold until the end of the war. From time to time the inmates were invited to the big house for tea or supper, and Laura also attended working parties to make bandages. Like other squire's ladies she continued to visit local cottagers to dispense charity and advice when needed, and at Christmas she and her husband distributed parcels and money gifts to their employees, much along pre-war lines.[30]

But not all estate owners were equally generous. When Lady Wemyss suggested turning Stanway into a hospital, her husband firmly rejected the idea. Instead he threatened to close the house altogether on economic grounds. So she had to content herself with 'helping at the local hospital' in Winchcombe and 'entertaining the wounded to lunch, tea and entertainments in the tithe barn'.[31]

Despite serious financial problems, Lady Warwick, too, became involved in the war effort from an early stage. Red Cross classes were held for local ladies in her drawing-room, and she

> supervised the Belgian refugees ... who waited in her tithe barn to be distributed among the houses of the neighbourhood. Territorials were trained in her park, infuriating her by their indifference to the footpaths. Later, as the food crisis grew, Lady Warwick ordered the keepers to thin the big herd of deer in the park, and ... venison, which the conservative labourers steadfastly refused to touch, was on sale for sixpence a pound.[32]

Interestingly, she refused to succumb to the wave of anti-German feeling which swept the country, and when German prisoners-of-war appeared in Essex she went out of her way to be friendly towards them. 'As an orthodox Socialist,' writes her biographer, 'Lady Warwick attributed the war, not to "the Germans" but to unfettered capitalism, militarism and the arms race throughout the world.'[33] As a child she had, of course, been taught by German governesses and had met many of the German friends and relations of her step-father, the Earl of Rosslyn. In adult life she had maintained many of those Teutonic links.

However, most country-house wives and daughters, like their counterparts in the humbler ranks of society, were infected with war fever and anti-German sentiments. In October 1914, Lady Laura Ridding noted with approval that 'a great move is at last being made to hunt out German spies'.[34] This was part of what the Prime Minister himself called a 'ridiculous spy fever'. In other cases, women became involved in army recruitment drives. Lady Tullibardine, for example, arranged a series of concerts in Scotland to support her husband's recruiting efforts in Perthshire.[35] And in North Wales, Antonia Gamwell remembered how she and her sister were so 'anxious to ... have a go at the Germans' that they borrowed a magic lantern and slides from a recruiting officer. They then set off in the family car to show these in the principality's isolated mountain villages. 'I think they were mostly of the Boer War because I remember the soldiers were all in scarlet and whether that impressed the boys or not I don't know, nor have I any recollection of how many we managed to recruit. But we did our best and I did the talking and my sister ... showed the slides, and that was my first step on behalf of the British in that war.'[36] Later, she, her mother and sister went to France, where they set up a hospital in an abbey near Paris, in association with the French Red Cross. Their car was turned into an ambulance, which Antonia drove, while her mother and sister helped with the nursing.

Another enthusiast for military recruitment was The Hon. Mrs Gell. She recalled holding a meeting for that purpose in a tent at her home in Derbyshire. 'One did not know in our remote part,' she wrote,

> how it would strike those who realised little of the great issues at stake. But, when the speeches were over, one after the other of the boys we had known from childhood shyly stepped forward and offered themselves, and, as we shook hands with them after they were enrolled, it was hard to congratulate them with a steady voice. It meant so much.[37]

Similar enthusiasm was displayed by Lady Glenconner in Wiltshire. She took on the role of an informal recruitment agent by visiting farms near her home in the Amesbury area. The aim was to persuade local agricultural workers to volunteer, and when she had succeeded in securing a few candidates, she speedily took them by car to Salisbury, where they were handed over to an official recruiting officer.[38]

Occasionally extra inducements were offered to encourage men to enlist. The Earl of Ancaster, for example, promised employees on his Lincolnshire and Rutland Estates that he would keep a job open for them when they returned, and would guarantee an income for the wives and families of the married men while they were away. The families of volunteers were, in addition, to live in their cottages, rent free and every man joining up would be given a bonus of £5. The ploy proved successful, for within days fourteen able-bodied men were accepted for enlistment.[39] When they departed for Lincoln barracks, amidst the applause of fellow villagers, the American-born Countess of Ancaster and the local clergyman provided each of them with tobacco and a pipe.

At Stanway, the Earl of Wemyss took a sterner line, threatening with dismissal 'all servants outside & in' who did not enlist. Those who cooperated would have their positions kept open for them and would receive half pay while they were 'away with the colours'. But Lady Wemyss considered this approach unacceptable and she was able to persuade her husband to withdraw his dismissal threat. 'Those who give their lives should have the grace and glamour of doing so freely and not be driven like sheep to the slaughter,' she wrote. Soon after she made a recruiting speech of her own, excusing the Earl's belligerence by arguing that he had given notice to the men

> not out of any wish to threaten or coerce but in order to make it easy for you to do what he thought it your duty to do – in order to make everyone realise and understand the extreme gravity and importance of the situation in which we are now placed.[40]

Her intervention had the desired effect, with twelve men leaving the security of Stanway at the end of August for an uncertain future fighting for King and country. Within two months she was helping to organise a memorial service at Stanway church after the first of them was killed. Afterwards she 'gave the poor parents & the little brothers & sisters coffee and beef'.[41]

Some chronically impoverished families, like the Yorkes at Erddig, reduced their male domestic staff ostensibly on patriotic grounds but in reality as a way of cutting back on their outgoings. Instead they recruited cheaper women servants and lads who were too young to join up – or they did without. As early as November 1914, Philip Yorke told his elder son that he had just employed a new hall boy:

The other has left to become a soldier, for I advise all who reach the age of sixteen to go & do so, & I will never keep any lad after he becomes of age to serve his King & Country. This one … is only fifteen, so he may be here for nearly two years.[42]

Mrs Cornwallis-West, the former Lady Randolph Churchill, also encouraged butlers to join up by publicly expressing her preference for female servants.

In the later stages of the war, even well-to-do households experienced servant difficulties. During March 1916, May Harcourt faced problems when the chauffeur was called up and the butler suffered a breakdown in health. 'I have a load of domestic worries but no doubt will weather the storm somehow! It is a gt. bore losing one's Butler, as somehow it is the last male servant one expected to be bereft of.'[43] Likewise at the Duke of Richmond's Goodwood, where an indoor staff of over twenty had been kept before the war, numbers dropped to twelve in 1917, of whom only three were male. This was clearly the result of conscription and the availability of alternative well-paid war work. By 1920, however, the total had again reached twenty-one, which was not far short of the pre-war average.[44] Household expenditure at Goodwood was also cut back as a result of war-time restrictions, falling from £8,922 in 1913 to £3,248 in 1916; by 1921 it had once more topped £8,000, although given the inflation of the war years, in real terms that was much less than the pre-war average.[45]

These wartime reductions would certainly have won the approval of *Country Life*, which not only advised employers to dispense with male servants but also to economise in other directions. 'The rich ought to live more sparingly, so that they may not consume food that might otherwise be available for the poor. Let it be fully understood that indulgence in luxury is not only a foolishness but a crime,' it admonished sternly on 15 August 1914. It was as part of the same approach that London social life was much curtailed, with the large town houses of the aristocracy closed for the duration of the war or, often enough, converted to other uses. Nevertheless, Sonia Keppel was able to come out in the New Year of 1918 'in full debutante style', despite working in a forces canteen.[46]

Many wives and daughters of county families were anxious to support the war effort through their own activities. Hence the future Lady Curzon ran a night canteen at Waterloo Station and Lady Victoria Bentinck, daughter of the Duke of Portland, and Lady Horner worked in munitions factories, the latter helping in the canteen. Other women set up charities to assist families experiencing financial difficulties because of the war. One group formed the National Milk Hostels

Committee to supply milk from their own farms to distressed families. Characteristically great care was taken to ensure that only those in genuine need received the milk.[47] More ambitiously, the Duchess of Westminster started a Red Cross hospital in the former Casino at Le Touquet, Lady Dudley established an Australian Hospital nearby, and in London, Lady Lowther organised food and clothing parcels for Belgian prisoners in Germany. Lady Helen Manners even qualified as an anaesthetist and served in France and Italy.[48] Already by the middle of 1916, the Duchess of Westminster's hospital had treated over seven and a quarter thousand officers and men, with the first patients admitted on 4 November 1914, during the first Battle of Ypres.[49]

Some women, like The Hon. Mrs Gell and Lady Horner, arranged village sewing parties to provide 'comforts' for the troops, or attended Red Cross classes. At Mells, Lady Horner

> had a big Work Party for the village, and we started making shirts and socks, and sharing all the news ... We used to sit in the Loggia and sew, and I read aloud ... I think the fact of working for their men, and hearing all the latest news I could get for them, was a great comfort to them all.[50]

The Primrose League, too, shared in the general mood by establishing a special Needlework Committee, with Lady Milman as chairman. By the early summer of 1918 it claimed to have sent out more than 176,000 garments from its headquarters.[51]

One enthusiastic Primrose Leaguer was Beatrice Cartwright, daughter of a Northamptonshire county family. She lived near Brackley and by the autumn of 1914 had not only started a branch of the Red Cross and formed a local sewing party, but had taken over the management of a twenty-bed convalescent home in the area. Among other activities she was organiser of the Soldiers' and Sailors' Families Association for the division.[52] Such ventures were an extension of her pre-war charitable and political interests, when Liberal opponents had unkindly said of her,

> Beware! Beware! the Primrose Dame,
> The cottages among,
> She comes with blankets on her Arm
> And blarney on her tongue.[53]

Even the home-loving Louisa Yorke joined Red Cross classes in Wrexham and took up bandage making. On 9 November 1916, she proudly told her elder son that she had 'made three bandages which involved about three yards of feather stitching' at the working depot attached to Wrexham War Hospital.[54] From time to time soldiers from the hospital were entertained at Erddig, where they were given tea and allowed to play croquet and bowls in the garden, or to take boats out on the lake.[55]

Elsewhere women like the reclusive spinster Rosalie Chichester of Arlington Court, Devon, accepted figurehead positions. Miss Chichester was the only female member of the Devon Appeal Tribunal of the War Agricultural Committee, which was concerned to release more men for active service by 'combing out' those in deferred occupations. She was also local organiser of a campaign to recruit women into the newly established Land Army to replace male workers. Finally, in May 1918 she was a founder member of the local branch of the Women Citizens' Association, a non-party, non-sectarian body concerned with the study of political, social and economic issues of the day and with the securing of adequate representation of women in community affairs. In no case, however, did she take an active part in the public deliberations of these organisations, even though she was a regular attender.[56] It seems likely that she was invited to join primarily because she was a major landowner in the area and, as such, had a status, which required recognition.

It was the younger women who gained most from the widening of opportunities for independent employment which the war offered. The old system of chaperonage had virtually broken down and for the first time in their lives many girls were able to fulfil personal aspirations. Mothers complained 'about how impossible their daughters had become', but the young women themselves saw things differently. 'What a blessing it is to have regular work cut out for one!' declared an enthusiastic volunteer. 'I hope we shall never go back to the times when all we had to plan at breakfast was how to amuse ourselves during the day.'[57] These sentiments were echoed by Joan Poynder, only child of Sir John Dickson-Poynder of Hartham Park, Wiltshire. She had long had a 'passion for independence ... and I knew that I wasn't going to get much in the pre-war days except through marriage ... But luckily I got it immediately by pretending I was much older and going in for nursing.'[58] She joined the Red Cross and after a period nursing in six hospitals in England she managed to get to a French hospital, even though at nineteen she was below the regulation age for such work.

Monica Grenfell was also determined to strike out for herself; she wrote of the 'enthusiasm, even exultation' with which she and her friends greeted the outbreak of the war. On 19 August 1914, she became a probationer at the London Hospital and three months later was accepted as a probationer at the British Hospital at Wimereux.

She was the only probationer in the 123-bed hospital, all the rest of the staff being fully trained.[59] During the previous London Season she had attended forty balls, but such light-hearted frivolity was a world away from her arduous daily round on the Western Front as 1914 drew to a close.

There were other initiatives as well. Lady Cynthia Colville, although married with young children, nonetheless spent one and a half years as a temporary correspondence clerk in the Ministry of Pensions.[60] Edith Sitwell, newly escaped from the claustrophobic atmosphere of Renishaw, took a similar post in Chelsea for a wage of 25s a week, plus two shillings war bonus. 'This I did partly out of patriotism, partly because I had to earn the money in order to live.'[61]

Some upper-class ladies became involved in the promotion of various quasi-military uniformed women's organisations. Each was, according to Arthur Marwick,

> an odd, but not necessarily ineffective mixture of Girl Guides, County Charity, and Territorial Army. First in the field were the Women's Emergency Corps, founded by The Hon. Evelina Haverfield, the Women's Volunteer Reserve, sponsored by the Marchioness of Londonderry, the Marchioness of Titchfield, and the Countess of Pembroke and Montgomery, and Mrs Dawson Scott's Women's Defence Relief Corps. The khaki uniforms and felt hats which The Volunteer Reserve women designed for themselves provided the basic model for the various women's auxiliary corps subsequently set up.[62]

Of these organisations, the most important was the Women's Legion, formed by Lady Londonderry in July 1915 as a development of the earlier Women's Emergency Corps and Women's Volunteer Reserve. Despite civil service doubts as to its efficiency it was officially recognised by an Army Council Instruction in February 1916. Legion members were eventually divided into four sections, covering cookery and canteen duties; motor transport; ambulance work; and agriculture. Lady Londonderry's object was 'to replace working men by working women'. To this end she sought 'to instil into all [the] members that Patriotism, if it is to be anything more than a name, must express itself in service to the State'.[63] The largest group comprised those engaged as cooks and waitresses at military establishments. By 1917 they numbered about 30,000. The second largest section – the motor transport grouping – provided women to work as army drivers and mechanics. Eventually both of these sections were merged into the Women's Army Auxiliary Corps.[64] The recruits, meanwhile, were mainly from a working-class or lower middle-class background; only the organisers were upper-class.

In practice, most female volunteers from county families took up canteen or nursing duties even if, as with Lady Diana Manners and her friend, Venetia Stanley, youngest child of Lord Sheffield, their stint of caring for the sick was frequently combined with a feverish social life.

Diana Manners began scheming to become a nurse at the front soon after hostilities broke out. 'Women were taking Red Cross hospitals and dressing-stations to France, and they were taking their daughters and their daughters' friends,' she recalled. 'I wrote to the Duchess of Sutherland and Lady Dudley and the Duchess of Westminster and others.'[65] Millicent, now Dowager Duchess of Sutherland, had indeed left England four days after the declaration of war to work with the French Red Cross. She was in Belgium immediately after the German invasion and was in Namur when it was occupied. By a mixture of influence and determination she was able to return to England, and there wrote an account of her experiences entitled *Six Weeks at the War*. Then, nothing daunted, she returned to the fray shortly after with the Millicent Sutherland Ambulance. In addition to her ambulance work, Millicent set up a temporary hospital, first on the outskirts of Dunkirk and then moving to Calais. The hospital was sited in huts and tents among the sand dunes at Calais, and by January 1916 had eight wards, equipped to deal with a hundred patients; by August 1917 this had increased to 160 beds and among other things, the hospital began using a new treatment for septic injuries.[66] However, the Duchess's zeal was not always appreciated. Lord Crawford complained that she and the Duchess of Westminster were particularly prone to overspend and then to expect the Red Cross to help them out. They also exploited their contacts with senior military and political figures, and were so keen to keep their hospitals filled that they 'carried off invalids ... like latter-day "body snatchers"'.[67] Millicent's sister, Lady Angela Forbes (who in private life was Lord Wemyss's mistress) also worked first in a voluntary hospital in Paris and then organised a canteen for soldiers in transit at Boulogne. This she supervised from her pre-war villa at Le Touquet. Later her canteens spread to Etaples, and she claimed that on one occasion, early in the Battle of the Somme, she herself fried 800 eggs between 4 a.m. and 7 a.m. Despite official disapproval (her influence was said to be 'not a good one with the troops'), her canteens fed about four and a half million men during the war.[68]

But none of these ladies was prepared to accept Lady Diana. Indeed, Lady Dudley warned that for an attractive girl to mix with soldiers so far from home was an almost certain invitation to be raped. Her mother, the Duchess of Rutland, was also firmly opposed to her going abroad, so she reluctantly embarked upon a training course at Guy's Hospital. As a preliminary she went to the kitchen at her London home, 'and saw a hare's insides taken out to prepare me for operations'.[69]

Lady Diana remained at Guy's for several months, until her mother decided to acquire a French château which she could convert into a hospital. She withdrew her daughter from Guy's to prepare for this, but after lengthy negotiations the scheme fell through when the Red Cross refused to sanction it. The duchess then proposed converting her own elegant town house into an officers' hospital and this time the Red Cross gave its approval. The venture went ahead under the name of the Rutland Hospital, with Lady Diana as one of the VAD (Voluntary Aid Detachment) nurses:

> The golden drawing-room – a real room-of-all-work – became a ward for ten patients. The ballroom held another twelve. The centre-skylit salon was the dining and club room, The walls were hung with glazed linen, the floors covered in linoleum. My mother's bedroom was equipped as an operating theatre, divided by glass from sterilising-machines and administrative desks. Sister White and two trained nurses … were engaged … There were to be several VADs.[70]

Although Lady Diana was reasonably competent, she found it difficult to take her nursing duties seriously. Often her time was only partially occupied and friends would arrive 'laden with chestnut-cream cakes and sherry for our elevenses'. Many off-duty hours were spent at parties, and she frequently returned from these in the early hours of the morning. Relations with her mother grew increasingly strained, with the duchess spending much time away from London running a convalescent home at Belvoir, her country house. Lady Diana also began to experiment with drug-taking, especially chloroform and morphia.[71] It was doubtless this kind of conduct that led the Countess of Warwick – herself no prude – to condemn the 'very large company of young women' to whom the war represented 'little more than a new sensation':

> Unfortunately the people I have in mind have not been content to devote themselves to brainless frivolity … they [have] invaded the sanctuary of the hospital nurse … I have known some who have danced till 3 a.m. and have presented themselves at the hospital at eight o'clock! … The social butterflies … acquired a trifling and superficial knowledge of a nurse's work, and then set their social influence to work in order to reach some of the base hospitals where they might sample fresh

experience … To sit at the end of a bed and smoke cigarettes with a wounded officer does not develop the efficiency of a hospital … it is intolerable that … any girl of good family who assumes a uniform she has not won the right to wear should pose as the representative of a sisterhood she is not worthy to associate with.[72]

Despite these strictures, however, even pleasure-seeking girls like Lady Diana Manners were unable to avoid the tragic side of the war. Most of her pre-war admirers were killed at the front; and years later she remembered the passage of days 'heavy with one's own heart and the hearts of others'. 'Looking back on these nightmare years of tragic hysteria, it is frightening to live them again in memory … The young were dancing a tarantella frenziedly to combat any pause that would let death conquer their morale.'[73] Meanwhile the Rutland Hospital itself was expanding to take another twelve officers, and more girls and 'young widows I knew came to work as VADs'.

Furthermore, in spite of their faults and frivolities, there is little doubt that most of the patients welcomed the ministrations of their high-society nurses. When The Hon. Lionel Tennyson returned to London as a wounded officer he found himself in the hands of Lady Carnarvon and Lady Ridley. He considered their hospital was 'the best in London … No attention was too much trouble, the nursing was wonderful, and the food given us exquisitely cooked and served.'[74] At the Duchess of Leinster's private hospital in Bryanston Square, Second Lieutenant Peter Mason could remember awakening from a drugged sleep, two days after his operation, to find the ducal butler standing at the foot of the bed and enquiring what he wanted for dinner that evening. 'Lamb Cutlets Reform, and perhaps half a bottle of Bollinger' was the butler's own suggestion.[75] No ordinary military hospital could match that.

Elsewhere agricultural activities occupied the wives and daughters of some county families. Among them was the Countess of Airlie, who at the beginning of the war had handed over the greater part of her Scottish home, Cortachy Castle, to the Red Cross. Subsequently she embarked upon various tasks in London in connection with the Army Nursing Board and the VAD Selection Committee. She also had arduous spells on duty as a lady-in-waiting to Queen Mary. But, despite this she continued to manage the Cortachy estate, and when in residence devoted much time to teaching such workers as she could recruit 'the rudiments of farming and gardening necessitated by the national drive for food production. "My entire horizon was bounded by potatoes," she wrote. "Every vine house was stuffed full of them; even the little hut at the back of the gardens was stacked with potato boxes from the floor to the roof.'"[76] One of her daughters gained employment exercising army remount horses and died tragically as the result of a fall within a fortnight of the Armistice.

The Hon. Mrs Gell of Hopton, Derbyshire, was another agricultural enthusiast. She and her husband not only attended village meetings equipped with supplies of vegetable seeds, but they ploughed up a section of the park to grow potatoes, and 'reinforced our vegetable garden in every way'. She was active in the Women's Central Agricultural Committee in London and gave talks to villagers on how to utilise their gardens to the best advantage. Just how warmly they welcomed advice from this self-appointed 'expert' it is impossible to say, but, nothing daunted, Mrs Gell also arranged preliminary training schemes for land girls. With her encouragement, Swanley Horticultural College, of which she was a governor, began to run short courses for women to train as dairymaids, so they could replace the male 'milkers' who were enlisting in the services.[77]

Not all of these well-meaning arrangements were a success. One which was not was the agricultural section of Lady Londonderry's Women's Legion. This had been formed at the end of 1915 with the aid of a £200 promotional grant from the Board of Agriculture, but its attempts to train females for farm work proved sadly ineffective. As early as March 1916, a Board of Agriculture official minuted wearily, 'We can't prevent Lady Londonderry starting her organisation wherever she likes & if she gets ... the work done we need not complain.'[78] Six months later the tune had become much sharper, with the Board's secretary sourly observing that it was

all very well for say, the local duchess to be brought into a new movement at its inception, mainly because her name is of value in an advertisement and because her purse is useful to provide the necessary funds, but when the movement has once been started, unless the duchess has the good sense to efface herself as quickly as possible and allow the project to be carried on by the people who are primarily interested in it, in nine times out of ten the scheme is bound to fail.[79]

Eventually the work of the Women's Legion was terminated by the Board of Agriculture on grounds of inefficiency, with feelings between the two parties reaching crisis point in October 1917 over the deficiencies of the Rutland branch its major sector. On 6 October, the board's travelling inspector for women's land work reported gloomily that she had 'found not only in Rutland but also in neighbouring counties ... our work has been discredited because of the bad management of the Women's Legion. For instance in Northampton the word is anathema, and held up as an example of absolute incompetence.'[80] The leading figure in Rutland was a Miss Brocklebank, who in pre-war days had been principally noted as an enthusiastic rider to hounds. Although the inspector found her personally 'very agreeable … she [had] the dangerous fault which so often attends riches, of plunging into enterprises regardless of cost, or her own capacity to carry them through'.[81] In the end the Marchioness of· Londonderry was persuaded to restrict the legion's 'agricultural' endeavours to fruit bottling and horticulture, although its Oakham training centre continued to offer three months' training courses in dairy farming, gardening and herb growing. The fee was 25s a week and, according to an advertisement in *Country Life*, 'good posts' were available to those who completed the training satisfactorily.[82]

In Worcestershire the legion also took a number of small-scale initiatives. Thus the branch president, Lady Hindlip, employed two legion members to run a milk supply scheme in her home village, while other lady volunteers collected fruit and vegetables from cottagers for use in the legion's bottling and preserving enterprise. The cottagers were paid market prices for their products, and while this may have benefited them, it scarcely tackled the major labour and production problems which existed in British agriculture during the First World War.

Other ineffective voluntary attempts to provide women for land work involved Mrs Dawson Scott's Women's Defence Relief Corps and the National Political League, which was condemned for its use of unspecified 'mischievous' methods. Small wonder that in 1917 the Board of Agriculture condemned the mass of uncoordinated private schemes which existed. 'The country is full of these irresponsible training[?] centres for women, and they are doing great mischief.'[83] However, its own slowness in developing a coherent national recruitment campaign for female land workers was partly to blame, in that this had encouraged Lady Londonderry and her friends to try to make good the deficiency.

These activities apart, the lives of country-house ladies were changed in many other ways as the war progressed. Not only was there the constant anxiety about menfolk at the front, and the burden of grief when a loved one was killed or injured, there were also, often enough, the problems of declining incomes, shortages, and even the lack of domestic servants to be overcome. In September 1916 when Lady Selborne visited Lord and Lady Grey in Northumberland, she found them 'living in a tiny corner of the house, using the housekeeper's room as a dining room, with hardly any servants'.[84] Her daughter, Lady Howick, who had a convalescent home on her property, was ingeniously using a succession of recuperating patients to act as unofficial servants. One, a chauffeur in civilian life, met Lady Selborne at the railway station with the family car, and others were at work in the gardens.[85] Elsewhere a lady's maid remembered sadly how, early in 1915 her mistress, a widow with two daughters, was so badly hit financially by the war that she had to close her country house. As a result the servants were dismissed and 'the family went to a private hotel far away.[86]

Nor were the well-to-do able to escape other uncomfortable consequences of the war such as the fuel scarcities which became particularly acute in 1918. On the fourth anniversary of the outbreak of hostilities, Lady Laura Ridding referred to the 'food, clothing, travelling, coal privations, paper privation' which the nation was enduring. 'The cutting of timber [for industrial purpose] is tragic ... during the war's four years a million acres of English woods will have been cut down'. Two months later her sister-in-law, the Countess of Selborne, wrote to her husband from Bath to advise him how to eke out dwindling coal stocks at their London home by burning old newspapers:

> Get Patty to try this experiment. Instead of sending the waste paper to the Salvation army put it in a tub of water. Every evening take it out, squeeze it into convenient sized lumps and let it dry. The harder & tighter it is squeezed the longer it will burn. As soon as it is dry get her to burn it in her little open grate & see how it does.
>
> If it succeeds we would make the maids do it every day with all the waste paper & would get some sort of a press to make the blocks with.[87]

It was doubtless with this kind of situation in mind that that the makers of the 'Edwardian' chimney pot advised readers of *Country Life* that their product would not only prevent down draught but would save coal as well.[88]

Even after the war, difficulties continued. Lady Ridding was still bewailing the fuel shortage at the end of March 1919:

> Every household (being short of labour & coal) has to live in a crowded way with social rooms shut up. Here I have had no upper housemaid for two months. No using of servants Hall, dining room, drawing-room or spare bedrooms. No bedroom fire for myself except on extremely icy nights and we are entirely using *coal dust* – as when I inspected the coal cellar, I found that we were eating dangerously into our store, & my ration only allows me five tons of coal before Sep: 30.[89]

Food shortages were another problem, especially before the introduction of rationing, despite the fact that most landed families benefited from having their own home farm and kitchen garden. 'We have had some excitement in Wrexham with regard to the Butter in the Market,' wrote Louisa Yorke in December 1917. 'I wish we ... could all get our proper share. I often go four days & even more without any sugar & I hate it.' Compulsory sugar rationing was eventually introduced in January 1918, but the meagre half-pound per person per week allowed was very different from consumption patterns in country houses before the war. Compulsory rationing of meat, butter, and margarine followed over a large part of southern England in February 1918 and was converted to a national scheme by the middle of July. Even this caused some initial difficulties. 'Will you tell Patty that no ration books have come to me,' wrote Lady Selborne anxiously to her husband from the Bath hotel where she was staying in late October 1918. 'She had better get on to Blackmoor [the Selborne's country house] on the phone, & if they are not there, send ... telegrams to Trimmer.'[90]

Lady Laura Ridding was a good deal more scathing about the ration books. 'The minute, complicated contradictory instructions issued with them will be a "Greats Examination Test" of the Nation's brainpower & patience,' she wrote acidly in her diary. 'And my book is shelved for want of paper, doomed by the Food Controller for all their [sic] maddening books of riddles.'[91]

Taxation and rising interest rates made increasingly serious inroads into the living standards of many landed families. Interest rates rose from 3.5 per cent to 6 per cent over the war years, and presented a serious problem for those who had run up debts or had mortgaged estates in the 'depression' years before 1914.[92] Income tax also increased, and whereas this had, for example, taken barely four per cent of gross rentals on the Wilton and Savernake estates before the war, by 1919 it was absorbing more than a quarter. The burden of all direct taxes combined (land tax, rates, and income tax) had climbed from nine per cent to thirty per cent of the rental of these estates.[93] Death duties were another crippling burden on many properties, especially when an owner's death was quickly followed by that of his heir, killed at the front. That was true of the Wyndhams at Clouds, with George Wyndham dying suddenly in 1913 and his son and heir, Percy, killed in France on 14 September 1914. A similar situation applied to the Shiffners at Coombe Park, Hamsey, with Sir John Shiffner dying relatively young in the spring of 1914 and his eldest son and heir being killed at the front in 1918 about a month after his nineteenth birthday (and two months after his marriage). In 1915, the Amesbury Abbey estate was put on the market after the death of its owner, Sir Edmund

Antrobus, was followed closely by that of his only son in battle.[94] While at Hawarden, where the young squire (who was William Gladstone's grandson) was killed, the duties paid at his death were six times the old-style succession duties levied on his predecessor's estate in 1891. Since taxation had also quadrupled over the same period, the net result was that by 1918 the new owner was spending four-fifths of his rental income on rates, taxes, and maintenance, leaving only a small portion for living and annuities. Small wonder that in the immediate aftermath of the war outlying parts of the Gladstone estate were sold for the then substantial sum of £112,000.[95]

These, then, were the conditions of financial uncertainty in which an increasing number of landowners began to contemplate the sale of part of their property as the war drew to an end. Sales had, indeed, begun to rise noticeably in 1917, but it was following the Armistice in November 1918 that the process accelerated. Between 1918 and 1921 around a quarter of the land of England changed hands in an unprecedented surge of activity.

Among the sellers at this time was the Countess of Warwick, who had been seriously in debt since the 1890s. Some sales had occurred at that time and in 1909–10 she had had to appear in court when certain of her creditors had sued her for non-payment of amounts owed. However, in this new phase she disposed of more than half the land she had inherited. The first to go was part of her Northamptonshire and Leicestershire property, in September 1918. But it was in 1919 that the major sales took place, with over 5,000 acres – almost a third of her inheritance – sold off in Essex alone. Other sales followed in Leicestershire, and as a result Lady Warwick secured during these twelve months the large sum of £222,572 (the present-day equivalent would be perhaps thirty times that amount). Yet, so great were her financial difficulties that even this could not solve them.[96] Throughout their youth she and her husband had known only wealth and privilege and in old age they were unable to adjust to the changed conditions. In 1921 she even announced in the press that she was 'unable to afford a car'. Her husband died three years later in straitened circumstances and her son followed in 1928, a victim of chronic alcoholism.[97]

The problems faced by the Warwicks were experienced, to varying degrees, by other landowners. In 1919 the Duke of Marlborough claimed in dramatic tones that the 'old order' was doomed, while the *Estates Gazette* referred to a 'revolution in landowning'.[98] *Country Life* joined in the lament, commenting on the way the countryside was 'changing from month to month. Estates are in process of disruption.'[99]

Often houses were sold for conversion into schools and institutions, or were purchased by businessmen. In 1921, Lord Willoughby de Broke sold Compton Verney to Joseph Watson, a soap-boiler and racehorse owner, who was created Lord Manton shortly afterwards.[100] At Wonston Lady Ridding referred sourly to the new owners of Norton Manor. The Thompsons were 'Darlington shipowners – the husband looks horribly unattractive ... [a] bullet-headed very rich Northerner'.[101] Before the war the estate had been owned by the Hamptons, but, whatever Lady Ridding's opinion, Mr Thompson remained at Wonston as one of its principal landowners and by 1927 had become a magistrate.

The proliferation of estate sales was a clear indication of the declining fortunes of many old established county families. A number were able to retrench and to adapt to their altered circumstances, perhaps by the men lending the prestige of their name to a company board or by investing in a commercial undertaking. This was, of course, an extension of trends in operation before 1914, when a growing number of peers during the agricultural depression years had taken on company directorships as a way of supplementing landed income. But whereas there had been 167 peers holding company directorships in 1896, that had risen to 232 by 1920. Railways, assurance and insurance companies, and ventures overseas were the most popular outlets. Seventy-four peers in 1920 (including established industrialists) were directors of four companies or more.[102] Meanwhile, their daughters were more willing than before to seek husbands outside the ranks of the traditional aristocracy and gentry. Some women also began to follow careers of their own.

It would be inaccurate to see the pre-1914 routine of the 'lady of the manor', with her charitable duties and carefully regulated social round, as having been entirely destroyed by the war. But there can be little doubt that that position had been seriously undermined, and in the succeeding decades this process was to intensify. The old certainties once enjoyed by country-house wives and daughters had died, along with the husbands, sons, and brothers of so many of them. In the years that lay ahead they had to adjust to the changed circumstances as gracefully as they could.

Notes

1 Ladies in Landed Society

1. Entry in the diary of Louisa Yorke for 2 July 1902, at Clwyd Record Office, D/E/2816.
2. Cecil Woodham Smith, *Florence Nightingale* (1955 edn), 41–2.
3. Dorothy Henley, *Rosalind Howard, Countess of Carlisle* (1958), 31.
4. Jennifer Ellis ed., *Thatched with Gold: The Memoirs of Mabell Countess of Airlie* (1962), 30.
5. Caroline Grosvenor, 'Moor Park' in Susan Tweedsmuir, *The Lilac and the Rose* (1952), 109.
6. G. M. Trevelyan, *Grey of Fallodon: Being the Life of Sir Edward Grey, Afterwards Viscount Grey of Fallodon* (1943 edn), 7.
7. Revd C. Kingsley, 'The Country Parish' in *Lectures to Ladies On Practical Subjects* (1855), 53.
8. Pat Jalland, *Women, Marriage and Politics 1860–1914* (1988 edn.), 63.
9. Lady Maud Cecil to William, Viscount Wolmer (later the Earl of Selborne), 7, 8 and 14 August 1883 at the Bodleian Library, Oxford, MS. Selborne Adds. 1, ff. 5, 9, 10 and 22.
10. Quoted in Angela Lambert, *Unquiet Souls: The Indian Summer of the British Aristocracy, 1880–1918* (1984), 72.
11. Susan Tweedsmuir, op. cit., 74.
12. Jessica Gerard, 'Lady Bountiful: Women of the Landed Classes and Rural Philanthropy' in *Victorian Studies*, Vol. 30, No. 2 (Winter 1987), 194.
13. Constance Leconfield, *Random Papers*, collected by her daughters-in-law and privately published at Petworth House, Sussex (*c.* 1938), 75.
14. Margaret Blunden, *The Countess of Warwick* (1967), 42.
15. Margaret Blunden, op. cit., 59.
16. Violet Powell, *Margaret, Countess of Jersey* (1978), 53.
17. Leonore Davidoff, *The Best Circles* (1986 edn), 46.
18. George Ewart Evans, *Where Beards Wag All* (1970), 123.
19. George Ewart Evans, op. cit., 122. Jessica Gerard, 'Lady Bountiful', 198.
20. Frances, Countess of Warwick, *Afterthoughts* (1931), 242.
21. Jennifer Ellis ed., op. cit., 29.
22. See, for example, entry in the diary of her sister, Cecilia, for 29 July 1877. Cecilia herself was an enthusiastic member of the choir – see diary entries for 27 Jan. and 19 and 25 Aug. 1877, in Carrington Diaries MS. Film 1097 at the Bodleian Library.
23. Susan Tweedsmuir, op. cit., 79.
24. Lord Suffield, *My Memories 1830–1913* (1914), 75.
25. Quoted in Pat Jalland, op. cit., 48.
26. Pat Jalland, op. cit., 47–8.

27. Diary of Lady Constance Primrose, entry for 6 April 1867, at West Sussex Record Office, Petworth House MSS. 1681. Henry Wyndham had a successful interview with Constance's mother, the Duchess of Cleveland, on 5 June.

28. Quoted in Angela Lambert, op. cit., 72.

29. The Dowager Countess of Jersey, *Fifty-one Years of Victorian Life* (1922), 66–7.

30. Quoted in Jessica A. Gerard, 'Family and Servants in the Country-House Community in England and Wales 1815–1914' (University of London Ph.D. thesis, 1982), 198.

31. Mrs George Cornwallis-West, *The Reminiscences of Lady Randolph Churchill* (1908), 124–6.

32. Maureen E. Montgomery, *Gilded Prostitution: Status, Money, and Transatlantic Marriages 1870–1914* (1989), 200 and 213.

33. L. E. O. Charlton, *The Recollections of a Northumbrian Lady 1815–1866* (1949), 29. Lawrence Stone and Jeanne Fawtier Stone, *An Open Elite? England 1540–1880* (1984), 98.

34. Lady Maud Selborne's Childhood Recollections in MS. Eng. misc. e. 964 at the Bodleian Library, f. 7.

35. Diana Mosley, *A Life of Contrasts* (1977), 6.

36. Alice Fairfax-Lucy ed., *Mistress of Charlecote. The Memoirs of Mary Elizabeth Lucy* (1990 edn), 137.

37. Viola Bankes, *A Kingston Lacy Childhood*, Collected by Pamela Watkin (1986 edn), 8.

38. Caroline Grosvenor, 'Moor Park', in Susan Tweedsmuir, op. cit., 120.

39. Adam Badeau, *Aristocracy in England* (1886) quoted in Jessica Gerard, 'Family and Servants', 37.

40. Maureen E. Montgomery, op. cit., 92–3.

41. Leonore Davidoff, op. cit., 50–51.

42. Margaret Wyndham to her mother, Lady Leconfield, 20 November 1912, in Petworth House MSS. 1648 at West Sussex Record Office.

43. Margaret Wyndham to Lady Leconfield, 28 October 1912, giving her plans up to 3 December.

44. Gervas Huxley, *Lady Elizabeth and the Grosvenors: Life in a Whig Family, 1822–1839* (1965), 171. Theodora was married in March 1877, when her mother was almost eighty.

45. Violet Powell, op. cit., 171.

46. Lady Muriel Beckwith, *When I Remember* (1936), 15.

47. Francesca M. Wilson, *Rebel Daughter of a Country House, The Life of Eglantyne Jebb, Founder of the Save the Children Fund* (1967), 33, 35 and 209.

48. Lawrence Stone and Jeanne Fawtier Stone, op. cit., 118–19.

49. Geoffrey H. White and R. S. Lea eds, *The Complete Peerage*, Vol. 12 (1959), 682.

50. Heather A. Clemenson, *English Country Houses and Landed Estates* (1982), 17. John Bateman, *The Great Landowners of Great Britain and Ireland*, 4th edn, (1883), *passim*.

51. David Cannadine, *The Decline and Fall of the British Aristocracy* (1990), 11.

52. F. M. L. Thompson, 'Life After Death: How Successful Nineteenth-century Businessmen Disposed of Their Fortunes' in *Economic History Review*, 2nd Series, Vol. 43, No. 1 (Feb. 1990), 41–42.

53. Legacy Duty Register at the Public Record Office, I.R.26.8016 for 1901, f. 142.

54. Legacy Duty Register at the Public Record Office, I.R.26.4841 for 1894, f. 1841.

55. F. M. L. Thompson, *English Landed Society in the Nineteenth Century* (1963), 99. The Monson son married in 1869.

56. Quoted in Maureen E. Montgomery, op. cit., 113.

57. Gregory D. Phillips, *The Diehards: Aristocratic Society and Politics in Edwardian England* (1979), 36–7.

58. Gregory D. Phillips, op. cit., 37.

59. Quoted in Maureen E. Montgomery, op. cit., 98.

60. Maureen E. Montgomery, op. cit., 167.

61. Consuelo Vanderbilt Balsan, *The Glitter and the Gold* (1973 edn), 36.

62. Maureen E. Montgomery, op. cit., 146–50. Consuelo Vanderbilt Balsan, op. cit., 36–40.

63. Maureen E. Montgomery, op. cit., 126–7.

64. Quoted in Maureen E. Montgomery, op. cit., 114.

65. Consuelo Vanderbilt Balsan, op. cit., 68 and 94.

66. David Green, *The Churchills of Blenheim* (1984), 137.

67. Quoted in Ray Strachey, *The Cause* (1978 edn), 401–3 and 415. Cecil Woodham-Smith, op. cit., 38.

68. Jessica A. Gerard, 'Family and Servants', 195.

2 Growing Up in a Country House

1. Lady Maud Selborne's Childhood Recollections at the Bodleian Library, MS. Eng. misc. e. 964.
2. Quoted in Jessica A. Gerard, 'Family and Servants in the Country-House Community in England and Wales 1815–1914'. (University of London Ph.D. thesis, 1982), 154. Ann Estella, Countess Cave, *Odds and Ends of My Life* (1929), 3.
3. Quoted in Adeline Hartcup, *Children of the Great Country Houses* (1986 edn), 81.
4. Jessica A. Gerard, 'Family and Servants', 156.
5. Jennifer Ellis ed., *Thatched with Gold: The Memoirs of Mabell Countess of Airlie* (1962), 30.
6. Jennifer Ellis ed., op. cit., 29.
7. Diaries of Lady Carrington at the Bodleian Library, Oxford, MS. Film 1097.
8. Diaries of Lady Carrington, entry for 17 August 1877. In a further entry on 24 August, she noted, 'I walked over to Thorpe to see my child & family. Looked over her whole wardrobe.' And on 4 September, shortly before they went to Scotland for the shooting, she went to 'see Frida's child & then mine'.
9. Lucy Cohen, *Lady de Rothschild and Her Daughters 1821–1931* (1935), 102–3.
10. Jessica A. Gerard, 'Family and Servants', 212. The Hon. Mrs E. M. L. Gell, *Under Three Reigns* (1927), 13.
11. Jessica A. Gerard, 'Family and Servants', 213.
12. Jessica A. Gerard, 'Family and Servants', 275. Susan Tweedsmuir, *The Edwardian Lady* (1966), 66–7.
13. Quoted in Pat Jalland, *Women, Marriage and Politics 1860–1914* (1988 edn), 9.
14. Pat Jalland, op. cit., 9.
15. Adeline Hartcup, op. cit., 26. Nigel Nicolson, *Portrait of a Marriage* (1990 edn), 10–11.
16. Viola Bankes, *A Kingston Lacy Childhood*, Collected by Pamela Watkin (1989 edn), 24.
17. Jessica A. Gerard, 'Family and Servants', 272.
18. Susan Tweedsmuir, *The Lilac and the Rose* (1952), 64–65.
19. May Harcourt to her step-mother-in-law, Lady Harcourt, 30 October [1909] in MS. Harcourt dep. 648, ff. 30–31 at the Bodleian Library, Oxford.
20. May Harcourt to Lady Harcourt, 13 Aug. 1909, loco cit., f. 26.
21. May Harcourt to Lady Harcourt, 27 Jan. 1905 in MS. Harcourt dep. 647, f. 151.
22. Anne Chisholm, *Nancy Cunard* (1981 edn), 31.
23. Anne Chisholm, op. cit., 31–2.
24. Osbert Sitwell, *Left Hand, Right Hand!* (1945), 92.
25. Sarah Sedgwick, 'Other People's Children' in *The Day Before Yesterday*, Noel Streatfeild ed. (1956), 18–19.
26. May Harcourt to Lady Harcourt, 14 August 1908, MS. Harcourt dep. 648, f. 10.
27. John Bailey ed., *The Diary of Lady Frederick Cavendish*, Vol. 1 (1927), 5–6.
28. Sarah Sedgwick, op. cit., 19.
29. Nigel Nicolson, op. cit., 60. Vita was nine when she drew up this list of toys.
30. Viola Bankes, op. cit., 9–10.
31. L. E. O. Charlton, *The Recollections of a Northumbrian Lady 1815–1866* (1949), 28–31.
32. Lady Muriel Beckwith, *When I Remember* (1936), 25.
33. Sarah Sedgwick, op. cit., 16–17.
34. Nigel Nicolson, op. cit., 59–60.
35. Frances, Countess of Warwick, *Life's Ebb and Flow* (1929 edn), 19.
36. Frances, Countess of Warwick, op. cit., 18–19.
37. Frances, Countess of Warwick, op. cit., 18.
38. Lady Maud Selborne's Childhood Recollections, loco cit., ff. 3 and 16.
39. Winston S. Churchill, *My Early Life* (1965 edn), 12–13. Thea Thompson, *Edwardian Childhoods* (1981), 216 for the comment by Joan Poynder.
40. Jessica A. Gerard, 'Family and Servants', 209–211.
41. The Dowager Countess of Jersey, *Fifty-one Years of Victorian Life* (1922), 8.
42. May Harcourt to Lady Harcourt, 30 Oct. 1901, in MS. Harcourt dep. 647, f. 78. Ann Estella, Countess Cave, op. cit., 1–2.
43. Edith Sitwell, *Taken Care Of* (1965), 26.
44. Edith Sitwell, op. cit., 41.
45. Adeline Hartcup, op. cit., 74.
46. May Harcourt to Lady Harcourt, 15 Nov. 1901, in MS. Harcourt dep. 647, f. 89.

47. Edith Sitwell, op. cit., 40.

48. Pat Jalland, op. cit., 9.

49. John Bailey ed., op. cit., Vol. 1, 14–15.

50. John Bailey cd., op. cit., Vol. 1, xiii.

51. Lady Leconfield's Diary, Sept. 1877–Jan. 1878 at West Sussex Record Office, Petworth House MSS. 1683.

52. Entry in Lady Leconfield's Diary for 23 Oct. 1877.

53. Lady Leconfield's Diary for May 1876–Feb. 1877, Petworth House MSS. 1682.

54. *The Times*, 28 June 1939.

55. Francesca M. Wilson, *Rebel Daughter of a Country House: The Life of Eglantyne Jebb, Founder of the Save the Children Fund* (1967), 33.

56. Victoria Glendinning, *Edith Sitwell: A Unicorn Among Lions* (1986 edn), 30. Osbert Sitwell, *The Scarlet Tree* (1949), 6–7.

57. The Dowager Countess of Jersey, op. cit., 10. Violet Powell, *Margaret, Countess of Jersey* (1978), 11.

58. Reminiscences of Mrs Dorothy H. J. Wright 00510/06 in the Department of Sound Records, Imperial War Musuem. Mrs Wright (née Beresford-Peirse) declared that she 'was not academic. I adored outdoor things.'

59. Quoted in Jessica A. Gerard, 'Family and Servants', 269–70.

60. John Bailey ed., op. cit., Vol. 1, 46–7.

61. Lucy Masterman ed., *Mary Gladstone: Her Diaries and Letters*, 2nd edn, (1930), 1–2.

62. John Bailey ed., op. cit., Vol. 1, 31–3.

63. Letters from Sarah Cole to Lady Leconfield, 1871–1880 in Petworth House MSS. 1624.

64. May Harcourt to Lady Harcourt, 5 Jan. 1902, in MS. Harcourt dep. 647, ff. 96–7.

65. Viola Bankes, op. cit., 19–20.

66. Jessica A. Gerard, 'Family and Servants', 251.

67. Thea Thompson, op. cit., 217.

68. Jessica A. Gerard, 'Family and Servants', 228.

69. Frances, Countess of Warwick, *Life's Ebb and Flow*, 13–14. Margaret Blunden, *The Countess of Warwick* (1967), 17.

70. Adeline Hartcup, op. cit., 35.

71. Lucy Masterman ed., op. cit., 2.

72. John Bailey ed., op. cit., Vol. 1, 7–8.

73. John Bailey ed., op. cit., Vol. 1, 36–7, entry for 5 June 1856.

74. Viola Bankes, op. cit., 29.

75. Viola Bankes, op. cit., 29–30.

76. Reminiscences of Mrs Dorothy H. J. Wright in the Department of Sound Records, Imperial War Museum.

77. Charles Roberts, *The Radical Countess: The History of the Life of Rosalind Countess of Carlisle* (1962), 10.

78. Cecil Woodham-Smith, *Florence Nightingale* (1955 edn), 36.

79. Jennifer Ellis ed., op. cit., 33.

80. Thea Thompson, op. cit., 224–5.

81. Consuelo Vanderbilt Balsan, *The Glitter and the Gold* (1973 edn), 25.

82. Loelia, Duchess of Westminster, *Grace and Favour* (1961), 70.

83. John, Duke of Bedford, *A Silver-plated Spoon* (1960 edn), 24. Josephine Kamm, *How Different From Us* (1958), 200.

84. May Harcourt to Lady Harcourt, (n.d. 1912) in MS. Harcourt dep. 648, f. 72.

85. Cynthia Asquith, *Haply I May Remember* (1950), 222–4.

86. Francesca M. Wilson, op. cit., 54.

87. Jessica A. Gerard, 'Family and Servants', 216 and 268.

88. Quoted in Pat Jalland, op. cit., 13.

89. Adeline Hartcup, op. cit., 59. Princess Louise was the only one of Queen Victoria's daughters to marry outside royal circles.

90. Pat Jalland, op. cit., 15.

91. Jennifer Ellis, op. cit., 65.

92. Thea Thompson, op. cit., 218.

93. Violet Powell, op. cit., 8.

94. Diary of Constance Primrose for 1856 in Petworth House MSS. 1680.

95. Constance, Lady Battersea, *Reminiscences* (1922), 105.

96. Margaret Blunden, op. cit., 124.

97. V. Sackville-West, *The Edwardians* (1960 edn), 91. The book was first published in 1930.

98. Constance, Lady Battersea, op. cit., 108.

3 'Coming Out' & Marriage

1. The Hon. Mrs E. M. Gell, *Under Three Reigns* (1927), 48–9.

2. Frances, Countess of Warwick, *Life's Ebb and Flow* (1929 edn), 32.

3. Frances, Countess of Warwick, op. cit., 25–8. Adeline Hartcup, *Children of the Great Country Houses* (1986 edn), 116.

4. Violet Powell, *Margaret, Countess of Jersey* (1978), 28–9. The Dowager Countess of Jersey, *Fifty-one Years of Victorian Life* (1922), 61–3.

5. Jessica A. Gerard, 'Family and Servants in the Country-House Community in England and Wales 1815–1914' (University of London Ph.D. thesis, 1982), 162. Margaret Blunden, *The Countess of Warwick* (1967), 23. Millicent, wife of the 4th Duke of Sutherland, was married on her seventeenth birthday in 1884. Denis Stuart, *Dear Duchess: Millicent Duchess of Sutherland 1867–1955* (1982), 36.

6. John Bailey ed., *The Diary of Lady Frederick Cavendish*, Vol. 1 (1927), 113 (entries for 2 and 4 April 1861).

7. Diana Cooper, *The Rainbow Comes and Goes* (1958), 94.

8. See Lady Carrington's diaries at the Bodleian Library, MS. Film 1097.

9. Jennifer Ellis ed., *Thatched With Gold: The Memoirs of Mabell, Countess of Airlie* (1962), 36.

10. *Etiquette for Ladies: A Complete Guide to the Rules and Observances of Good Society* (1900), 16.

11. Maureen E. Montgomery, *Gilded Prostitution: Status, Money, and Transatlantic Marriages 1870–1914* (1989), 100–101, quoting the views of an American correspondent of the time named George Smalley.

12. Quoted in Jennifer Ellis ed., op. cit., 41.

13. Robert Rhodes James, *Rosebery: A Biography of Archibald Philip, Fifth Earl of Rosebery*, (1964), 1.

14. Viscountess Ridley, *Cecilia: The Life and Letters of Cecilia Ridley (1819–1845)* (1958), 23.

15. John Bailey ed., op. cit., Vol. 1, 73.

16. John Bailey ed., op. cit., Vol. 1, 75–6.

17. John Bailey ed., op. cit., Vol. 1, 79.

18. John Bailey ed., op. cit., Vol. 1, 82.

19. John Bailey ed., op. cit., Vol. 1, 85.

20. Constance Battersea, *Reminiscences* (1922), 108–10.

21. Cynthia Asquith, *Remember and Be Glad* (1952), 58–9.

22. The Hon. Mrs E.M. Gell, op. cit., 60. Jennifer Ellis ed., op. cit., 40.

23. John Bailey ed., op. cit., Vol. 1, 89.

24. Diary of Constance Weld for 1874 at Dorset Record Office, D/WLC. D/WLC.D.10/F. 109.

25. John Bailey ed., op. cit., Vol. 1, 263.

26. Diary of Constance Weld, entry for 18 May 1874.

27. Diary of Lady Carrington (née Cecilia Harbord) at the Bodleian Library, entries for May–July 1877.

28. Leonore Davidoff, *The Best Circles* (1986 edn), 42. Susan Tweedsmuir, *The Edwardian Lady* (1966), 32.

29. Lady Muriel Beckwith, *When I Remember* (1936), 159–61.

30. Susan Tweedsmuir, op. cit., 26.

31. Constance Primrose's Diary for 1867, entry for 2 April, in Petworth House MSS. 1681 at West Sussex Record Office.

32. Diary of Constance Weld for 1874, entry for 9 June.

33. Osbert Sitwell ed., *Two Generations* (1940), 265.

34. Quoted in Pat Jalland, *Women, Marriage and Politics 1860–1914* (1988 edn), 23.

35. Jean Robin, *Elmdon: Continuity and Change in a North-west Essex Village 1861–1964* (1980), 141. Merlin Waterson, *The Servants' Hall* (1980), 6.

36. V. Sackville-West, *The Edwardians* (1960 edn), 105.

37. Alice Fairfax-Lucy ed., *Mistress of Charlecote: The Memoirs of Mary Elizabeth Lucy* (1990 edn), 76.

38. Information obtained at Charlecote Park in August 1990. Alice Fairfax-Lucy ed., op. cit., 80.

39. Alice Fairfax-Lucy ed., op. cit., 94–108.

40. Georgina Battiscombe, *Mrs Gladstone: The Portrait of a Marriage* (1956), 16.

41. Lady Carrington's diary for 1877 at the Bodleian Library.

42. Lord Carrington's diary for 1898 at the Bodleian Library, MS. Film 1103, entry for 24 March 1898.

43. Lady Carrington's diary for 1878, MS. Film 1097, entry for 31 July, 1878.

44. Lady Carrington's diary for 1878, entry for 9 August 1878.

45. Quoted in Jessica A. Gerard, op. cit., 197.

46. Katherine Everett, *Bricks and Flowers* (1951), 43–4.

47. David Thomas, 'Social Origins of Marriage Partners of the British Peerage in the Eighteenth and Nineteenth Centuries' in *Population Studies*, Vol. 26, No. 1 (March, 1972), 102 and 106. For the 2nd Duke of Westminster, in his time the richest man in England, see Leslie Field, *Bendor The Golden Duke of Westminster* (1986 edn). *The Complete Peerage* noted that in 1883 Lord Leconfield was one of the twenty-eight noblemen who possessed above 100,000 acres of land in the United Kingdom; he ranked 24th in order of acreage, though 10th in order of income.

48. Hon. Vicary Gibbs and H. A. Doubleday ed., *The Complete Peerage*, Vol. 5, (1926), 780.

49. David Thomas, op. cit., 106 and 108.

50. David Cannadine, *The Decline and Fall of the British Aristocracy* (1990), 347. Y. Cassis, 'Bankers in English Society in the Late Nineteenth Century' in *Economic History Review*, 2nd Series, Vol. 38, No. 2 (May 1985), 218.

51. Maureen E. Montgomery, op. cit., 89, 90, 222–4.

52. Maureen E. Montgomery, op. cit., 79.

53. Susan Tweedsmuir, *The Lilac and the Rose* (1952), 82.

54. Consuelo Vanderbilt Balsan, *The Glitter and the Gold* (1973 edn), 55.

55. May Harcourt to Lady Harcourt, 23 December 1904 at the Bodleian Library, MS. Harcourt dep. 647, f. 142.

56. David N. Thomas, 'Marriage Patterns in the British Peerage in the Eighteenth and Nineteenth Centuries' (London University M. Phil. thesis, 1969), 129.

57. David Thomas, 'Social Origins of Marriage Partners', 109.

58. David Cannadine, op. cit., 348. J. M. Bulloch, 'Peers Who Have Married Players' in *Notes and Queries*, Vol. 169 (1935), 92–94. Trevor Lummis and Jan Marsh, *The Woman's Domain: Women and the English Country House* (1990), 130.

59. Quoted in Pat Jalland, op. cit., 26.

60. The Earl of Bessborough ed., *Lady Charlotte Guest: Extracts from her Journal 1833–1852* (1950), 69.

61. The Earl of Bessborough ed., op. cit., 71.

62. Pat Jalland, op. cit., 75 and 85–6 and Lady Selborne to her daughter, Lady Howiek, at Hampshire Record Office, letter dated 15 Sept. 1906 in 9M68/130.

63. Lady Carrington's diary for 1906 at the Bodleian Library, MS. Film 1100, entries for 13, 15, 16 February, 26 March, 5 and 7 April, 1906. Lord Carrington's diary for 1905 and 1906 at the Bodleian Library, MS. Film 1105, entries for 12 Dec. 1905 and 18 and 24 March, 1906.

64. Lord Carrington's diary for 1899 at the Bodleian Library, MS. Film 1103, entry for 7 February.

65. Osbert Wyndham Hewett, *Strawberry Fair: A Biography of Frances, Countess Waldegrave 1821– 1879* (1956), 115.

66. Robert Rhodes James, op. cit., 84–5.

67. Lucy Cohen, *Lady de Rothschild and her Daughters, 1821–1931* (1935), 169 and 180. Constance's sister, Annie, had also married a Christian in 1873; he was the Hon. Eliot Yorke, a younger son of the Earl of Hardwicke.

68. May Harcourt to Lady Harcourt in MS. Harcourt dep. 648, letter dated 14 August 1908, f.11. The bride, Lady Gwendeline Bertie, was a Roman Catholic but her husband, Captain John Churchill, younger son of Lord Randolph Churchill, was not.

69. Maureen E. Montgomery, op. cit., 96.

70. Pat Jalland, op. cit., 63–4.

71. Quoted in Pat Jalland, op. cit., 68.

72. Lord Leconfield to Lady Leconfield, 7 December 1899, in Petworth House MSS. 1658 at West Sussex Record Office.

73. Maud Yorke to Lady Leconfield, 23 December 1899, in Petworth House MSS. 1658. Mary was married on 18 December.

74. Pat Jalland, op. cit., 41.

75. Pat Jalland, op. cit., 66–7.

76. Pat Jalland, op. cit., 66–7 and 71.

77. David Verey, *The Diary of a Victorian Squire* (1989), 50.

78. Pat Jalland, op. cit., 70.

79. Elinor Glyn, *Romantic Adventure* (1936), 56–8.

80. Merlin Waterson, op. cit., 86–90.

81. Diary of Louisa Yorke at Clwyd Record Office, D/E/2816, entry for 30 and 31 May, 1902.

82. Pat Jalland, op. cit., 69.

83. The Hon. Mrs Hugh Wyndham ed., *Correspondence of Sarah Spencer, Lady Lyttelton 1787–1870* (1912), 397.

84. L. E. O. Charlton, *The Recollections of a Northumbrian Lady 1815–1866* (1949), 76 and 104–6.

85 L. E. O. Charlton, op. cit., 115–119.

86. Revel Guest and Angela V. John, *Lady Charlotte: A Biography of the Nineteenth Century* (1989), 12–13.

87. Revel Guest and Angela V. John op. cit., 13.

88. Lady Colin Campbell, *Etiquette of Good Society* (1893), 91.

89. Pat Jalland, op. cit., 30.

90. Calculated from a sample of 550 married or widowed peers and baronets in Burke's *Peerage and Baronetage*, 72nd edn (1910).

91. Letter from May Burns to Lady Harcourt in MS. Harcourt dep. 647, 20 April 1899, f. 9.

92. Diary of Constance Primrose for 1867 at West Sussex Record Office.

93. May Harcourt to Lady Harcourt, 8 July and 11 August, 1899 in MS. Harcourt dep. 647, f. 14 and f. 18.

94. John Bailey ed., op. cit., Vol. 1, 222–3.

95. Diary of Constance Primrose for 1867. Constance Leconfield, *Random Papers* (privately published *c.* 1938), 34, at West Sussex Record Office.

96. Pat Jalland, op. cit., 42–3.

97. Margaret Blunden, op. cit., 37–8.

98. Lady Carrington's diary for 1878 MS. Film 1097, entry for 18 July 1878.

99. John Bailey ed., op. cit., Vol. 1, 229 (entry for 30 July 1864).

100. Consuelo Vanderbilt Balsan, op. cit., 64.

4 Wives & Mothers

1. Pat Jalland, *Women, Marriage and Politics 1860–1914* (1988 edn), 30.

2. May Burns to Sir William Harcourt, Bt., 14 Nov. 1898, in MS. Harcourt dep. 669, f. 2 in the Bodleian Library.

3. John, Duke of Bedford, *A Silver-plated Spoon* (1960 edn), 24–5.

4. John, Duke of Bedford, op. cit., 25.

5. John: Duke of Bedford, op. cit., 26.

6. Jennifer Ellis, ed., *Thatched with Gold: The Memoirs of Mabell Countess of Airlie* (1962), 54. Lady Airlie admitted that although she admired her mother-in-law, she was 'never at ease with her in the early years of my marriage'.

7. Gervas Huxley, *Lady Elizabeth and the Grosvenors: Life in a Whig Family 1822–1839* (1965), 33.

8. Gervas Huxley, op. cit., 35.

9. Gervas Huxley, op. cit., 23–4.

10. Gervas Huxley, op. cit., 54.

11. *Etiquette for Ladies: A Complete Guide to the Rules and Observances of Good Society* (1900), 77.

12. *Etiquette for Ladies*, 76–7.

13. Jessica A. Gerard, 'Family and Servants in the Country-House Community in England and Wales 1815–1914' (University of London Ph.D. thesis, 1982), 199.

14. Lady Maud Cecil to William Palmer, Viscount Wolmer, 21 Oct. 1883 in MS. Selborne Addl. 1, f. 62 in the Bodleian Library. She added that she thought she had impressed her view on his mind 'already but here it is set down in black & white, in order that you may never be able to complain of my differing with you, when I am your wife. There is nothing like plain speaking on these occasions.'

15. Lady Selborne to her daughter, Mabel, Lady Howick, 24 May 1909 at Hampshire Record Office, 9M68/186.

16. Quoted in Jessica A. Gerard, op. cit., 239.

17. Owen Chadwick, *Victorian Miniature* (1960), 68–70.

18. The Earl of Bessborough ed., *Lady Charlotte Guest: Extracts From Her Journal 1833–1852* (1950), 117–18.

19. Quoted in Jessica A. Gerard, op. cit., 165.

20. Mrs Isabella Beeton, *The Book of Household Management* (1861), 1.

21. See Lady Carrington's diary for 1878 and 1879 on MS. Film 1097 at the Bodleian Library, entries for 7 and 8 Nov., 1878 and 3 May, 1879.

22. Osbert Sitwell, ed., *Two Generations* (1940), 75–76.

23. Lady Muriel Beckwith, *When I Remember* (1936),24.

24. Cecil Woodham-Smith, *Florence Nightingale 1820–1910* (1955 edn), 53.

25. P. Blackwell, 'An Undoubted Jewel: A Case Study of Five Sussex Country Houses 1880–1914' in *Southern History*, Vol. 3 (1981) 191.

26. Nancy Mitford, *The Stanleys of Alderley 1851–1865* (1939), 348.

27. Alice Fairfax-Lucy ed., *Mistress of Charlecote: The memoirs of Mary Elizabeth Lucy* (1990 edn), 40.

28. Shiffner MSS. at East Sussex Record Office: Recipes, &c. Shiffner MSS. 1355. Stock and dairy account Shiffner MSS. 1526. Personal Income and Expenditure Shiffner MSS. 1529. Personal and household accounts of Lady Elizabeth Shiffner, Shiffner MSS. 1534.

29. Pat Jalland, op. cit., 235. Nigel Nicolson, *Portrait of a Marriage* (1990 edn), 55.

30. P. Blackwell, op. cit., 187.

31. Consuelo Vanderbilt Balsan, *The Glitter and the Gold* (1973 edn), 62. Marchioness of Bath, *Before the Sunset Fades* (1957), 9 and 28.

32. L. E. Jones, *Victorian Boyhood* (1955), 12–13 and 72.

33. Diary of Louisa Yorke for 1902 at Clwyd Record Office, D/E.2816, entries for 1 July, 17 July, 5 Sept., and 11 Nov.

34. Diary of Louisa Yorke for 1907, D/E.2816, entries for 9 Sept. and 3 Dec.

35. Diary of Louisa Yorke for 1904, D/E.2816, entry for 28 March.

36. Quoted in Jessica A. Gerard, op. cit., 222.

37. John Bailey ed., *The Diary of Lady Frederick Cavendish*, Vol. 1 (1927), 263 (entry for 17 May 1865).

38. John Bailey ed., op. cit., Vol. 2, 36 (entry for 13 July 1867).

39. Noel Streatfeild ed., *The Day Before Yesterday* (1956), 91.

40. Edith Sitwell, *Taken Care Of* (1965), 64.

41. Mrs [Sarah] Ellis, *The Wives of England: Their Relative Duties, Domestic Influence, and Social Obligations* (n.d. *c.* 1843), 24.

42. John Bailey ed., op. cit., Vol. 1, 284 (entry for 9 Sept. 1865).

43. Revel Guest and Angela V. John, *Lady Charlotte: A Biography of the Nineteenth Century* (1989), 39 and 131.

44. Revel Guest and Angela V. John, op. cit., 130.

45. Georgina Battiscombe, *Mrs Gladstone: The Portrait of a a Marriage* (1956), 41.

46. Pat Jalland, op. cit., 192.

47. John Bailey ed., op. cit., Vol. 1, 270–1 (entry for 20 June 1865).

48. Lucy Cohen, *Lady de Rothschild and Her Daughters, 1821–1931* (1935), 31–2.

49. Consuelo Vanderbilt Balsan, op. cit., 81 and 84–5.

50. May Harcourt to Lady Harcourt, 6 Jan. 1902 in MS. Harcourt dep. 647, at the Bodleian Library, ff. 100–101.

51. Leonore Davidoff, *The Best Circles* (1986 edn), 61.

52. Noel Streatfeild ed., op. cit., 119.

53. Cynthia Asquith, *Remember and Be Glad* (1952) 4 and 6.

54. Diary of Louisa Yorke for 1902, entry for 3 August.

55. Diary of Louisa Yorke for 1909, D/E.2816, entry for 17 Oct.

56. The Marchioness of Bath, op. cit., 29.

57. Noel Streatfeild ed., op. cit., 100.

58. Jessica A, Gerard, op. cit., 205.

59. Lady Clodagh Anson, *Book: Discreet Memoirs* (1932) 362–3.

60. Revel Guest and Angela V. John, op. cit., 283.

61. Quoted in Jessica A. Gerard, op. cit., 26.

62. Revel Guest and Angela V. John, op. cit., 33.

63. Revel Guest and Angela V. John, op. cit., 33.

64. Alice Fairfax-Lucy ed., op. cit., 38–9.

65. May Harcourt to Lady Harcourt, 15 June 1908, in MS. Harcourt dep. 648, f. 3.

66. Quoted in Janet Horowitz Murray, *Strong Minded Women, and Other Lost Voices From Nineteenth-century England* (1984), 143–4.

67. Margaret Blunden, *The Countess of Warwick* (1967), 41. Janet Horowitz Murray, op. cit., 144.

68. See, for example, an entry in her diary for 15 Aug., 1880: 'Sent for Dr Brodie who made me stay in bed.' On 4 March 1881, she noted that she was 'not at all well', and early the following morning Alexandra was born. Lady Carrington's diary for 1880/8.1, MS. Film 1097 at the Bodleian Library.

69. Lady Carrington's diary for 1895, MS. Film 1100 at the Bodleian Library.

70. Consuelo Vanderbilt Balsan, op. cit., 52.

71. Quoted In Maureen E. Montgomery, *Gilded Prostitution: Status, Money, and Transatlantic Marriages 1870–1914* (1989), 199.

72. Maureen E. Montgomery, op. cit., 192. W. C. D. and C. D. Whetham, *The Family and the Nation* (1909), 138–9.

73. W. C. D. and C. D. Whetham, op. cit., 139.

74. Maud Yorke to Lady Leconfield in Petworth House MSS. 1658 at West Sussex Record Office, letter dated December 1899. Trevor Lummis and Jan Marsh, *The Woman's Domain: Women and the English Country House* (1990), 194.

75. Maud Yorke to Lady Leconfield in Petworth House MSS. 1658, 23 Dec. 1899.

76. Lady Leconfield's diary for 1877 in Petworth House MSS. 1683, entries for 4 and 5 Oct.

77. Lady Clodagh Anson, op. cit., 363. Violet Powell, *Margaret, Countess of Jersey* (1978), 52. Revel Guest and Angela V. John, op. cit., 283. Gervas Huxley, op. cit., 22.

78. Pat Jalland, op. cit., 154.

79. Dorothy Henley, *Rosalind Howard Countess of Carlisle* (1958), 105–6.

80. Frances Horner, *Time Remembered* (1933), 84.

81. John Bailey ed., op. cit., Vol. 1, 47–57 (entries for 7, 27 and 28 Feb., 19 June, and 13–16 August 1857).

82. May Harcourt to Lady Harcourt, 30 Oct. 1901, in MS. Harcourt dep. 647, ff. 77–8.

83. May Harcourt to Lady Harcourt, 20 March 1901, MS. Harcourt dep. 647, f. 66.

84. May Harcourt to Lady Harcourt, 22 July 1906, MS. Harcourt dep. 647, ff. 215–6 and Pat Jalland, op. cit., 168.

85. Pat Jalland, op. cit., 159.

86. Lady Selborne to Mabel, Lady Howick, 24 April 1908 at Hampshire Record Office, 9M68/l63.

87. Lady Selborne to Lord Selborne, 10 June 1914 in MS. Selborne Adds. 3, f. 158 in the Bodleian Library.

88. Lady Selborne to Lord Selborne, 4 Aug. [no year given] in MS. Sciborne Adds. 3, ff. 155b–155c.

89. Dorothy Henley, op. cit., 99–100, 115 and 134–5.

90. Dorothy Henley, op. cit., 87.

91. Diary of Louisa Yorke for 1903, D/E.2816, entries for 10 and 30 July.

92. Consuelo Vanderbilt Balsan, op. cit., 141–2.

93. Lady Leconfield's diary for 1891, entries for 5, 7 and 21 Jan. in Petworth House MSS. 1685, for example.

94. [Ethel A.P. Grenfell, Baroness Desborough,] *Pages From a Family Journal 1888–1915* (1916), 27. Angela Lambert, *Unquiet Souls: The Indian Summer of the British Aristocracy* (1985), 76.

95. Angela Lambert, op. cit., 76.

96. Pamela Horn, *The Victorian Country Child* (1990 edn), 214. 'Fortieth Annual Report of the Registrar General of Births, Deaths and Marriages' in *Parliamentary Papers 1878–79*, Vol. 19, lxxvii, for the period 1867–1876. Thus in Herefordshire, where 10.9 per cent of babies born in 1897 died before the end of their first year, in 1867–76 the figure had been 11.8 per cent; in Buckinghamshire the respective figures were 10.9 per cent and 13.3 per cent.

97. Gervas Huxley, op. cit., 25.

98. Gervas Huxley, op. cit., 26.

99. Gervas Huxley, op. cit., 29.

100. Alice Fairfax-Lucy ed., op. cit., 58–9, 62–3 and 75.

101. Georgina Battiscombe, op. cit., 5–6.

102. Quoted in Dorothy Thompson, *Queen Victoria: Gender and Power* (1990), 59.

103. Osbert Sitwell, *The Scarlet Tree* (1949), 16–17.

104. Leonore Davidoff, op. cit., 54–5.

105. M. H. E., A *Manual of Etiquette tor Ladies and Gentlemen* (n.d. *c.* 1908), 75.

106. Alice Fairfax-Lucy, op. cit., 76.

107. Robert Rhodes James, *Rosebery: A Biography of Archibald Philip, Fifth Earl of Rosebery* (1964), 3

and 14.

108. John Bailey ed., op. cit., Vol. 2, 265–6.
109. Alice Buchan, *A Scrap Screen* (1979), 93.

5 The Role of 'Lady Bountiful'

1. Anthony Trollope, Framley Parsonage (1957 edn), 15.
2. Alice Fairfax-Lucy, *Mistress of Charlecote: The Memoirs of Mary Elizabeth Lucy* (1990 edn), 20.
3. Lady Leconfield's diary for 1891 in Petworth House MSS. 1685 at West Sussex Record Office.
4. Quoted in Jessica Gerard, 'Lady Bountiful: Women of the Landed Classes and Rural Philanthropy' in *Victorian Studies*, Vol. 30, No. 2 (Winter 1987), 193.
5. Consuelo Vanderbilt Balsan, *The Glitter and the Gold* (1973 edn), 104–5.
6. Lady Clodagh Anson, *Victorian Days* (1957), 96–7.
7. Lady Clodagh Anson, op. cit., 80.
8. George Ewart Evans, *Where Beards Wag All* (1970), 123.
9. Lucy Cohen, *Lady de Rothschild and Her Daughters 1821–1931* (1935), 73.
10. Lucy Cohen, op. cit., 99.
11. Jessica Gerard, 'Lady Bountiful', 190. Jessica A. Gerard, 'Family and Servants in the Country-House Community in England and Wales 1815–1914' (University of London Ph.D. thesis, 1982), 226.
12. Quoted in Pamela Horn, *The Rise and Fall of the Victorian Servant* (1990 edn), 44.
13. Pamela Horn, op. cit., 44.
14. Pamela Horn, op. cit., 43.
15. 'Second Report of the Royal Commission on the Employment of Children, Young Persons and Women in Agriculture', *Parliamentary Papers 1868–69*, Vol. 13, Evidence, 355–6.
16. Margaret Blunden, *The Countess of Warwick* (1967), 79–81.
17. Francesca M. Wilson, *Rebel Daughter of a Country House* (1967), 26 and 30–1.
18. Viscountess Milner, *My Picture Gallery 1886–1901* (1951), 83.
19. Viscountess Milner, op. cit., 84.
20. Quoted in Brian Harrison, 'For Church, Queen and Family: The Girls' Friendly Society 1874–1920' in *Past and Present*, No. 61 (Nov. 1973), 114.
21. Jessica Gerard, 'Lady Bountiful', 195. Lucy Masterman ed., *Mary Gladstone, Her Diaries and Letters* (1930), 115. (Diary entry for 13 Feb. 1877).
22. The Hon. Mrs E. M. Gell, *Under Three Reigns* (1927), 73–4.
23. John, Duke of Bedford, *A Silver-plated Spoon* (1959 edn), 24 and 27. Anne Summers, *Angels and Citizens: British Women as Military Nurses* (1988), 73–90.
24. Lady Louisa Knightley's Diary for 1879/80 at Northamptonshire Record Office, K.2898, entry for 16 June 1879.
25. Lady Knightley's Diary for 1889/91 at Northamptonshire Record Office, K.2904, entry for 9 Jan. 1889, for example. *The Times*, 7 Feb. 1914.
26. Cynthia Asquith, *Remember and Be Glad* (1952), 152–3.
27. Caroline Dakers, *The Countryside at War* (1987), 82–3.
28. Jean Robin, *Elmdon: Continuity and Change in an Essex Village, 1861–864* (1980), 162.
29. Revd C. Kingsley, 'The Country Parish' in *Lectures to Ladies on Practical Subjects* (1855), 53–5.
30. Jessica Gerard, 'Lady Bountiful', 203.
31. D. Haworth and W. M. Comber eds, *Cheshire Village Memories* (1969), 54.
32. Jessica Gerard, 'Lady Bountiful', 200.
33. Lee Holcombe, *Victorian Ladies at Work* (1973), 6, 10 and 103. 'First Report of the Royal Commission on the Employment of Children, Young Persons and Women in Agriculture', *Parliamentary Papers 1867–8*, Vol. 17, Evidence, 286. *The Times*, 21 Oct. 1905.
34. Quoted in Jessica Gerard, 'Lady Bountiful', 186.
35. Frances Horner, *Time Remembered (1933)*, 75–6 and 85. *A Pattern of Hundreds: Buckinghamshire Federation of Women's Institutes* (1975), 17.
36. John Burnett ed., *Destiny Obscure* (1984), 291–2.
37. Alice Buchan, *A Scrap Screen* (1979), 105–6.
38. Christmas Beef and Flour on the Cholmondeley estate, 1902–1914 at Cheshire Record Office, DCH/SS/30.
39. G. E. Mingay ed., *The Victorian Countryside* (2 vols.) (1981), 595.
40. David Verey, *The Diary of a Victorian Squire: Extracts from the Diaries and Letters of Dearman and Emily Birchall* (1989), 231. In the spring of 1883, Clara Birchall, the eldest sister, had contracted

scabies, apparently as a result of her cottage visiting. David Verey, op. cit., 147.

41. Personal and household accounts of Lady Elizabeth Shiffner at East Sussex Record Office, Shiffner MSS. 1529 and 1534.

42. A Late Resident, [Mrs H. Grote], *Some Account of the Hamlet of East Burnham, Co. Bucks* (1858). The pamphlet was intended for private circulation and is in the Bodleian Library. I am indebted to Raphael Samuel for this reference. See, for example, p. 44.

43. [Mrs. H. Grote] op. cit., 49.

44. Jessica Gerard, 'Lady Bountiful', 206.

45. Cecil Woodham-Smith, *Florence Nightingale* (1955 edn), 41–2.

46. Cynthia Asquith, op. cit., 152 and 155.

47. Denis Stuart, *Dear Duchess: Millicent Duchess of Sutherland 1867–1955* (1982), 40, 57, 68, and 91–5.

48. Lady Knightley's Diary for 1869/71 at Northamptonshire Record Office, K.2893, entry for 24 Oct. 1869. Jessica Gerard, 'Lady Bountiful', 189.

49. Lady Knightley's Diary for 1875/77, K.2896, entry for 8 April 1876.

50. John Bailey ed., *The Diary of Lady Frederick Cavendish* (1927), Vol. 2, 80 (entry for 26 Feb. 1870).

51. Diary of Constance Flower, Lady Battersea, at the British Library, Add. MSS. 47,933, entries for 2 and 11 Feb., 1879.

52. Diary of Constance Flower, entry for 7 Feb. 1880.

53. Diary of Constance Flower, entry for 10 Feb. 1879.

54. Charles Roberts, *The Radical Countess: The History of the Life of Rosalind Countess of Carlisle* (1962), 63.

55. Charles Roberts, op. cit., 40, 43 and 67.

56. Julia Cartwright ed., *The Journals of Lady Knightley of Fawsley* (1915), 1, 181 and 182.

57. Julia Cartwright, op. cit., xi–xix.

58. Lady Knightley's diary for 1869/71, entry for 4 May 1870, for example.

59. Agnes L. Money ed., *History of the Girls' Friendly Society* (1905), 3. Mary Heath-Stubbs, *Friendship's Highway: Being the History of the Girls' Friendly Society, 1875–1935* (1935), 4.

60. M. L. W. *What is the GFS?* (1884 pamphlet), 3.

61. Brian Harrison, op. cit., 109. *Annual Report of the Girls' Friendly Society for 1899*, 11. The Annual Reports of the Society are preserved at GFS headquarters in London.

62. Lady Knightley's Diary for 1875/77, entry for 5 April 1876.

63. Lady Knightley's Diary for 1879/80, entry for 22 April 1879 and Julia Cartwright, op. cit., 290.

64. Lady Knightley's Diary for 1884/85 at Northamptonshire Record Office, K.2901, entry for 22 May 1885, for example. Mary Heath-Stubbs, op. cit, 70, 72 and 286. Discussions on emigration began in November 1883 and the Society established a special Emigration department in 1885.

65. Brian Harrison, op. cit., 114.

66. *Friendly Leaves*, Vol. 11 (March, 1886), 76. Copies of this journal are preserved at GFS headquarters.

67. Brian Harrison, op. cit., 131.

68. *Friendly Leaves*, Vol. 11 (Sept. 1886), 234.

69. Brian Harrison, op. cit., 114.

70. Cecil Woodham-Smith, op. cit., 41.

71. Nightingale MSS. at the British Library, Add. MSS. 47,714, Report on King's College Hospital, 1863.

72. Mary Stocks, *A Hundred Years of District Nursing* (1960), 92–93. Monica E. Baly, *A History of the Queen's Nursing Institute* (1987), 49–50.

73. Pamela Horn, *Victorian Countrywomen* (1991), 212–3.

74. Mary Stocks, op. cit., 100.

75. Mary Stocks, op. cit., 100–101. *Report on the Rural District Branch of Queen Victoria's Jubilee Institute for 1893* at the British Library, Cup. 401.1.3.

76. *Queen Victoria's Jubilee Institute for Nurses: Rural District Branch: Report of the Central Committee for 1891: List of Vice-Presidents*, at the British Library, Cup.401. 1.3.

77. Queen Victoria's Jubilee Institute for Nurses: Inspector's Reports for Boxgrove and Westhampnett, Sussex, at the National Archives, PRO.30/63/416.

78. Pamela Horn, *Victorian Countrywomen*, 216.

79. Report for 1903 of Queen Victoria's Jubilee Institute for Nurses: Minutes of the Council, preserved at the Queen's Nursing Institute, London. In 1902 there were 950 Queen's Nurses on the roll and this had risen to 1,024 by 1903, but in each year 169 nurses had resigned. Of these, 21

in 1902 and 25 in 1903 left to get married, while 73 and 77, respectively, left for 'Home Duties and other work', and the rest left to go to other nursing jobs; because of poor health; because they were unsuitable, or had died.

80. Queen Victoria's Jubilee Institute for Nurses: Rural District Branch, Hampshire Centre, at the National Archives, PRO.30/63/126, letter from Lady Selborne to the Central Midwives Board, n.d. (c. 1908).

81. Betty Cowell and David Wainwright, *Behind the Blue Door: The History of the Royal College of Midwives* 1881–1981 (1981), 47.

82. May Harcourt to Lady Harcourt, 30 Nov. n.d. (probably C. 1903), at the Bodleian Library, Harcourt MSS. MS. Harcourt dep. 647, f. 190.

6 Leisure & Pleasure

1. Cynthia Asquith, *Remember and Be Glad* (1952), 78.

2. The Hon. Mrs E. M. Gell, *Under Three Reigns* (1927), 15–16. Phyllida Barstow, *The English Country House Party* (1989), 9.

3. Christopher Simon Sykes, *Country House Camera* (1980), 13–14. Maurice Baring, *The Puppet Show of Memory* (1922), 59.

4. Alethea Adeane to her aunt, Lucy Hare, 18 and 28 May, 1850, in DSA/154 at Cheshire Record Office.

5. Elizabeth Cartwright-Hignett, *Lili at Aynhoe* (1989), 40. Earlier, on 28 December 1834, Lili had noted that writing letters was 'a great comfort and consolation when one finds oneself far from one's own'. (Ibid., 29).

6. Diary of Constance de Rothschild in the British Library, Add. MSS. 47,928, entry for 10 March 1874.

7. Nigel Nicolson, *Portrait of a Marriage* (1990 edn), 62. For details of the Duchess of Sutherland's literary activities see Dems Stuart, *Dear Duchess: Millicent Duchess of Sutherland* 1867–1955 (1982), 80 and 107.

8. Mitchell A. Leaska and John Phillips ed., *Violet to Vita: The Letters of Violet Trefusis to Vita Sackville-West* (1989), 25 and 40–1.

9. Information at Lacock Abbey and in Lacock churchyard, where there are several family memorials.

10. Jessica A. Gerard, 'Family and Servants in the Country-House Community in England and Wales 1815–1914' (University of London Ph.D. thesis, 1982), 237 and 238.

11. Gervas Huxley, *Lady Elizabeth and the Grosvenors: Life in a Whig Family, 1822–1839* (1965), 33 and 35.

12. Gervas Huxley, op. cit. 36.

13. Diary of Lady Carrington (the former Cecilia Harbord) at the Bodleian Library, MS. Film 1097, entries for 30 and 31 July 1877, for example.

14. Cynthia Asquith, op. cit., 114–5.

15. May Harcourt to Lady Harcourt, 28 Dec. 1904, in MS. Harcourt dep. 647, ff. 145–6.

16. Entry in Louisa Yorke's diary for 22 Feb. 1909, D/E.2816 at Clwyd Record Office.

17. John van der Kiste, *Queen Victoria's Children* (1990 edn), 144.

18. Cynthia Asquith, op. cit., 119.

19. Louisa Yorke's diary for 1904, D/E.2816 at Clwyd Record Office.

20. Lady Elizabeth Shiffner's diary for 1887 at East Sussex Record Office, MSS. Shiffner 869. The Bulteel girls of Pamflete, Devon, were also excellent cricketers, according to a relative. Maurice Baring, op. cit., 58.

21. Lady Knightley's diary for 1888/90 at Northamptonshire Record Office, K.2904, entry for 2 Jan. 1889.

22. Lady Clodagh Anson, *Victorian Days* (1957), 272.

23. Lady Clodagh Anson, op. cit., 271.

24. Florence Nightingale, 'Cassandra' in Ray Strachey, *The Cause* (1978 edn), 397.

25. Florence Nightingale, op. cit. 404,

26. Pat Jalland, *Women, Marriage and Politics 1860–1914* (1988 edn), 16–17.

27. The Marchioness of Cranborne to Lady Edward Cecil, 3 Nov. 1899, in Violet Milner MSS. at the Bodleian Library, U.1599.C.77/4.

28. Lady Knightley's diary for 1880/82 at Northamptonshire Record Office, K.2899.

29. Victoria Glendinning, *Edith Sitwell: A Unicorn Among Lions* (1986 edn), 16.

30. Alice Fairfax-Lucy, *Mistress of Charlecote: The Memoirs of Mary Elizabeth Lucy* (1990 edn), 84 and

leaflet on *St Leonard's Church*, Charlecote (n.d.) obtainable at the church.

31. Alice Buchan, *A Scrap Screen* (1979), 47.
32. Susan Tweedsmuir, *The Lilac and the Rose* (1952), 97.
33. Susan Tweedsmuir, op. cit., 98–9.
34. L. E. O. Charlton, *The Recollections of a Northumbrian Lady 1815–1866* (1949), 160 and 176–7.
35. Mrs George Cornwallis-West, *The Reminisences of Lady Randolph Churchill* (1908), 60–61.
36. Mrs George Cornwallis-West, op. cit., 18.
37. Viscountess Milner, *My Picture Gallery 18 86–1901* (1951), 112–3.
38. Diary of Constance Weld for 1874 at Dorset Record Office, D/WLC.D.10/F.109, entries for 6,7, 8, 9 and 10 Jan. and 28 Jan. 1874.
39. Frances Horner, *Time Remembered* (1933), 85. Lady Knightley's diary for 1885/87 at Northamptonshire Record Office, K.2902, entries for 7 March 1886 and 13 Jan. 1887, for example. Julia Cartwright ed., *The Journals of Lady Knightley of Fawsley* (1915), 337 (entries for 23 Jan., 6 March and 9 March 1880).
40. Diary of Lady Knightley for 1869/70, K.2893, entry for 18 Aug. 1870.
41. Frances, Countess of Warwick, *Afterthoughts* (1931), 99.
42. The Marchioness of Londonderry, *Retrospect* (1938), 101.
43. Frances Horner, op. cit., 74.
44. Quoted in Georgina Battiscombe, *Mrs Gladstone: The Portrait of a Marriage* (1956), 18.
45. John Bailey ed., *The Diary of Lady Frederick Cavendish*, Vol. 1 (1927), 123–4 (entry for 31 Jan. 1862).
46. Margaret Blunden, *The Countess of Warwick* (1967), 44.
47. Denis Stuart, op. cit., 40 and 50–1. Lady Angela Forbes, *Memories and Base Details* (n.d. *c.* 1922), 84.
48. Pamela Horn, *Victorian Countrywomen* (1991), 54.
49. John, Duke of Bedford, *A Silver-plated Spoon* (1960), 26.
50. Reminiscences of Dorothy H. J. Wright at the Department of Sound Records, Imperial War Museum, 00510/06.
51. Mrs George Cornwallis-West, op. cit., 148–9.
52. Cynthia Asquith, op. cit., 130–1.
53. Frances, Countess of Warwick, op. cit., 38–40.
54. Leonore Davidoff, *The Best Circles* (1986 edn), 65. Gregory D. Phillips, *The Diehards: Aristocratic Society and Politics in Edwardian England* (1979), 19.
55. John Bailey ed., op. cit., Vol. 1, 134.
56. The Hon. Mrs E. M. Gell, op. cit., 58–9.
57. Frances, Countess of Warwick, op. cit., 42.
58. Angela Lambert, *Unquiet Souls: The Indian Summer of the British Aristocracy, 1880–1918* (1985 edn), 8.
59. Angela Lambert, op. cit., 8.
60. Diary of Lord Carrington for 1900 at the Bodleian Library, MS. Films 1103, entry for 3 July 1900.
61. David Cannadine, *The Decline and Fall of the British Aristocracy* (1990), 349.
62. Ralph Nevill ed., *The Reminiscences of Lady Dorothy Nevill* (n.d., *c.* 1906), 126–8.
63. John Bailey ed., op. cit., Vol. 1, 143 (entry for 12 July 1862).
64. Ralph Nevill ed., op. cit., 51–63.
65. Alice Fairfax-Lucy, op. cit., 61–72 and information obtained at Charlecote Park.
66. David Cannadine, op. cit., 371.
67. May Harcourt to Lady Harcourt, 7 Sept. 1905 in MS. Harcourt dep. 647, ff. 176–8.
68. The Countess of Cardigan and Lancastre, *My Recollections* (1909), 52–9.
69. Quoted in Phyllida Barstow, op. cit., 73.
70. Frances, Countess of Warwick, op. cit., 173.
71. Quoted in Christopher Simon Sykes, op. cit., 74.
72. Cynthia Asquith, op. cit., 165.
73. Cynthia Asquith, op. cit., 166.
74. Cynthia Asquith, op. cit., 12–14.
75. Quoted in E. W. Bovill, *English Country Life 1780–1830* (1962), 84–5.
76. Lady Knightley's diary for 1869/70, entries for 27 Nov. and 10 Dec. 1869.
77. Lady Knightley's diary for 1879/80, K.2898, entry for 31 Jan. 1879.
78. John Sutherland, *Mrs Humphry Ward: Eminent Victorian, Pre-eminent Edwardian* (1990), 187.

79. John Sutherland, op. cit., 188.

80. Margaret Blunden, op. cit., 64.

81. Margaret Blunden, op. cit., 88–9.

82. Gregory D. Phillips, op. cit., 20–21.

83. Frances, Countess of Warwick, op. cit., 42.

84. Margaret Blunden, op. cit., 77–8.

85. Margaret Blunden, op. cit., 71.

86. Allen Horstman, *Victorian Divorce* (1985), 118 and 134. *Annual Register for 1870* (1871), 168. Angela Lambert, op. cit., 43–4. *Burke's Peerage and Baronetage* (1910 edn), 1304.

87. Vita Sackville-West, *The Edwardians* (1960 edn), 19–20.

88. Nigel Nicolson, op. cit., 56–7.

89. Griselda Rowntree and Norman H. Carrier, 'The Resort to Divorce in England and Wales 1858–1957' in *Population Studies*, Vol. 11, No. 3 (March 1958), 201.

90. Jessica A. Gerard, op. cit., 24.

91. Allen Horstman, op. cit., 161. G. Rowntree and N. H. Carrier, op. cit., 92.

92. David Green, *The Churchills of Blenheim* (1984), 114–115.

93. Viscountess Milner, op. cit., 1.

94. Consuelo Vanderbilt Balsan, *The Glitter and the Gold* (1973 edn), 148.

95. Consuelo Vanderbilt Balsan, op. cit., 148–9.

96. Phyllida Barstow, op. cit., 51–2. Frances, Countess of Warwick, op. cit., 48 and 103–4.

97. Angela Lambert, op. cit., 66–7 and 79.

7 Politics, Power & Professionalism

1. Philippa Levine, *Victorian Feminism 1850–1900* (1987), 71.

2. Quoted in Pamela Horn, *Victorian Countrywomen* (1991), 52.

3. Patricia Hollis, *Ladies Elect: Women in English Local Government 1865–1914* (1987), 366.

4. Patricia Hollis, op. cit., 368. *Parish, District and Town Councils' Gazette*, 5 Jan., 1895.

5. Roger R. Sellman, *Devon Village Schools in the Nineteenth Century* (1967), 65.

6. Margaret Blunden, *The Countess of Warwick* (1967), 94–5.

7. Pamela Horn, op. cit., 52.

8. Mrs McIlquham, *The Enfranchisement of Women* (Women's Emancipation Union pamphlet, 1891) at the British Library, 8415g.63(16), 4. In the same pamphlet Mrs McIlquham claimed that, 'Every woman, except the Queen, is politically non-existent' (p. 5).

9. Anthony Trollope, *Phineas Finn* (1973 edn), 89. The book was first published serially between Oct. 1867 and May 1869.

10. John Bailey ed., *The Diary of Lady Frederick Cavendish*, Vol. 2 (1927), 22.

11. *The Nineteenth Century*, Vol. 26 (July 1889), 104–5 and (August 1889), 323–361. See also (June 1889), 781–5.

12. *The Nineteenth Century* (June, 1889), 782.

13. *The Nineteenth Century* (July 1889), 89 (comment by Mrs Fawcett).

14. Diary of Louisa Yorke of Erddig at Clwyd Record Office, D/E.2816, entry for 31 March 1904.

15. May Harcourt to Lady Harcourt, 26 Nov. 1909, in MS. Harcourt dep. 648 at the Bodleian Library, f. 32.

16. Blanche E. C. Dugdale, *Family Homespun* (1940), 106.

17. Maud Cecil to Viscount Wolmer in MS. Selborne Addl. 1 at the Bodleian Library, letters of 1, 19, 20 and 22 Oct. 1883, ff. 57, 59–60, 64 and 66. They were married on 27 Oct. Martin Pugh, *The Tories and the People 1880–1935* (1985), 48.

18. Frances, Countess of Warwick, *Afterthoughts* (1931), 45. Harold Macmillan, *The Past Masters* (1977 edn), 208, 210 and 216. Martin Pugh, op. cit., 45, however, suggests that the role of the hostesses began to diminish somewhat during the 1880s.

19. Denis Stuart, *Dear Duchess: Millicent Duchess of Sutherland 1867–1955* (1982), 57.

20. Martin Pugh, op. cit., 45. Brian Harrison, *Separate Spheres: The Opposition to Women's Suffrage in Britain* (1978), 82–3.

21. Brian Harrison, op. cit., 83.

22. Osbert Wyndham Hewett, *Strawberry Fair: A Biography of Frances Countess Waldegrave 1821–1879* (1956), 235.

23. Frances, Countess of Warwick, op. cit., 45.

24. Frances, Countess of Warwick, op. cit., 49 and 103–4.

25. Frances, Countess of Warwick, op. cit., xiv. Margaret Blunden, op. cit., 100, 168 and 178.

26. Margaret Blunden, op. cit., 173, 176 and 194.

27. Ralph Nevill, *The Remiscences of Lady Dorothy Nevill* ed. (n.d., c. 1906), 92.

28. Brian Harrison, op. cit., 83, 127–8. See also *Annual Report of the National League for Opposing Women Suffrage 1911–12: Oxford Branch* (1912), 4.

29. Lady Knightley's Diary for 1912 at Northamptonshire Record Office, K.2922, entry for 29 March 1912.

30. Lady Knightley's Diary for 1912, entry for 31 May.

31. *The Times*, 30 June 1913.

32. Lady Selborne to Lord Selborne, MS. Selborne Adds. 3 in the Bodleian Library, letter dated 7 Dec. 1911, f. 150. Sec also Maud Selborne, 'A Note on Women's Suffrage from the Common-sense Point of View' in *The Nineteenth Century*, Vol. 58 (Aug. 1905), 306–7.

33. Quoted in Pat Jalland, *Women, Marriage and Politics 1860–1914* (1988 edn), 211.

34. Martha Vicinus, *Independent Women: Work and Community for Single Women 1850–1920* (1985), 272.

35. Brian Harrison, op. cit., 162.

36. Martha Vicinus, op. cit., 274–5. L. E. Snellgrove, *Votes for Women* (1984 edn), 35. *Who Was Who*, Vol. 2 (1947), 655–6.

37. Mrs George Cornwallis-West, *The Remiscences of Lady Randolph Churchill* (1908), 87–8 and 95.

38. Pat Jalland, op. cit., 198.

39. *The Times*, 28 June 1939.

40. Susan Tweedsmuir, *The Edwardian Lady* (1966), 12–13.

41. Pat Jalland, op. cit., 197.

42. Martin Pugh, op. cit., 20–27.

43. Mrs George Cornwallis-West, op. cit., 98–9.

44. Lady Knightley's Diary for 1895 at Northamptonshire Record Office, K.2901, entry for 12 May 1885.

45. Martin Pugh, op. cit., 46–7.

46. Records of the Ladies' Grand Council of the Primrose League at the Bodleian Library, MSS. Primrose League 11, Cash Accounts for the Years 1888 and 1889; both show an expenditure of £500.

47. Minutes of the Ladies' Grand Council of the Primrose League, MSS. Primrose League 11, meetings on 15 Sept. 1886 and 1 May 1888. Second Report of the Ladies' Grand Council Executive Committee as at February, 1886 in MSS. Primrose League 10(1), f. 104.

48. Quoted In Pamela Horn, *Joseph Arch* (1971), 183.

49. Lady Dorothy Nevill, *Under Fire Reigns* (1910), 210–1.

50. Mrs George Cornwallis-West, op. cit., 100.

51. Charles Roberts, *The Radical Countess* (1962), 117–8. Martin Pugh, op. cit., 68.

52. Martin Pugh, op. cit., 52.

53. Charles Roberts, op. cit., 56–7.

54. Charles Roberts, op. cit., 122.

55. Martin Pugh, op. cit., 43. Diary of Constance Flower for 1880 at the British Library, Add. MSS. 47,933, entry for 12 March: 'got thro' a great deal of canvassing'. She had arrived in Brecon the previous day.

56. Diary of Constance Flower, entry for 1 April 1880.

57. Diary of Constance Flower, entry for 1 April 1880.

58. Diary of Constance Flower, entry for 1 April 1880.

59. Peter Gordon, 'Lady Knightley and the South Northamptonshire Election of 1885' in *Northamptonshire Past and Present*, Vol. 6, No. 5 (1981–82), 267. For early discussions on the franchise questions with her cousins see, for example, Julia Cartwright ed., *The Journals of Lady Knightley of Fawsley* (1915), 129.

60. Diary of Lady Knightley for 1884–1885, K.290 I, entry for 29 July 1885.

61. Diary of Lady Knightley, entry for 30 July 1885.

62. Diary of Lady Knightley, entry for 15 Sept. 1885.

63. Diary of Lady Knightley, entry for 19 Sept. 1885.

64. Diary of Lady Knightley, entry for 27 Nov. 1885.

65. Diary of Lady Knightley, entry for 27 Nov. 1885.

66. Diary of Lady Knightley, entry for 28 Nov. 1885.

67. Diary of Lady Knightley, entry for 28 Nov. 1885.

68. Diary of Lady Knightlcy, entry for 29 June 1886.

69. Diary of Lady Knightley, entry for 30 June 1886.

70. Diary of Lady Knightley for 1912, for example, entries for 10, 19 January, 15 Feb., 6 May and 25 July.

71. Lady Selborne to Lord Selborne in MS. Selborne Addl. 1, letter n.d. [June 1897], f. 147–149.

72. Lady Selborne to Lord Selborne in MS. Selborne Addl. 3, letter 7 Dec. 1910, f. 119.

73. Lady Selborne to Lord Selborne in MS. Selborne Addl. 3, 8 Dec. 1910, f. 122.

74. Pat Jalland, op. cit., 239.

75. Pat Jalland, op. cit., 240.

76. Lady Selborne to Lord Selborne in MS. Selborne Addl. 3, letter n.d. [1911], ff. 146–148.

77. Pat Jalland, op. cit., 244. See also Ann Estella, Countess Cave, *Odds and Ends of My Life* (1929), 159. Lady Cave helped with her husband's electioneering in 1906 for the first time: 'At that time I knew nothing of politics and cared less, but it was for the man I worked, because I knew what he and his work meant to the country.'

78. May Harcourt to Lady Harcourt, 3 Dec. 1910, in MS. Harcourt dep. 648, f. 50.

79. Harold Macmillan, op. cit., 213–4. John Grigg, *Nancy Astor: Portrait of a Pioneer* (1980), 72–7.

80. Mrs James de Rothschild, *The Rothschilds at Waddesdon Manor* (1975), 75–80.

81. Charles Roberts, op. cit., 137.

82. Charles Roberts, op. cit., 140.

83. Dorothy Henley, *Rosalind Howard, Countess of Carlisle* (1958), 138.

84. Dorothy Henley, op. cit., 137.

85. Edith Marchioness of Londonderry, *Frances Anne: The Life and Times of Frances Anne, Marchioness of Londonderry and her Husband Charles, Third Marquess of Londonderry* (1958), 268.

86. Edith Marchioness of Londonderry, op. cit., 269.

87. Jennifer Ellis ed., *Thatched with Gold: The Memoirs of Mabell Countess of Airlie* (1962), 96.

88. Jennifer Ellis ed., op. cit., 119.

89. Victoria Glendinning, *Edith Sitwell: A Unicorn Among Lions* (1983 edn), 12.

90. Pamela Watkin, *A Kingston Lacy Childhood: Reminiscences of Viola Bankes* (1989 edn), 35–36 and 117–8.

91. Viscountess Wolseley to Frances Wolseley, 30 July 1906 in Wolseley Papers 138 at Hove Reference Library. Marjory Pegram, *The Wolseley Heritage: The Story of Viscountess Wolseley and Her Parents* (1939), 165. Frances succeeded to the title Viscountess in 1913, on her father's death.

92. Typescript account of the establishment of the School of Gardening for Women, written by Viscountess Wolseley in *c*. 1924, in Wolseley Papers 196 at Hove Reference Library. The school seems to have petered out in the early 1920s. Frances died in December 1936, aged sixty-four.

93. Cynthia Asquith, *Haply I May Remember* (1950), 228–9.

94. Francesca M. Wilson, *Rebel Daughter of a Country House: The Life of Eglantyne Jebb, Founder of the Save the Children Fund* (1967), 54–5.

95. Francesca M. Wilson, op. cit., 149–50.

96. Francesca M. Wilson, op. cit., 56, 59, 65, 80–81, 90 and 174–5.

97. Lady Cynthia Colville, *Crowded Life* (1963), 62–3.

98. Diary of Elizabeth Mary Wilbraham (née Barnard) for 1858 at Cheshire Record Office, *DX/459*, entries for 2, 3 Feb. and 10 and 20 March, for example.

99. Kay N. Sanecki, *A Short History of Studley College* (1990), 4. Margaret Blunden, op. cit., 137.

100. Letter book of the Lady Warwick Hostel at Reading University Library, WAR.5/1/3, Edith Bradley warden, to Miss Astley-Sparke, Folkestone, 3 and 10 Jan. 1900, ff. 366 and 396. Pamela Horn, op. cit., 129. Kay N. Sanecki, op. cit., 7.

101. Kay N. Sanecki, op. cit., 17.

102. Quoted in Pamela Horn, op. cit., 71.

103. Letter book of the Lady Warwick Hostel, WAR.5/1/2, Edith Bradley to the Countess of Bective and the Countess of Kilmorry, 7 Aug. 1899, f. 481.

104. Register of Students at the Glynde School for Lady Gardeners, from 1903, in Wolseley Papers 182. Four of the first seven students recruited between March 1903 and Oct. 1904 were clergymen's daughters.

105. Pamela Horn, op. cit., 130.

106. Pamela Horn, op. cit., 130.

107. Pamela Horn, op. cit., 71.

108. Pamela Horn, op. cit., 116.

8 Epilogue: The Impact of War, 1914-18

1. Reminiscences of Mrs Dorothy Wright (née Beresford-Peirse) at the Imperial War Museum: Department of Sound Archives, 00510/06.
2. Diary of Lady Laura Ridding at Hampshire Record Office, 9M68/65.
3. [Ethel A. P. Grenfell, Baroness Desborough,] *Pages from a Family Journal 1888–1915* (1916), 439.
4. Margaret Blunden, *The Countess of Warwick* (1967), 245.
5. G. M. Trevelyan, *Grey of Fallodon: Being the Life of Sir Edward Grey, Afterwards Viscount Grey of Fallodon* (1943 edn), 261 and 266.
6. Diana Cooper, *The Rainbow Comes and Goes* (1958), 113–4.
7. Caroline Dakers, *The Countryside at War 1914–18* (1987), 26.
8. David Cannadine, *The Decline and Fall of the British Aristocracy* (1990), 81.
9. David Cannadine, op. cit., 83.
10. Lady Selborne to Lord Selborne, 1 Oct. 1914, in MS. Selborne Adds. 3, f.171 at the Bodleian Library.
11. Lady Selborne to Lord Selborne, 26 Sept. 1916 in MS. Selborne Adds. 4, f.18 at the Bodleian Library. See also Lady Laura Ridding's diary for 23 Jan., 19 Feb. and 13 March 1916. Not until 13 March did Lord Selborne receive confirmation via the German Red Cross that his son had been captured 'grievously wounded but died before reaching hospital'.
12. Lady Selborne to Lord Selborne, 24 Oct. 1918, in MS. Selborne Adds. 4, ff.27–8.
13. Angela Lambert, *Unquiet Souls: the Indian Summer of the British Aristocracy* (1985 edn), 172.
14. Caroline Dakers, op. cit., 88.
15. Lady Desborough's *Pages From a Family Journal* was privately printed by Eton College in 1916.
16. Quoted in David Cannadine, op. cit., 72.
17. P. Campion, *A Recent History of Hampshire, Wiltshire and Dorset* (n.d., c. 1922), under the heading 'Breamore House'. This book is not paginated.
18. Quoted in Philip Ziegler, *Diana Cooper: Thee Biography of Lady Diana Cooper* (1983 edn,), 95.
19. Violet Powell, *Margaret Countess of Jersey* (1978), 177–8.
20. Angela Lambert, op. cit., 188. Pamela Horn, *Rural Life in England in the First World War* (1984), 184–5.
21. Quoted in Pamela Horn, op. cit., 25.
22. Lady Laura Ridding's diary, entry for 12 Aug. 1914.
23. Quoted in David Cannadine, op. cit., 72.
24. Caroline Dakers, op. cit., 25 and 182.
25. Charles Roberts, *The Radical Countess* (1962), 50.
26. Pamela Horn, op. cit., 27–8.
27. P. Campion, *The Honourable Women of the Great War* (n.d., c. 1919), under 'The Duchess of Bedford'. This book is not paginated. John, Duke of Bedford, *A Silver-plated Spoon* (1959 edn), 29.
28. Diary of Lady Laura Ridding, entry for 24 April 1915.
29. Reminiscences of Mrs Dorothy Wright at the Imperial War Museum: Department of Sound Archives. Anne Summers, *Angels and Citizens, British Women as Military Nurses* (1988), 261.
30. Guy Slater ed., *My Warrior Sons: The Borton Family 1914–1918* (1973), 11, 14, 30, 37, 62, 71, 78, 87, 143 and 199.
31. Caroline Dakers, op. cit., 37.
32. Margaret Blunden, op. cit., 247.
33. Margaret Blunden, op. cit., 249.
34. Diary of Lady Laura Ridding, entry for 24 Oct. 1914.
35. David Cannadine, op. cit., 73. Pamela Horn, op. cit., 36.
36. Reminiscences of Antonia Marian Gamwell at the Imperial War Museum: Department of Sound Records, 000502/11.
37. The Hon. Mrs E. M. Gell, *Under Three Reigns* (1927), 260.
38. Pamela Horn, op. cit., 28.
39. Pamela Horn, op. cit., 30.
40. Caroline Dakers, op. cit., 26–7.
41. Caroline Dakers, op. cit., 42.
42. Philip Yorke to Simon Yorke, (n.d., c. 27 Nov. 1914), at Clwyd Record Office, D/E.2837.
43. May Harcourt to Lady Harcourt, n.d. (March 1916) in MS. Harcourt dep. 648, f. 96 at the Bodleian Library, Oxford.

44. Patricia Blackwell, 'The English Landed Elite in Decline: A Case Study of Five Sussex Country Houses, 1880–1914' (University of Sussex: Graduate History Division thesis, 1978), 15–16.

45. Patricia Blackwell, op. cit., 20.

46. F. M. L. Thompson, *English Landed Society in the Nineteenth Century* (1963), 328–9.

47. Arthur Warwick, *Women at War 1914–1918* (1977), 37. Frances Horner, *Time Remembered* (1933), 204.

48. Denis Stuart, *Dear Duchess: Millicent Duchess of Sutherland 1867–1955* (1982), 125. David Cannadine, op. cit., 73.

49. War Diary on No. 1 Red Cross (Duchess of Westminster's Hospital), Le Touquet at the Imperial War Museum Library, BRCS 23/2; in August 1915 the hospital was converted to receive officers only.

50. Quoted in Caroline Dakers, op. cit., 38.

51. *Primrose League Gazette*, June 1918, 6.

52. *Primrose League Gazette*, Oct. 1914, 12.

53. Jonathan Bradbury, *Government and County: A History of the Northamptonshire County Council 1889–1989* (1989), 19. Miss Cartwright became in 1919 the first woman *elected* to the County Council, as opposed to merely being co-opted.

54. Louisa Yorke to Simon Yorke, 9 Nov. 1916, D/E.2837 at Clwyd Record Office.

55. Louisa Yorke to Simon Yorke, 9 June 1915, D/E.2837 at Clwyd Record Office.

56. Trevor Lummis and Jan Marsh, *The Woman's Domain: Women and the English Country House* (1990), 162.

57. *Country Life*, 28 Dec. 1918. Angela Lambert, op. cit., 177.

58. Thea Thompson, *Edwardian Childhoods* (1981), 229.

59. Ethel Annie P. Grenfell, Baroness Desborough, op. cit., 442 and 494. Denis Stuart, op. cit., 124–5.

60. Lady Cynthia Colville, *Crowded Life* (1963), 92.

61. Edith Sitwell, *Taken Care Of* (1965), 79.

62. Arthur Marwick, op. cit., 38–9.

63. *War Service Legion and Women's Legion Reports, 1915–18* (1918), 11 and 13 in ARMY 1 at the Imperial War Museum Library.

64. *War Service Legion and Women's Legion Reports, 1915–18*, 11. *The Motor*, 19 March, 1918. Arthur Marwick, op. cit., 92.

65. Diana Cooper, op. cit., 117–8.

66. Denis Stuart, op. cit., 125–8 and 132–7.

67. David Cannadine, op. cit., 76.

68. Denis Stuart, op. cit., 131 and Lady Angela Forbes, *Memories and Base Details* (n.d. *c.* 1922), 174–5, 222, 250–1, 266–9, 270 and 273.

69. Diana Cooper, op. cit., 118.

70. Diana Cooper, op. cit, 135.

71. Philip Ziegler, op. cit., 71.

72. The Countess of Warwick, *A Woman and the War* (1916), 38–42.

73. Diana Cooper, op. cit., 142–3.

74. David Cannadine, op. cit., 76.

75. Lyn Macdonald, *The Roses of No Man's Land* (1984 edn), 39.

76. Jennifer Ellis ed., *Thatched with Gold: The Memoirs of Mabell Countess of Airlie* (1962), 133.

77. The Hon. Mrs E. M. Gell, op. cit., 260–262.

78. Minute by a Board of Agriculture official, 3 March 1916, at the National Archives, MAF.42/8/12027/L3.

79. Quoted in Pamela Horn, op. cit., 119.

80. M. E. Hobbs, Travelling Inspector to Miss Meriel Talbot, 6 Oct. 1917 at the National Archives, MAF.42/8/12027/L3.

81. M. E. Hobbs to Miss Meriel Talbot, 6 Oct. 1917, loco cit.

82. *Country Life*, 2 Nov. 1918, xxii.

83. Pamela Horn, op. cit., 118–120. *War Service Legion and Women's Legion Reports, 1915–18*, 51 and 75. See also 'The Marketing of Garden Produce' in *Country Life*, 30 March 1918, 330, for other examples of collective marketing and distribution by female volunteers, such as the Worcestershire Fruit and Vegetable Society, based upon Lord Coventry's estate, with his daughter, Lady Barbara Smith, as the driving spirit. Jam making, fruit pulping and apple drying industries were also set up.

84. Lady Selborne to Lord Selborne, 8 Sept. 1916 in MS. Selborne Adds. 4, f.16.

85. Lady Selborne to Lord Selborne, 6 Sept. 1916 in MS. Selborne Adds. 4, f. 13.

86. Pamela Horn, *The Rise and Fall of the Victorian Servant* (1990 revised edn), 223.

87. Lady Selborne to Lord Selborne, 27 Oct. 1918, in MS. Selborne Adds. 4, f. 35.

88. *Country Life*, 2 Nov. 1918, xxviii.

89. Diary of Lady Laura Ridding for Jan.–July 1919, 9M68/68 at Hampshire Record Office, entry for 23 March 1919, f. 6.

90. Lady Selborne to Lord Selborne, 28 Oct. 1918 In MS. Selborne Adds. 4, f. 37. Louisa Yorke to Simon Yorke, 7 Dec. 1917, D/E.2837 at Clwyd Record Office. Pamela Horn, *Rural Life in England*, 191.

91. Diary of Lady Laura Ridding, entry for 14 July 1918, 9M68/67 at Hampshire Record Office.

92. David Cannadine, op. cit., 93.

93. F. M. L. Thompson, op. cit., 328.

94. F. M. L. Thompson, op. cit., 328.

95. David Cannadine, op. cit., 98 and 107.

96. Margaret Blunden, op. cit., 262–3.

97. Margaret Blunden, op. cit., 281 and David Cannadine, op. cit., 402.

98. F. M. L. Thompson, op. cit., 330.

99. *Country Life*, 19 Oct. 1918, 342.

100. F. M. L. Thompson, op. cit., 333.

101. Diary of Lady Laura Ridding for Jan.–July 1919, entry for 11 March 1919, f. 5. See also Kelly's *Directory Hampshire* for 1920 and 1927.

102. Gregory D. Phillips, *The Diehards: Aristocratic Society and Politics in Edwardian England* (1979), 39 and 43. Hon. Vicary Gibbs and H. A. Doubleday ed., *The Complete Peerage*, Vol. 5 (1926), Appendix C, 780–3. Gibbs and Doubleday comment, 'It is an interesting sign of the times that Lady Rhondda should be second in the list as directing (of course as the representative of her late able father) no less than thirty-four undertakings, but she and the Dowager Lady Nunburnholme are by no means the only women to be found in the Directory of Directors.' (780).

Acknowledgements

I should like to thank all those who have assisted me with the preparation of this book by providing information and illustrations, or who have helped in other ways. In particular, my thanks are due to The Hon. Mrs Crispin Gascoigne for permission to quote from the Harcourt papers in the Bodleian Library, Oxford, and to Mrs I. Moon for permission to use the Sulham House photographs at the Museum of English Rural Life, University of Reading. My thanks are also due to Professor Peter Gordon, the Girls' Friendly Society, London (particularly Mrs J. Gould), the Queen's Nursing Institute, London, Hampshire County Museums Service, the Trustees of Studley College, the Trustees of the Imperial War Museum, and Mr John Peacock of Oxford. I have received much efficient assistance from staff at the various libraries and record offices at which I have worked and I am indebted to them all. These include the Bodleian Library, Oxford (particularly Mr Colin Harris), the British Library, East Sussex Library, the Library of the University of Reading particularly the National Archives, the Museum of English Rural Life, Reading, and the county record offices for Cheshire, Clwyd, Dorset, Hampshire, Northamptonshire, Oxfordshire and East and West Sussex.

As always, I owe a special debt of gratitude to my late husband. He has not only accompanied me on a number of research 'expeditions' but has helped in countless other ways. Without his assistance this book could not have been written.

Pamela Horn

Also available from Amberley Publishing

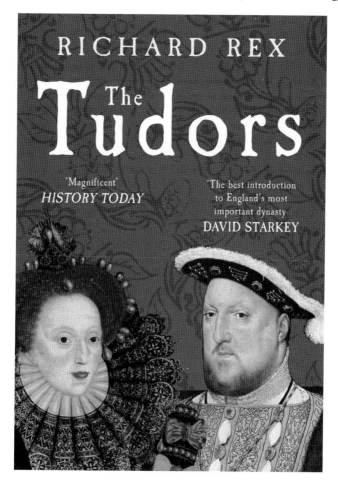

An intimate history of England's most infamous royal family

'The best introduction to England's most important dynasty' DAVID STARKEY
'A lively overview... Rex is a wry commentator on the game on monarchy' THE GUARDIAN
'Gripping and told with enviable narrative skill. This is a model of popular history... a delight' THES
'Vivid, entertaining and carrying its learning lightly' EAMON DUFFY

The Tudor Age began in August 1485 when Henry Tudor landed with 2000 men at Milford Haven intent on snatching the English throne from Richard III. For more than a hundred years England was to be dominated by the personalities of the five Tudor monarchs, ranging from the brilliance and brutality of Henry VIII to the shrewdness and vanity of the virgin queen, Elizabeth I.

£14.99 Paperback
143 illustrations (66 colour)
272 pages
978-1-4456-0280-6

Available from all good bookshops or to order direct
Please call **01453-847-800**
www.amberleybooks.com

Also available from Amberley Publishing

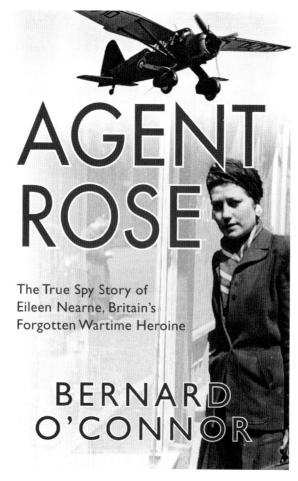

AGENT ROSE

The True Spy Story of
Eileen Nearne, Britain's
Forgotten Wartime Heroine

BERNARD O'CONNOR

The life and poignant death of one of Britain's bravest women

In September 2010 the body of Eileen Nearne was found in a flat in Torquay. With no known friends or relatives, a council burial was arranged. A police search of her belongings found wartime French currency, and wartime medals. Further investigation revealed that she was one of 40 women sent into France by the SOE, the Special Operations Executive, Churchill's top secret wartime 'spook' organisation. Her story and her poignant death as a recluse became an international media sensation.

£20 Hardback
50 illustrations
288 pages
978-1-4456-0838-9

Also available from Amberley Publishing

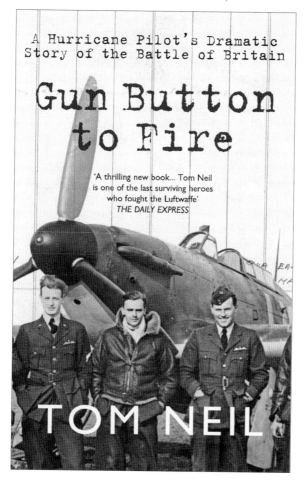

A Hurricane Pilot's Dramatic Story of the Battle of Britain

Gun Button to Fire

'A thrilling new book... Tom Neil is one of the last surviving heroes who fought the Luftwaffe'
THE DAILY EXPRESS

TOM NEIL

The amazing story of one of the 'Few', fighter ace Tom Neil who shot down 13 enemy aircraft during the Battle of Britain

'A thrilling new book... Tom Neil is one of the last surviving heroes who fought the Luftwaffe'
THE DAILY EXPRESS

'The best book on the Battle of Britain' SIR JOHN GRANDY, Marshal of the RAF

This is a fighter pilot's story of eight memorable months from May to December 1940. By the end of the year he had shot down 13 enemy aircraft, seen many of his friends killed, injured or burned, and was himself a wary and accomplished fighter pilot.

£9.99 Paperback
120 Photographs (20 colour)
320 pages
978-1-4456-0510-4

Available from all good bookshops or to order direct
Please call **01453-847-800**
www.amberleybooks.com

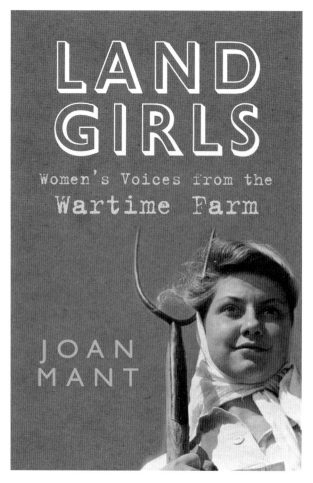

Also available from Amberley Publishing

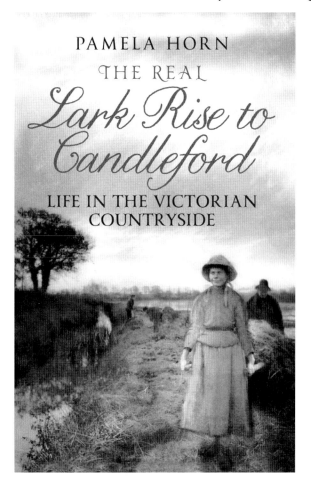

PAMELA HORN

THE REAL

Lark Rise to Candleford

LIFE IN THE VICTORIAN
COUNTRYSIDE

*An honest account of what life was really like for the rural community
in the Victorian Age*

The Real Lark Rise to Candleford demonstrates how deeply the labouring classes in rural areas were affected in
their ordinary lives by the great changes taking place around them.

Pamela Horn provides an insight into what life was really like for the rural community in the Victorian era,
for the real inhabitants of places like Lark Rise: small dwellings crowded with mouths that needed feeding;
long working days and low earnings; the trials and tribulations facing the young, the sick and the elderly. But
they had open space and this was the life they knew.

£12.99 Paperback
30 photographs
256 pages
978-1-84868-814-8

Available from from all good bookshops or to order direct
Please call **01453-847-800**
www.amberleybooks.com

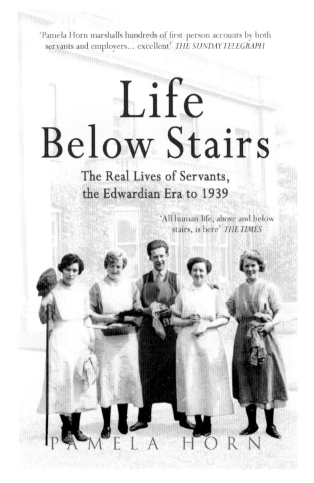

'Pamela Horn marshalls hundreds of first-person accounts by both
servants and employers... excellent' *THE SUNDAY TELEGRAPH*

Life
Below Stairs

The Real Lives of Servants,
the Edwardian Era to 1939

'All human life, above and below
stairs, is here' *THE TIMES*

P A M E L A H O R N

*'Pamela Horn marshalls hundreds of first-person accounts by both servants
and employers... an excellent book'* THE SUNDAY TELEGRAPH

By the end of the 1920s domestic service remained the largest female occupation in Britain. We view it
today as an undesirable job, owing to the class divide it has come to represent, and this is reflected in the
portrayals of mistresses and servants in books and on the screen in such dramas as *Upstairs Downstairs* and
Downton Abbey. But what do we really know about how girls felt when taking up these positions in other
people's houses, or how they were treated? Pamela Horn uses first-hand accounts and reminiscences, as well
as official records and newspaper reports, to extract the truth about the lives and status of men and women
in domestic service from 1900 to 1939.

£9.99 Paperback
40 photographs
192 pages
978-1-4456-1008-5